Ann Perkins

Portrait of Deborah Franklin.—*Photo courtesy American Philosophical Society*

Courage & Candlelight

the Feminine Spirit of '76

by Joseph J. Kelley, Jr. and Sol Feinstone

Stackpole Books

Published by
STACKPOLE BOOKS
Cameron and Kelker Streets
Harrisburg, Pa. 17105

Printed in U.S.A.

Library of Congress Cataloging in Publication Data

Kelley, Joseph J
  Courage and candlelight.

    1. Women in the United States--Biography. I. Fein-
stone, Sol, 1890-   joint author. II. Title.
HQ1418.K45   301.41'2'0973   73-23105
ISBN 0-8117-0452-1

To their own "Best of Wives—Best of Women"
ROSE FEINSTONE and ELEANOR E. KELLEY
the authors affectionately
dedicate this book

Contents

Whether on paper or in person, communications between these
married lovers generated sparks aplenty as they teased, scolded,
comforted, enlightened, and renewed each other.

Fiercely loyal to her husband despite the furor caused by his infidelity, this quiet but determined woman emerged from the
obscurity which she cheerfully embraced during his lifetime to
wage a relentless campaign to assure his proper place in American
history after his death.

While her famous husband traveled throughout the Colonies and
abroad on government business, attracting the attentions of pretty
women as he went, Benjamin Franklin's spunky wife endured the
pangs of loneliness and defended their house against angry mobs
at gunpoint.

Though her distracted behavior convinced Washington, Hamilton, and Lafayette that she was innocent of her husband's treason,
modern historians tend to believe that this lovely but enigmatic
lady was one of history's greatest dissemblers.

Commander in Chief Washington himself was not too busy to
acknowledge the flowery encomiums of the poetical prodigy and
self-educated slave, Phillis Wheatley, or to engage in an elegant
flirtation with the prolific poetess Annis Stockton.

After his idyllic marriage to Martha Wayles was ended by her
untimely death, an array of extraordinary women entered Jefferson's life, not the least intriguing of whom was the beautiful slave
girl, Sally Hemings.

A Beginning Word

Woman's role in the period of the American Revolution has either been quietly neglected or suffused with saccharine. Nineteenth-century historians molded her in the idealized image of their own time. So she was pictured as the model Victorian—long-suffering, patient, unthinking, a gentlewoman whose virtues bordered on the angelic.

Apart from the fact that relatively few normal women can meet such unrealistic standards in any age, it certainly was not characteristic of the eighteenth-century American girl. Shaped by the times in which she lived, she had a fierce streak of independence, a capability of courage often superior to males, and a loyalty to her principles which did not dissolve in tears.

The American Revolution was a civil war. It split the population of 2,500,000 in 1776 into roughly three equal parts: those who preferred long established links to Great Britain, and called themselves "The Good Americans"; those who preferred to remain neutral—a virtual impossibility in the intensity of emotions, and those who saw in stamps, sugar, and tea symbols of growing oppression by a distant government grown tyrannical. The Revolution was not only a political upheaval. It had far-reaching social repercussions. Dr. Benjamin Rush, groping on the fringes of latter-day psychiatry, attempted to measure the impact on the psyches of Philadelphians. All in all, the beginnings, middle, and end of the era stretched across the last forty years of the century.

But nineteenth-century romanticists filtered out the agony, cruelty, and hardships; figuratively squeezed the life out of the patriots, scrubbed their faces, dressed them neatly in buff and blue, and had them march nobly and unerringly toward a Heaven-ordained manifest destiny. It was just such a group of ladies in a patriotic society about 1900 who decided to honor the memory of Molly Pitcher. When they learned more about her, they went into a state of mild shock.

Everyone had heard about the heroic woman. In the blistering heat of June 1778, at the battle of Monmouth, she stoutly took over her fallen husband's gun and fired a few rounds at the redcoats. Such a heroine was tailor-made for dreamy nineteenth-century artists, who imaginatively portrayed her like Delacroix's celebrated goddess of liberty, with, of course, bosom more chastely covered. No one seemed to know her real name, and even Harper's *Encyclopedia of American History*, the formidable ten-volume work, listed her as "Molly Pitcher." Researchers, however, discovered that this was a generic name, affectionately applied to camp followers who brought water to slake the thirst of soldiers in combat. Digging a bit deeper they found the heroine was Mary Ludwig Hays, a husky twenty-one-year-old farm girl from near Carlisle, Pennsylvania, who had trudged along with her barber husband when he was called into service. The war had made nomads of many wives, who because of love, boredom, a craving for adventure, or the necessity for survival stayed close to their poorly paid spouses. Mary was tough and coarse-grained and had precisely the necessary guts and skill to meet the challenge of those few brief hours which made her immortal. At war's end, the couple returned to Carlisle; the husband died and she married one of his close friends and fellow soldiers. He was not much good for the young widow and her infant son; so she left him and by alternating as a nursemaid and washerwoman eked out enough to support herself and her child. Her second husband gave her nothing more than an additional name, McCauley. Gradually Mary adopted a new life style. She replaced her skirts with soldier's breeches, had her hair clipped mannishly close, and adopted the military tricorn hat. She waged an unending campaign for a pension from Pennsylvania and later the young Republic, drank and swore like a man, and was a notable figure around Carlisle until she died at age seventy-eight. Hardly the type genteel women would invite to tea, she would probably have punctuated such an invitation with a string of salty oaths. Long after they laid her to rest, the people of Carlisle commemorated her memory with a superb, life-size statue of the youthful Mary—a handsome, strong woman, sleeves rolled up, ramrod in hand—someone who commanded admiration even if the patriotic order of ladies did not agree.

The women in these pages did nothing quite as spectacular as Mary Hays, unless one is sufficiently broad-minded to look at Peggy Shippen Arnold through the objectivity of neutral glasses. But each had her private ordeal, and their lives illuminate a variety of aspects of the period.

What was it like to be married to Benjamin Franklin? Deborah Read Franklin, almost forgotten in the wake of her celebrated husband, gives a graphic picture in picturesque phonetically spelled letters. She was the same rough-cast, reliable type as Mary Hays, and picked up a gun to stave off the threat of a mob in Philadelphia. Content to spend her days in the shadow of the steeple of Christ Church, she was consigned to long years of loneliness.

Abigail Adams knew loneliness, too; but she had a full partnership with John, and this average-looking couple transformed themselves into idyllic lovers through the extraordinary reach of their minds and hearts. Where Deborah Franklin seemed unaware and unconcerned about the forces of history gathering about her, Abigail so sensed the significance of them that she raced little John Quincy Adams to a hill overlooking Boston harbor as the British and Americans maneuvered into a position of fatal confrontation. Her letters crackle with such electricity of thought and expression that the current still vibrates through the parchment. Her erudite husband was dazzled by the sweep of her sentences, and the relentless demands she made upon him and others for the full equality of women could provide a liberation movement with mottoes for years.

What was it like to be married to a traitor? At West Point the Revolutionary generals, all save one, are honored with a tablet giving their name, rank, birth, and death dates. The only exception is a nameless tablet which simply records a date of birth. So a nation shows its disdain for General Benedict Arnold. Peggy Shippen Arnold remains an enigma, veering between the compassionate view that she was a victim of her husband's treachery and that which regards her as a shrewd, consummate actress fully in league with her personal devil. Whatever the case, none can discount her courage; and this slender blonde, thought by some British officers to be the most beautiful woman in America, displayed admirable mettle in the long exile that was the aftermath of treason.

To the lovely Annis Boudinot Stockton of Princeton, New Jersey, life was a matter of metric verse. She translated everything from Washington to snow-covered trees into poetry. Marriage to the affluent and appreciative Richard Stockton made it easy to recreate Alexander Pope's gardens at Morven, their spacious estate; and her kindliness made it hard to refuse to join a circle where she rechristened everyone with classical names. Her blithe spirit never faltered in dark hours, and endeared her to many, including her impossibly self-righteous son-in-law, Benjamin Rush. Both of them marveled at the brilliance of Elizabeth Graeme Fergusson, whose dour home on the edge of Pennsylvania's Montgomery County almost mourns the ill-starred destiny that awaited her. So it was, too, with Phillis Wheatley, an ex-slave whose poetic talents charmed Boston and made her the darling of fashionable prewar

London society, but who died young in abject poverty, married to a man who could not cope with her mind or make enough to provide nourishment for her body.

Alexander Hamilton's wife, Betsey, came close to being everything the Victorians admired. Quiet, demure, loving wife and mother, she was content to stay shyly in the background of her husband's glittering career. But when Burr killed him in the needless duel, and political animosities and indifference threatened to obliterate his contributions to America, she embarked on an incredible crusade to insure his place in history, proving by works the depths of a love she never could quite put into words.

Through Sally Hemings we view the scene on southern plantations, but she touches the era through her master, Thomas Jefferson; and their relationship, wrapped in silence, still baffles his biographers. This attractive slave girl was his dead wife's half-sister, a not uncommon thing in that time and place. Theirs is a story without words, but he brought her to France virtually as a member of the family, educated her, and dressed her in excellent taste. We might attribute it to his generosity until we find her disdaining the freedom she could have had in a country that abhorred slavery to return to Monticello, where she later bore several sons who looked remarkably like Jefferson.

We have tried in these pages to show the reflections of a few women in their looking-glasses. Scores of others could have qualified, but this select company may afford the reader a better appreciation of what it was like to be a woman during one of the most momentous ages mankind has ever recorded.

A Partnership of Minds

Abigail and John Adams

In 1766, twenty-two-year-old Abigail Adams and her husband sat for their portraits by Benjamin Blyth, a young Salem artist. Her brown eyes seem glazed by the fixed pose—her straight nose a bit too regular and the lips a bit too perfect, with only a smudge of shadow to suggest the faintest of smiles. But her dark hair is attractively swept back from a patrician brow, and casually caught by a pink bow, and if the picture lacks animation it somehow suggests the subject had unusual qualities. All things considered, it is probably a fair representation of the features upon which John Adams looked with admiration and love.

The pastels were deceptive in one respect. Understandably the artist gave bloom to her complexion, but a tendency to illness often denied her such color. From childhood she had converted such indispositions into positive forces, reading far beyond the range of others, and tempering her thoughts with the wisdom learned from her mother and grandmother. Yet her vivacious and healthier sisters kept her personality from becoming blunted by too much maturity.

Adams had known the Smith family long before he came to court Abigail. Her sisters were prettier, but it was Abigail who most appreciated his sharp word sketches of characters encountered in his law practice.

He was nine years older—a sturdy farm-raised man with an encyclopedic mind. She enjoyed testing the mettle of her own opinions against his. No man ever overawed Abigail. "If man is the lord, woman is the lordess," she would say later in life, but it was an axiom which guided her from girlhood.

Their romance was as much an adventure of the mind as an affair of the heart, and within that realm they carved out an aristocracy of their own. They invested themselves, unconsciously perhaps, with the royal purple of intellectual snobbery; but since many New Englanders deemed themselves God's elect through other devices, this attitude was unique only in the fact that husband and wife—as they soon became—moved in tandem. Abigail's mother, leaning on the artificiality of lineage, felt John did not have the requisite breeding to be worthy of her daughter. Of course this was nonsense, and Abigail quickly disposed of the notion. "We are cast in the same mold," said she, and that was that.

It is hard to envision Adams as a passionate lover. He took himself seriously and was a fuss-budget, often prim and always a prude. Moreover he had an odd vanity. An intensive student of history, he constantly scanned the events of his day as if they were portents designed particularly to shape his destiny. To assume that men and events, at least within the sphere of his interest, were plotting to challenge his character, was a supreme example of egotism—not so much, perhaps, when he became president but certainly when he was a young, unknown lawyer.

His love letters to Abigail in the courting period were, nevertheless, filled with banter, as well as a high degree of sophistication. She responded in kind. If he was not cleverly casual like

Franklin, he was more at ease than Alexander Hamilton and Benedict Arnold in this sort of thing.

When they wanted to lift themselves above the calendar and put their love in the context of legend, she became his Diana, and he her Lysander—the choice of the Spartan general and admiral being perhaps a sop to Adams's perennial dreams of becoming a great military man. If she became moody, he chided her. "You tell me that you sometimes view the darker side of your Diana," she answered and asserted that her spells of depression came "more from a wrong head than a bad heart." When his law business kept him from being with her she wrote:

> I see you but cannot make myself visible to you—that tortures me, but it is still worse when I do not come for I am then haunted by half a dozen ugly sprights. One will catch me and leap into the sea, another will carry me up a precipice (like that which Edgar describes to Lear), then toss me down, and were I not then as light as gossamer I should shiver into atoms—another will be pouring down my throat stuff worse than the witches' broth in Macbeth.

Often he was hypercritical. She sharply cut him down to size: "Heigh day, Mr. what's your name? Who taught you to threaten so vehemently?"

Adams underwent the ordeal of getting inoculated against smallpox in Boston. The technique of making a small incision and inserting infected lint in it was the prelude to a period of minor misery for a few weeks. These were spent in isolation in a hospital, but between the fevers and nausea, he kept up his correspondence with her. The letters were handled gingerly by a Negro servant. Abigail watched as he clamped the paper between iron tongs and held it high above the fire. She described the ordeal to Adams: "Did you ever rob a Birds nest? Do you remember how the poor Bird would fly round and round, fearful to come nigh, yet not know how to leave the place—just so they say I hover round Tom whilst he is smoking my Letters." He seemed light-hearted, kidding her about a "buxom lass" she sent to visit him—

a friend who had been immunized from the pox—and had he been more presentable and not in the hospital garb, he would "have infallibly taken a game of romps" with her. He had promised himself to take the deacon's daughter, Polly Palmer, "romping very soon." Abigail dismissed such male chauvinism with a brush of the pen, and congratulated him on withstanding "the distemper like an oak." However, she had hoped "this purgation of Lysander would have set us on a level and rendered him a sociable creature, but ill luck, he stands it like an oak, and is as haughty as ever." His imperious attitude in company made others uneasy, she felt, and while she absolved him of conceit, "for sauciness no mortal can match him, no, not even his Diana."

He countered with a catalog of her shortcomings, half humorous, half serious. When he objected to her crossing her legs, she said he had no business paying attention to her "Leggs." The "parrot-toed" walk she affected, she felt could be cured by a "dancing master"; but she readily admitted she could not sing and was inclined to sit with bowed head because of bashfulness.

Still they both knew they were meant for each other. Mrs. Smith, despite her family connections, had to work at her sewing to supplement the salary of her minister husband, and was unable to enlist his help in trying to veer the determined Abigail away from marriage. The couple chose October 25, 1764, as their wedding date, and wrestled with nervous stomachs which made them both uncomfortably ill. Abigail was ordered to bed by the family physician and she felt "extremely weak and . . . low spirited . . . hardly myself." But they managed to rally themselves for the ceremony, and the bride's father, with a tinge of nonchalance, chose as his sermon text: "For John came neither eating nor drinking, and they say, He hath a devil."

They set up housekeeping in the frame saltbox house in Braintree, Massachusetts, where he was born. A little more than nine months later he could write:

> On the 14 day of July of this Year 1765, Mrs. Adams presented me with a Daughter and in her Confinement in her Chamber, I

was alone in [the Parlour below] my Office of Evenings and Mornings.

Like any country lawyer most of his cases at the outset were of homespun trivia, arguments over cattle, hats, trespass, and other phases of pastoral life. He traveled within a radius of forty miles, trying his cases before dull, unlettered magistrates against men who called themselves "lawyers," but were wholly untrained, in back rooms filled with smoke and lounging louts. The vituperation and rancor sickened him, and the pettiness "seemed to have wrought an entire metamorphosis of the human Character." When he could relax in the quiet of the country night he thought of important issues like the Stamp Act, which Britain had devised as a measure to recoup some of the heavy expenses incurred in the French and Indian War. In Abigail he had an appreciative audience, and she would listen intently to his explanations of why he felt Parliament and the Ministry in London were violating the colonists' rights as free Englishmen. She, moreover, could ask intelligent and searching questions. Along with the few attorneys who had some professional qualifications, he was invited to join a "sodality" formed by Jeremiah Gridley, a leading Boston practitioner, designed to deepen their knowledge of the law. Their weekly meetings in homes and taverns, over a cordial glass of wine or tankard of ale, sharpened their sensitivities to constitutional rights, and Adams infused such high theories into the pedestrian matters that filled his days. Thus the Stamp Act and similar laws made Americans look deeper into the humdrum of daily routine for the traces of individual nobility they would subsequently assert with pride in the Declaration of Independence.

Besides scribbling off learned letters to the newspapers, Adams became a selectman and thus trod the periphery of politics. Then, almost miraculously, through Gridley, he was plucked from anonymity to share with Gridley and James Otis the task of arguing against the Stamp Act before the governor and council. Thus was Adams projected into prominence and launched on his public career.

It was Abigail who bore the brunt of the decision. Her doughty husband had courage. "Facts are stubborn things," he liked to tell juries, and he was every bit as stubborn in presenting his version of the facts. His diary entry for Sunday, December 22, 1765, simply notes:

> At Home, with my family. Thinking.

The next day he went to Boston, and the diary bubbles with details of the men with whom he met, the gist of the conversations, and the inevitable character sketches: "Otis is fiery and fev'rous. His Imagination flames, his Passions blaze. He is liable to great Inequalities of Temper—sometimes in Despondency, sometimes in a Rage." On December 24:

> Returned from Boston. Spent the afternoon and Evening at Home.

And the following day, Christmas, began:

> At Home. Thinking, reading, searching, concerning Taxation without Consent.

The details were recounted. What Lord Coke said. What the ancient statutes of Henry VIII and Henry VII indicated. Then Abigail and he "Drank Tea at Grandfather Quincys" after dining at home, and listened to Grandmother Quincy "as merry and chatty as ever, with her Stories out of the News Papers." Day's end offered this quiet scene:

> Spent the Evening at Home, with my Partner and no other Company.

The arguments over the stamp tax had produced violence along with logic. John Hancock suggested some of the foes of the colonists' position should be beheaded—a stark and grim reminder of a practice in England which never gained a foothold in America. As Abigail and her husband attended church services, they listened closely for the political sentiments of the ministers, mulling over the biblical texts they chose and scanning every word of the lengthy sermons.

Things quieted down when the controversial act was repealed in 1766. Abigail bore a son, John Quincy, in the new saltbox house the couple built just a stone's throw from Adams's original home. That was in 1767 and by 1770, another daughter and two more boys had been born—the second girl, Susan, dying in infancy in 1770. For a time they lived in Boston, closer to the scene of Adams's growing practice. As selectman he had to serve as overseer of the poor for a term, and this took him into places of poverty. So it opened an urgent train of new thought. He discussed with Abigail the need to ensure their four children would have good educations to equip them for the business of life. She agreed. Then the political pot began to boil again with confrontations between the crown and the province. Hancock's sloop was seized for trying to evade customs duties, and the Sons of Liberty were incensed by the arbitrary way in which the situation was handled. Incident after incident occurred, and finally the friction between Bostonians and the British Army exploded in the "Massacre"; three were killed and two mortally wounded. The date was March 5, 1770.

No lawyer of stature could be found to defend English Captain Preston and the accused soldiers until Adams was asked. He did so without hesitation, deeming it his duty—but not without a sense of dramatics. Given the mood of the people, it was a high risk, for win or lose he felt his practice would suffer. There were reactions, some bitter, more disgruntled; but there were no reprisals, no rocks thrown against his Brattle Street windows. And even before the case came to trial his friends nominated him for election to the Massachusetts Assembly, and he won by a large margin.

Abigail, plagued by migraine headaches, weakened by her successive pregnancies, and distraught—as was he—over the death of little Susan, felt the tensions he was experiencing. Service in the colonial legislature meant further subtraction from the time the busy Adams could spend with her and his growing family, but she resolutely supported his decision to accept. By the early months of 1771, with Preston's trial happily ended by acquittal and the sole convictions returned against a few of the soldiers on the reduced charge of manslaughter, Adams decided to move his wife and children back to Braintree. Her health seemed progressively worse, and he—constantly fussy about his own, an almost chronic complainer—was glad for the surcease, temporary though it was, from busy Boston. In the spring country air, he contemplated a farewell to politics. Neither he nor anyone else took the threat seriously. It was simply a bit of self-indulgence. Despite his "feeble" condition, he went back to his Boston office and was soon caught up in the tide of affairs. Devoted to his wife and children, Adams soon felt the need of them in Boston; so after sixteen months at Braintree, he brought the family to Brattle Street.

If the Stamp Act provisions were a bit obscure to most Americans, tea was not. For a good number of years merchants up and down the coast made a tidy profit in selling smuggled Dutch tea, and since the revenue laws were lightly enforced until 1765, the heavily taxed English tea was at a considerable disadvantage. The East India Tea Company, in which a number of wealthy Britons had stock, was on the verge of bankruptcy—largely through mismanagement but partially, at least, because it could not compete with the untaxed Dutch tea. In May of 1773 Parliament moved to bail out the corporation by offering a refund on the tax paid when tea left England, so the only duty involved would be the nominal threepence per pound when it arrived in American ports. This would drive the price down below what the smuggled Dutch tea commanded, as well as the price of tea legally imported from other sources. To ensure a market for East India tea, consignees were designated in New York, Charleston, Philadelphia, and Boston. Bristling with British troops, Boston was particularly vulnerable. The Sons of Liberty, spurred by member merchants who saw their profit margin threatened, spread the word that the consignees were enemies of America; these hapless individuals in the three cities other than Boston quickly resigned. In Boston they were safely secluded in Castle William under the protection of the royal governor.

The threepence import duty was at the heart of the problem. As voracious tea drinkers, Americans had been particularly indignant when Parliament levied the tax. Even though the shipper was required to pay it, the tax was passed on to the consumer.

For those who challenged the right of Parliament to levy taxes on the Colonies, the tea tax was as obnoxious as the more visible and direct stamp tax. The East India Company had urged its repeal. It had no interest in the debates over the issue of taxation; it simply wanted to recoup its American markets. But Lord North refused. By accepting cheaper tea, the Americans, he thought, would be accepting the principle of Parliamentary supremacy with every sip.

By law such tea ships had twenty days in which to discharge their cargoes and pay the American duty. Only then could they be given clearance to sail for home. Otherwise their cargoes could be seized and they would be forced to leave without any tea or cash.

So Lord North was betting on American thirst, American merchants were betting on patriotism to protect their more profitable ventures, and the Sons of Liberty and similar groups were teaching and threatening those tea drinkers who were weighing their thirst against principles. If the East India tea was not permitted to land, part of the problem would be resolved. If, on the other hand, the resisting colonists managed to keep the ships at bay for twenty days, the authorities could move in, seize the cargoes, and sell them on the open market, further depressing it and applying the proceeds to pay the salaries of royal government officials in the provinces. In late November 1773 three East India vessels arrived in Boston, and with no prospect of being able to unload, lay dismally at anchor awaiting developments.

Abigail wrote to her friend Mercy Warren:

> The tea, that baneful weed, is arrived. Great and I hope effectual opposition has been made to the landing of it . . . the proceedings

of our citizens have been unified spirited and firm. The flame is kindled and like lightning it catches from soul to soul. Great will be the devestation if not timely quenched or allayed by some more lenient measures.

She feared unless the governor backed down

many, very many of our heroes will spend their lives in the cause . . . [My heart] beats at every whistle I hear and I dare not openly express half my fears.

The governor had no intention of backing down. The masters of the ships asked to be allowed to sail away with cargoes intact, but British warships blocked any thoughts they might have had of leaving without clearance. If the Sons of Liberty achieved a victory by blocking the discharge, they now were confronted with the reality that on December 17, the customs officials could seize the tea. Thus on the night of December 16 they resolved the dilemma by dressing as Indians, boarding the *Dartmouth*, which had been the first to put into port and whose twenty days would expire on the morrow, and dumped 342 chests of tea, valued at $90,000, into the harbor.

The Adamses watched 1774 arrive with full expectation that Boston would feel the force of British wrath. Abigail's sickness through the early winter prompted John to send her and the children back to Braintree, where he thought the sea air might help her recovery. He felt miserable himself, bothered by one of the heavy colds he so frequently caught. The combination of things got him down. They, he wrote Abigail, "have put my utmost philosophy to the trial. . . . We live, my dear soul, in an age of trial." He did not hold out much hope for the future of Boston. "It must expire. . . . Our principal consolation is that it dies in a noble cause. The cause of truth, of virtue, of liberty and of humanity." To be sure, he optimistically expected it would rise again "to greater wealth, splendor and power than ever." Meantime he suggested they better economize, but not to a point where they refused to share what they had, to a degree, with less fortunate people. When he was chosen as a delegate to the first Continental Congress to be convened in Philadelphia in September 1774, he worked diligently to earn as much as he could so that Abigail and the children would be financially secure during his absence.

He broadened his law circuit in search of cases, and both he and Abigail got a foretaste of the separation the Philadelphia trip would mean. Expecting to find sentiment strong for the colonial cause, he discovered to his dismay the people were either tepid or Tory. There was so little business he could write to her as often as three times a day. "My fancy, wishes and desires are at Braintree, among my field, pastures, and meadows, as much as those of the Israelites were among the leeks, garlic and onions of the Land of Goshen." His thoughts were "continually with you and in the neighborhood of you, and with your little prattling Nabby, Johnny, Charley and Tommy. . . . Pray remember me to my dear little babes, whom I long to see running to meet me and climb upon me." Clients were scarce, but "I will not lie down in despair. If I cannot serve my children by the law, I will serve them by agriculture, by trade, by some way or other."

Then with his remarkable prescience of history he urged her to put his letters "up safe and preserve them. They may exhibit to our posterity a kind of picture of the manners, opinions, and principles of these times of perplexity, danger and distress."

On August 10, 1774, he set out for Philadelphia. A letter from Abigail caught up with him before he reached Princeton. Already she felt the loneliness, she told him, mingled with fears for the future. Then as if to relieve the torment she must have known he would feel, brightened a bit to say she had "taken a very great fondness for reading Rollins Ancient History," and let little John Quincy read aloud to her in hopes he would also "entertain a fondness for it." Still she could not avoid the press of the present. The parched earth was such "my poor cows will certainly . . . petition . . . you, setting forth their grievances and informing you that they have been deprived of their ancient privileges." She thought September "perhaps may be of as much importance to Great Britain as the Ides of March were to Caesar."

He apologized for not having written, absorbed as he had been in meeting delegations along the way. He missed her and the children:

> Train them to virtue. Habituate them to industry, activity and spirit. Make them consider vice as shameful and unmanly. Fire them with ambition to be useful. . . . Fix their ambition upon great and solid objects, and their contempt upon little, frivolous and useless ones. It is time, my dear, for you to begin to teach them French. Every decency, grace and honesty should be inculcated in them.

Abigail hardly needed such admonitions. Trying to maintain a farm and care for the youngsters and the household, she would have been justified in protesting; but he was merely recording what they talked about so often and was echoing sentiments she shared. Nor did she think it unusual when he suggested in October that she exhort the Braintree militia to "exercise every day in the week if they will, the more the better. Let them furnish themselves with artillery, arms and ammunition. Let them follow the maxim which you say they had adopted, 'In times of peace prepare for war.' But let them avoid war if possible—if possible, I say." The idea of war and peace pivoting on the decisions of the Braintree militia would seem amusing if one was not conscious of the storm a few men triggered by the Boston Tea Party, and before that, the "Massacre." Less than a year later the power of a few was to be further demonstrated at Lexington and Concord.

Missions like this exhilarated Abigail. If she mildly enjoyed "Tittle-tattle" in his letters, she was more interested in the policies and personalities of the Continental Congress. For the time being, Adams told her he was so swamped with required reading of pamphlets, newspapers, and other research, she was to ask Paul Revere, who rode post between Boston and Philadelphia, for more details.

At the moment history was not being made in Braintree, and she could indulge her personal feelings:

> My much beloved friend—I dare not express to you, at three

hundred miles distance, how ardently I long for your return. I have some very miserly wishes, and cannot consent to your spending one hour [in Boston] till, at least I have had you twelve. The idea plays about my heart, unnerves my hand, whilst I write; awakens all the tender sentiments that years have increased and matured . . . The whole collected stock of ten weeks' absence knows not how to brook any longer restraint, but will break forth and flow through my pen.

She enclosed letters from Nabby and John Quincy. The seven-year-old boy was hesitant about his penmanship.

Mamma says you will accept my endeavors, and that my duty to you may be expressed in poor writing as well as good. I hope I grow a better boy and that you will have no occasion to be ashamed of me when you return. Mr. Thaxter says I learn my books very well. He is a very good master. I read my books to Mamma. We all long to see you. I am, sir, your dutiful son.

Through debates Adams found "nibbling and quibbling," the Congress finally adopted a course of action. It agreed to a Declaration of Rights, a humble but firm petition to George III, and the machinery for a boycott on British goods. This last feature was to become effective in September 1775, if the English showed no inclination to improve relations. Through articles of association the Colonies bound themselves to act in concert on nonimportation, and volunteer vigilante committees dubbed "Associators" would ensure that the average citizen complied. If circumstances required, the Congress agreed to meet in Philadelphia again the following May, but as Adams headed home on October 28, 1774, "in a very great Rain," he penned homage to "the happy, the peacefull, the elegant, the hospitable, and polite City of Phyladelphia" and added, "It is not very likely that I shall ever see this Part of the World again."

That he made no mention in his diary of his tenth wedding anniversary on October 25, but five days after jotted "My Birthday, I am 39 Years of Age" is not significant. There was no doubt in his mind that Abigail was the best thing that ever happened to him, and he charted his course to Braintree to avoid, as much as possible, the ceremonial dinners and entertainments enthusiastic groups planned.

The personal happiness of reunion overshadowed everything else. Adams promised himself that as soon as the current crisis was over he would withdraw from politics: "I have neither fortune, leisure, health, nor genius for it." He was home with Abigail when word came the following April about the confrontation on Lexington green, and with all the blustery ambition of an amateur strategist he raced out to inspect the situation. He returned to Braintree in such an excited condition, he was running a fever. That coupled with other "alarming symptoms" put him in bed. Abigail nursed him to a sufficient state of recovery where he could manage to leave for Philadelphia the next month, although she admitted as he departed her "very insensible and heroic" smile shielded "a heart of lead." He wrote to her with a fair degree of frequency on the way, his spirits heightened by anticipation of mighty events, but mingled philosophy with minutiae, knowing her taste for exalted thoughts. Like her he was curious about what God's plan called for, but mildly rebuked himself by adding: "It is arrogance and presumption . . . to pretend to penetrate far into the designs of Heaven. The most perfect reverence and resignation becomes us." Still he felt within bounds to surmise that the suffering Boston was experiencing was part of the Divine scheme to solidify the Colonies. "It will plead with all America with more irresistable persuasion than angels trumpet-tongued." He did not think Abigail and the children were in imminent danger, but should it come he offered an unnecessary suggestion, take them and "fly to the woods."

On June 15, 1775, the Continental Congress chose one of its delegates, George Washington, to be commander in chief of the Continental Army it had voted on May 31. On June 17 Abigail, with eight-year-old John Quincy by her side, raced up Penn's Hill near their home, to watch the scene at Bunker and Breed's hills. From this vantage point, commanding as it did a fine view of Boston harbor, mother and son were eyewitnesses to the sights and sounds of musketry and cannon. Within a week Washington stopped to pay his respects. Abigail was impressed. She hastily wrote John:

> You had prepared me to entertain a favorable opinion of him, but I thought the half was not told me. Dignity with ease and complacency, the gentleman and the soldier look agreeably blended in him. Modesty marks every line and feature of his face. Those lines of Dryden instantly occurred to me:

> "Mark his majestic fabric; he's a temple
> Sacred by birth, and built by hands divine;
> His soul's the deity that lodges there,
> Nor is the pile unworthy of the god."

Braintree suddenly found itself a center of action. Abigail opened the doors to tired troops who mingled with refugees from Boston, pausing for "a day, a night, a week." While there was an ample supply of meat, coffee, sugar, and pepper were all but gone. She assured her husband they could manage, even if it meant living on whortleberries and milk, but she desperately needed pins and asked him to find some in Philadelphia. But she wanted something much more. His letters had been brief and cryptic. "They let me know that you exist, but some of them contain scarcely six lines." The secrecy rule imposed by Congress on its proceedings should not bar "sentimental effusions of the heart. I am sure you are not destitute of them. Or are they all absorbed in the great public? Good night. With thoughts of thee I close my eyes. Angels guard and protect thee."

He was moved by her letter describing Bunker Hill. She had written:

> The day—perhaps the decisive day—is come, on which the fate of America depends. My bursting heart must find vent at my pen . . . A particular account of these dreadful but, I hope, glorious days will be transmitted to you, no doubt, in the exactest manner . . . I think I am very brave, upon the whole. If danger comes near my dwelling, I suppose I shall shudder. We want powder but, with the blessing of heaven, we fear them not.

He replied:

> You are a heroine, and you have reason to be. For the worst that
> can happen can do you no harm. A soul as pure, as benevolent,
> as virtuous and pious as yours has nothing to fear, but everything
> to hope and expect from the last of human evils.

Congress adjourned for the month of August and Adams hurried to Braintree. His "brave" Abigail had nursed his brother until
he died from a mysterious malady, but with British armies still
poised against untrained Americans, the death was measured with
affectionate realism against more imminent dangers. When he left
again for Philadelphia, Abigail was confronted with a major crisis. Dysentery and smallpox swept down on Braintree, felling her
and little Tommy, and before she was half-recovered, it proved
fatal to her mother and a little serving girl. Still weak, she had
been tireless in trying to bring them through, but "turkey rhu-
barb" and the other "medicines" she asked John to dispatch from
Philadelphia were unavailing. She buried them in October, sustained only by her faith and the realization that she and her son
had been spared. Her letters to John recited the lamentations of
the Old Testament, as if in writing them she was endeavoring to
convince herself of their ancient truth. In six short weeks she had
lost five "near connections, laid in the grave . . . I cannot over-
come my too selfish sorrow. Yea, though He slay me, I will trust
in Him, said holy Job. What though His corrective hand hath
been stretched against me; I will not murmur."

From Philadelphia he tried to comfort her, but said: "If I
could write as well as you, my sorrow would be as eloquent as
yours, but, upon my word, I cannot."

But death, all too commonplace, did not absorb Abigail's
time. Like her husband she was conscious they were both part of
a much larger design, and her anxieties about matters in Philadelphia swiftly transcended grief.

> I wish I knew what mighty things were fabricating. If a form
> of government is to be established here, what one will be as-

sumed? Will it be left to our assemblies to choose one? And will not many men have many minds? And shall we not run into dissensions among ourselves?

She told her husband she was

> more and more convinced that man is a dangerous creature; and that power, whether vested in many or a few, is ever grasping, and, like the grave cries, "Give, give!" The great fish swallow up the small; and he who is most strenuous for the rights of the people, when vested with power, is as eager after the prerogatives of government.
>
> How shall we be governed so as to retain our liberties? . . . Who shall frame these laws? Who will give them force and energy? When I consider these things . . . I feel anxious for the fate of our monarchy, or democracy, or whatever is to take place.

She found herself in "a labyrinth of perplexities" but guessed that righteousness and justice would eventually make "order rise out of confusion." Then she paused, "I believe I have tired you with politics." She realized nothing pleased him more. He was proud of her mental prowess.

To his diary he confided he heard that "an English Gentleman . . . a Man of Penetration, tho of few Words . . . was pleased with Mrs. Adams, and thought her, the most accomplished Lady he had seen since he came out of England." He prefaced the entry by saying it was "for my Wife, who will be peeping here sometime or other, and come across it" and added, "Down Vanity, for you don't know who this Englishman is."

She could have used the compliment immediately. Her morale was sagging under the "nunnery" at Braintree. She was lonely without him, and the nights seemed interminable:

> My pen is always freer than my tongue. I have written many things to you I suppose I never could have talked. My heart is made tender by repeated afflictions; it never was a hard heart.

He tried to cheer her by suggesting the next time he made the trip to Philadelphia she accompany him with "Master Johnny."

He envied Hancock who had his wife, Dorothy, with him. They both knew it was wishful thinking. His late brother's little daughter had now come to live at Braintree.

Adams tried to quiet her restlessness by suggesting more topics for the children's education. Geography was one of the specifics. He thought they should learn to become cosmopolitan, and could acquire useful knowledge by drawing maps and making sketches of distant cities, castles, and the like, but principally places in America. In the next breath he was extolling the greatness of New England, and his cautions against provincialism were scattered to the winds. "New England must produce the heroes, the statesmen, the philosophers, or America will make no great figure for some time." "If we mean to have heroes, statesmen and philosophers," she tartly replied, "we should have learned women." She reminded him that in all the grandiose talk about education, women were virtually ignored, and hoped "some more liberal plan might be laid for the benefit of the rising generation." She was aware her ideas were revolutionary in their own right, but knew he had

> a mind too enlarged and liberal to disregard the sentiment. If much depends, as is allowed, upon the early education of youth, and the first principles which are instilled take the deepest root, great benefit must arise from literary accomplishments in women.

"Your sentiments," he answered, "of the importance of education in women are agreeable to my own."

But when she asked him to buy her a copy of Lord Chesterfield's letters, which were being widely discussed in Boston, he politely refused. Like Congreve's plays they were "stained with libertine morals and base principles," and he knew she would not want them in her library. At thirty-one, Abigail thought she was old enough to make up her own mind as to what she wanted to read. Half in jest, half in earnest, she suggested that while Congress was mulling about independence, they should give some thought to independence for women, and draft some laws that

would not put "such unlimited power into the hands of husbands." Men, she felt, liked to be tyrants, and the delegates would
be well advised if "attention should be paid to the rights of the
ladies who might otherwise foment a rebellion and not . . . hold
ourselves bound by any laws in which we have no voice or representation."

Adams answered:

> I cannot but laugh. We have been told that our struggle has
> loosened the bonds of government everywhere, that children and
> apprentices were disobedient; that schools and colleges were
> grown turbulent; that Indians slighted their guardians, and Ne-
> groes grew insolent to their masters. But your letter was the first
> intimation that another tribe were grown discontented. This is
> rather too coarse a compliment, but you are so saucy, I won't
> blot it out.

Male supremacy, he thought, was an illusion.

> We are obliged to go fair and softly, and, in practice, you know
> we are the subjects. We have only the name of masters, and
> rather than give up this, which would completely subject us to
> the despotism of the petticoat, I hope General Washington and
> all our brave heroes would fight.

Abigail was not to be put off so lightly. She tried to enlist
Mercy Warren in her campaign to "put it out of the power of the
arbitrary and tyrannic to injure us with impunity by establishing
some laws in our favor upon just and liberal principles." To John
she replied:

> I cannot say I think you are very generous to the ladies; for,
> whilst you are proclaiming peace and good will to men, eman-
> cipating all nations, you insist upon retaining an absolute power
> over wives.

She reminded him that

> notwithstanding all your wise laws and maxims, we have it in our

power, not only to free ourselves, but to subdue our master, and, without violence, throw both your natural and legal authority at our feet.

John got too absorbed in Congressional affairs to continue the debate, but he did manage to get leave in December and made the trek from Philadelphia to Braintree in ten days, something of a record, but one achieved by putting aside his Puritan objections to traveling on Sundays. Amid the joys of reunion he took time to answer, somewhat condescendingly, trenchant observations Mercy Warren had made about the matter of governments. He thought women were inclined to be too idealistic about the goodness of men's nature—"men," of course, being used in the generic sense. But Mrs. Warren, like Abigail, was too scholarly to be dismissed lightly; and her theory about a strong, unicameral legislature and a weak executive received a lengthy examination under his pen.

It was a busy, brief vacation. No one could surpass John as a good husband and father or Abigail as a warm, bright wife and mother. Back once more in Philadelphia, he sent her a copy of Thomas Paine's *Common Sense*, just off the presses. Since Paine was unknown, there was wide speculation that either Franklin or Adams himself had written it. "I could not have written anything in so manly and striking a style," John told Abigail, but the modesty was counterbalanced in a letter to James Warren: "He is a keen writer but very ignorant of the science of government."

Still the force of Paine's sentences "charmed" Abigail, who felt no one with "an honest heart . . . who wishes the welfare of his country, and the happiness of posterity, can hesitate one moment at adopting them." If Paine swashbuckled his way over more sober "political principles," he matched the kind of rhythm to which her own thoughts marched.

In March 1776 she once more ran up Penn's Hill, lured by the "incessant roar" of American and British batteries. The noise was

one of the grandest in nature . . . the true species of the sublime!

> . . . but oh! the fatal ideas which are connected with the sound!
> How many of our dear countrymen must fall!

She stayed up until midnight as the firing rattled the windows.

> I sometimes think I cannot stand it. I wish myself with you, out
> of hearing so I cannot assist them . . . I am too much agitated to
> write as I ought, and languid for the want of rest.

She imagined Boston was being leveled in fulfillment of John's prophecy about its martyrdom, but in the morning when all was quiet, it looked serene and unscathed. She was half-disappointed that the only result was that Washington had occupied Dorchester Heights. All the "muster and stir . . . I would not have suffered all I have for two such hills." Howe reacted differently. He was astounded at the swift stroke by which Washington made his position impregnable—trenches dug under the cover of night and fire that would have taken Englishmen three months. On March 17 Abigail saw the impact of the general's strategy, as from her own hill she watched "upwards of a hundred and seventy sail" carry Howe's army out of Boston.

Adams thought her letters, rather than his, should be preserved. In her vivid descriptions she caught the skirts of her own emotions, and scenes came alive for him in distant Philadelphia. There was none of the restraint Puritan discipline dictated. She invoked poets and philosophers to bear witness to her feelings. He was transfixed by the sheer beauty and intelligence of her letters, and incorporated passages, without credit, in his own correspondence and speeches.

When his spirits flagged because his fellow-delegates did not respond to his recommendations, he praised her "capacity to comprehend" as "the choice blessing" of his life. "There are very few people in this world," he confided to her, "with whom I can converse. I can treat all with decency and civility. . . . But I am never happy in their company." Diligent student though he was of Clarendon's technique in politics, he never quite learned the basic premise that politics is the art of accommodation. The self-righteousness of his Puritanism battered against the immobility of some of his colleagues, and he reacted almost like Moses when he beheld the Israelites worshipping the golden calf. "I have a very tender, feeling heart—this country knows not, and never can know, the torments I have endured for its sake." As a compassionate wife she listened, possibly unconvinced by his climactic cry, "Let me have my farm, family and goose quill and all the honors and offices this world has to bestow may go to those who deserve them better and desire them more. I court them not." His spirits revived when the Declaration of Independence was approved, and he turned once more to the quaint character sketches of tradesmen, his barber, and average Philadelphians who had been overshadowed for so many months in his letters by the loom of history. He dreamed of walking with his wife "over to the common, the plain and the meadow . . . Charles in one hand and Tom in the other . . . Abby on your right hand and John on my left, to view the corn fields, the orchards, etc."

"Oh, that I could annihilate space!" she wrote back. "My heart is like a feather and my spirits dancing." His letters were "a feast to me" and she had cried over them. "Nor dare I describe how earnestly I long to fold to my fluttering heart the object of my warmest affections; the idea soothes me. I feast upon it." But she did not "ruminate upon the happiness we might enjoy, lest absence become intolerable."

"I want to hear you think or see your thoughts," he pleaded. "The conclusion of your letter makes my heart throb more than a cannonade would. You bid me burn your letters. But I must forget you first."

Thus the portly, pompous Adams and his austere Abigail, unromantic figures to all but each other, spun their testament of love. It mattered not whether she was talking of pedestrian farm business or giving clinical accounts of the fearsome smallpox inoculations she and the children "took" while John was involved in the tremulous question of independence. Somehow, with a few words, she made them rise from stark realism to rare loveliness. "My anxiety for your welfare will never leave me," she said, almost too weak to hold a pen, "but with my parting breath. 'Tis more important to me than all the world contains." She worried lest his clothes "should go to rags, having nobody to take any care of you in your long absence." To keep him from worrying, she had "slyly" gone into Boston with the children on July 12, and in Hancock's mansion underwent the dread ordeal of inoculation. He scolded her gently, "This might be a kind Intention, and if the design had succeeded, would have made me very joyous. But the secret is out, and I am left to conjecture." He felt "like a savage to be" away "while my family is sick at Boston. But it cannot be avoided . . . I am in the midst of scenes of business which must not stop for anything." There were some anxious moments. "I hang upon Tenterhooks," he wrote on July 27. "Fifteen days since, you were all inocculated and I have not yet learned how you have fared. But I will suppose you all Better and out of Danger. Why should I torture myself when I cant relieve you?" Charles, one of the younger boys, had gone into a coma and for forty-eight hours hovered between life and death, but the crisis was passed when he heard of it. Abigail knew where his duty lay. America was "a secondary god, the first and greatest parent"; and she was proud of his role "when I reflect that a person so nearly connected with me has had the honor of being a principal actor in laying a foundation for its future greatness." The Declaration had been read publicly in King Street to great crowds, some of whom ripped the royal coat of arms from the Massachusetts State House and tossed it into a bonfire. "Thus ends royal authority in this state," Abigail announced in her letter.

Now he felt free to discuss some of the problems of the proposed confederation of states. How should they vote? Should the larger and more populous get a proportionately larger vote than the smaller? Or should each be entitled to just one vote? "You love to pick a political bone so I will throw it to you." She pondered it while asking him if he could find some tea for her migraine.

Few civilians outside the Congress were better informed on what was taking place. Adams described the men, the issues, and the setting. He wished he could have with him "my best, my dearest, my wisest friend in this world," for it would make him "proud and happy as a bridegroom." As always, she was pleased with the impractical dream, but told him the war had drained manpower from Braintree and expected that women would have to harvest the crops: "I believe I could gather corn and husk it, but I should make a poor figure at digging potatoes."

Then he found himself immersed in a deluge of work and there were long gaps in his correspondence. "I have been here, untill I am stupefied. If I set down to write even to you, I am at a Loss what to write," he said on October 7, 1776. He understood her worries at not hearing more frequently, and was more troubled about it than she, but there was just nothing he could do about it. Four days later, he got leave, and jocularly wrote: "I suppose your ladyship has been in the twitters for some time past because you have not received a letter by every post, as you used to do. But I am coming to make my apology in person."

He had been away a long time, and saw firsthand the impact of war as she had described it. With few teachers left, education had been neglected. "The poorer children . . . range the streets, without schools, without business, given up to all evil." Inflation was taking its toll. Her prayers were "for peace and tranquility. All my desire and ambition is to be esteemed and loved by my partner, to join with him in the education and instruction of our little ones, to sit under our own vines in peace, liberty and safety."

That was still a distant dream, for by November Washington, retreating across New Jersey from heavy losses sustained in New York, was heading for the cold comfort of Bucks County, Pennsylvania, uncertain whether he could save Philadelphia from the pursuing British.

In December the prospect became so real Congress adjourned to Baltimore, but Washington made his famous crossing of the Delaware and inflicted major defeats on the enemy at Trenton and Princeton. These events transpired without disturbing Adams's holiday, and before he headed south after the New Year to go to Baltimore, he was able to count two months and nine days he shared with Abigail and his children. "My good genius, my guardian angel," he exulted from the road, "whispers to me that we shall see happier days, and that I shall live to enjoy the felicities of domestic life with her whom my heart esteems above all earthly things."

With danger averted, Congress came back to Philadelphia, and Adams saw, in February, signs of an early spring, which made his "longing imagination" encompass "my little farm and its dear inhabitants" and wistfully sitting "with her who has all my heart by the side of the brooks" and listening to "the prattle of my children." Spring held no such promise for Abigail, who discovered she was pregnant. All of her pregnancies had been hard, magnifying the normal fears of death in childbirth. It also magnified her loneliness, and she tried to conjure him in her dreams. "I visit you almost every night," she wrote, "or you me, but waking the agreeable delusion vanishes—'like the baseless fabrick of a vision.'" The children, she said, delighted in his letters to them, but little Tommy, the youngest, had been heartbroken because he hadn't received one—not so much an oversight as due to the fact that he could not yet read. The little fellow talked about being a general. Adams sent him a note: "I believe I must make a physician of you," and then went on to explain why in sentences better suited to a nineteen-year-old. If he could not put things simply to children, he at least never spoke down to them, and made them reach to understand him.

He told ten-year-old John Quincy he must read Thucydides in the original Greek, but might borrow Hobbes's translation from his library to help in the process. The child replied:

> I love to receive letters very well much better than I love to write them, but I make but a poor figure at composition, my head is much too fickle; my thoughts are running after birds' eggs, play and trifles, till I get vexed with myself.

Thus did two future presidents communicate in the persons of father and son.

As summer approached Abigail became more anxious to have John by her side. "Is it weakness?" she asked him, but never one to dwell long on the uncertain future, she expressed her indignation at present prices: "A Dollor now is not eaquel to what one Quarter was two years ago," and she flatly said she would buy no new clothes even if it meant returning to the fashions of Eve.

"You will have Patience with me," he pleaded, explaining it was impossible to be with her when the baby was due, and reasserting his oft-expressed determination to quit public life. During the night of July 8, 1777, Abigail was taken with "a shaking fit," and she had the frightening prescience "that a life was lost." An affectionate letter from John came the next day and on the tenth a "fine looking" baby girl was born dead. Just as he mourned throughout life for their second daughter who died before she was a year old, so now he mingled his thanksgiving for Abigail's safety with sadness for the little girl lost: "Is it not unaccountable, that one should feel so strong an Affection for an Infant, that one has never seen, nor shall see? Yet I must confess to you, the Loss of this sweet little Girl, has most tenderly and sensibly affected me."

Abigail apparently deemed it best not to let sorrow unnerve her. It could only add to the burden of her husband; so she wrote the precious infant seemed as "transitory as the morning cloud" and set about to cheer an absent husband. "If you will come home and turn farmer I will be dairy woman [and] we will grow wealthy." But Philadelphia heat and the endless demands of work sapped his strength. "I am wasted and exhasted in mind and body, but if I can possibly endure it, will hold out the year." He soliloquized about the three years that had passed since he took the coach to Philadelphia "in quest of adventures—and adventures I have found" but at what a price. "What have I not suffered? What have I not hazarded. . . . Never was [a] wretch more weary of misery than I am of the life I lead, condemned to the dullest servitude, separated from all that I love, and wedded to all that I hate. Digging in a potato yard upon my own garden and living in my own family would be to me paradise. The next time I come home shall be for a long time" but, as if to put temptation behind

him, he would not "leave the field until the campaign is ended."
She gave him solace:

> I feel my sufferings amply rewarded in the tenderness you ex-
> press for me. . . . It is almost thirteen years since we were united,
> but not more than half that time have we had the happiness of
> living together. The unfeeling world may consider it in what light
> they please. I consider it as a sacrifice to my country, and one of
> my greatest misfortunes, for you to be separated from my chil-
> dren, at a time of life when the joint instructions and admoni-
> tions of parents sink deeper than in maturer years.

Adams and his wife had no time to commiserate, for in September
the British were again poised for the conquest of Philadelphia;
and when they opened their fall campaign in 1777 by defeating
Washington at Brandywine and again at Germantown in October,
Adams and the Congress were forced to flee to York, Pennsylvania.
He told her not to worry, but with so many of the eminent figures
from the Congress of 1776 gone—Jefferson back to Virginia, Franklin to France—she saw no valid reason why he should have to remain. A dream had frightened her, for in it she saw him return to
Braintree "but met me so coldly that my heart ached half an hour
after I waked." "I cannot consent to your tarrying much longer,"
she wrote,

> I shall send you word by and by and by, as Regulus' steward did,
> that whilst you are engaged in the Senate your own domestic
> affairs require your presence at home, and that your wife and
> children are in danger of wanting bread. If the Senate of America
> will take care of us, as the Senate of Rome did of the family of
> Regulus, you may serve them again, but unless you return, what
> little property you possess will be lost.

She told him however gloomy the picture might be

> We possess a spirit that will not be conquered. If our men are all
> drawn off and we should be attacked, you would find a race of
> Amazons in America.

And if anyone sued for peace with England, "an army of women would oppose him."

During the tense days before Congress evacuated Philadelphia Abigail asked John for a map of the area so she might follow the military movements. Preoccupied with pressures of the moment, Adams asked his fellow delegate from Massachusetts, James Lovell, to get one. When it arrived under Lovell's frank, Abigail grew alarmed, fearing that something might have happened to her husband. Once that shock was passed, she got another, for the accompanying letter contained this curious passage, explaining why he mailed it directly instead of merely giving it to her husband:

> I could not with delicacy have told him *to his face* that your having given your heart to *such* a man is what, most of all, makes me yours.

Under the thin veil of praise for Adams Lovell waxed warm for Abigail. Two years younger than John, Lovell, a skilled linguist and mathematician, had gone from Harvard to the faculty of his father's South Grammar (now Boston Latin) School. He had first come into public notice with an address on the first anniversary of the Boston Massacre, which clearly put him on the side of the patriots and directly opposed to his father's loyalist views. The school was closed by the British on April 19, 1775, and when the confrontation heated up, Lovell was charged with espionage in March 1776, and carried off as a prisoner to Halifax. In November he was exchanged and received a rousing welcome from Bostonians. The wave of enthusiasm sent him to the Continental Congress, where he took his seat in February 1777. Since the various state delegations often lodged in the same house and frequently dined together, he undoubtedly heard much about Abigail. The map gave him the opportunity to find how sophisticated this legendary woman was, and, better still, provided him with the possibility of an interesting affair.

For all her idyllic devotion to Adams, Abigail was lonely, and if her Puritan ancestry occasionally acted as a brake, it never was her complete guideline. As she grew older she became prettier and increasingly sensuous, and her bold intelligence drew a number of admiring young men to the parlor at Braintree. One such, her handsome first cousin, John Thaxter, seems to have spent a good part of his leisure time in her company. She frequently took advantage of his bachelorhood to talk quite explicitly about the delights of marriage, possibly for her own amusement because of his natural reserve, possibly for titillation. In any event Thaxter never tried to test her and thereby left a tantalizing question unanswered.

Lovell was something else. Caustic, fond of the double entendre, and totally uninhibited, he both puzzled and pleased her. She sent him a brief note of thanks and, in reporting the receipt of the map to John, described the Lovell letter as "very polite." Having breached the wall at Braintree, however, Lovell began to write quite regularly, even appropriating one of Adams's pet names for Abigail, "Portia," and brazenly asking Adams to intercede with "Portia" on his behalf if she got angered by some of his pithy paragraphs. On such occasions he assumed the mask of innocence, and it is doubtful that Abigail disclosed the contents. Adams got leave from Congress in November 1777, and rode out of York on a circuitous route home to keep clear of the British-occupied Philadelphia area. Washington was camped at Whitemarsh, some twenty miles north of the city, and on December 19 would move his troops into Valley Forge. Lovell promised to keep John posted on developments in Congress, thus preserving good relations with the master of Braintree while pursuing his curious courtship, by correspondence, of its mistress.

Adams, back by his "blissful fireside, surrounded by a wife and a parcel of chattering boys and girls," was determined not to stand for re-election to Congress. He picked up his law practice again and was beginning to make up lost income when Congress tapped him to replace Silas Deane as one of the three commissioners to France. Lovell enthusiastically urged him to accept, and Adams put the question to Abigail. She agonized, saying that he had only been home a few weeks, but she "found his honor and reputation much dearer to me than my own pleasure and happiness." The departure date was set for February 1778, aboard the new twenty-four-gun frigate *Boston*; the couple decided John Quincy should accompany his father.

The long ocean voyage, made doubly hazardous by British warships, proved fascinating for Adams and his son, since the *Boston* took a prize and barely escaped being captured herself by three enemy frigates, and then, nearing Europe, slipped by two heavily gunned ships in bright moonlight. Abigail, bracing herself for a more extended absence from John, wrote within a few days after he sailed to John Thaxter. She expressed concern over letting John Quincy accompany his father for fear of the influence France might have upon him. Characteristically, however, she concluded, "to exclude him from temptation would be to exclude him from the world in which he is to live, and the only method which can be pursued is to fix the padlock upon the mind." Then she asked him to convey a message to Lovell that since, as a congressman, he helped take her husband from her, she expected he would keep her informed on what was taking place in Congress. "I feel very lonely and miss you exceedingly," she told Thaxter.

Lovell, who had written a particularly ardent letter before Adams departed, had asked him to "become a reconciling advocate for me with your dear lovely Portia," blaming it all on the ink—"that black and mischievous liquor." Adams was bemused. Now Lovell had an invitation from Abigail herself to reestablish communications. He was soon busy with his lusty pen. Abigail professed to be shocked each time, and received in return such hurt exclamations as "Amiable though unjust Portia! doubly unjust!—to yourself, and to me." "Must I only write to you in the language of gazettes?" He was bored with his colleagues, "he-creatures, drudging, plodding politicians," but told her that if she found his pen offensive, he would content himself with "secret admiration."

Abigail was not quite ready to dismiss him. "I begin to look upon you as a very dangerous man . . . a most ingenuous and a public flatterer." Still she admitted she read his letters "with a pleasure which the communicative manner of your writing must always give to your correspondence." Everything after the word "pleasure" is meaningless jargon, and both of them knew it. Thus inspired, Lovell congratulated her in July 1778, a safe distance away from the day she kissed Adams good-bye, on not being pregnant. "I will take pleasure in your escape" from Adams's "rigid patriotism."

Somewhat conditioned by now, Abigail gave him leave "to make use of whatever expressions he pleases," since "the talent for which I formerly censured . . . is natural to him . . . nor would I rob him of the pleasure he takes in thus indulging" in flattery because of his proficiency. Tongue in cheek, he lamented he had ever, by carelessness, caused "a pressure to your lovely palpitating bosom" and added that, reading her most recent letter in "a grave assembly," he almost exclaimed "audibly . . . 'gin ye were mine ain thing how dearly would I love thee!" Having made his point, he admitted that a second reading did not warrant such a happy interpretation, but he was content to forget that in favor of his first impressions. In a more sinister stroke he consoled her for the long silence from John by telling her he was certain her husband was using his spare moments in cultural pursuits and was concentrating only on "the mistress of his happiness, *a Portia.*"

An English newspaper reaching Boston carried an item that Adams had arrived in France and thus relieved the tension triggered by the false rumor of his capture. Earlier when the tale was still current she had reaffirmed her faith in a letter to him:

> Were it not for this [her faith] I would be miserable and over-whelmed by my fears and apprehensions . . . Difficult as the day is, cruel as this war has been, separated as I am on account of it from the dearest connection in life, I would not exchange my country for the wealth of the Indies, or be any other than an American, though I might be queen or empress of any nation upon the globe . . . Beneath my humble roof, blessed with the society and tenderest affection of my dear partner, I have en-

joyed as much felicity and as exquisite happiness as falls to the
share of mortals.

She was less rhapsodic when his first letters, written in the haste
and confusion of getting settled in France, arrived. They were
brief, and she was angry:

> Could you, after a thousand fears and anxieties, long expectation
> and painful suspense, be satisfied with my telling you that I was
> well, that I wished you were with me, that my daughter sent her
> duty, that I had ordered some articles for you, which I hoped
> would arrive, etc. etc.? By heaven, if you could, you have
> changed hearts with some frozen Laplander, or made a voyage to
> a region that has chilled every drop of your blood!

Then three more expansive letters came and she hastened to
amend her earlier pique, saying she touched them to her heart
and "soothed myself to rest with the tender assurances of a heart
all my own." But he got her bitter blast first and cried out:

> For God's sake, never reproach me again with not writing or
> with writing scrips. Your wounds are too deep. You know not,
> you feel not, the dangers that surround me nor those that may be
> brought upon our country. Millions would not tempt me to write
> you as I used. I have no security that every letter I write will not
> be broken open and copied, and transmitted to Congress and to
> English newspapers . . . There are spies upon every word I utter,
> and every syllable I write. Spies planted by the English, spies
> planted by stock jobbers, spies planted by selfish merchants, and
> spies planted by envious and malicious politicians . . . My life
> has been often in danger, but I never considered my reputation
> and character so much in danger as now. I can pass for a fool,
> but I will not pass for a dishonest or mercernary man. Be upon
> your guard, therefore, I must be upon mine, and I will.

She had been anxious to know something of court life—the manners, the styles, and attitudes—as well as, as he put it, "all the
mysteries of the politics of Europe, and all the intrigues." These
last he brushed aside testily on the grounds that he just did not

know enough about them. As to queries on fashions and mores, he overreacted:

> For mercy sake don't exact of me that I should be a boy till I am seventy years of age. That kind of correspondence will do for young gentlemen and ladies under twenty . . . but old men, borne down with years and cares, can no more amuse themselves with such things than with toys, marbles and whirligigs. If I ever had any wit it is all evaporated—if I ever had any imagination it is all quenched. Pray consider your age and the gravity of your character, the mother of six children, one of them grown up, who ought never to be out of your sight, nor ever to have an example of indiscretion set before her. . . . If I were to tell you all the tenderness of my heart, I should do nothing but write to you. I beg of you not to be uneasy.

The crisis passed, and their happiness in each other was reasserted. John and John Quincy returned to Braintree in August 1779, and Abigail exulted, but her happiness was once more interrupted. Massachusetts had asked his help in drafting a constitution. That much she could stand, for he was not too far from home. Then Congress beckoned again, naming him minister plenipotentiary to negotiate treaties of peace and commerce with Great Britain. He was asked to go to Holland, and the nature of the mission was so secret that not even Franklin in Paris was to know about it. This time, in addition to John Quincy, he took his son Charles and John Thaxter as his personal secretary. So less than four months had been spent at home.

No sooner had their ship put out to sea than Abigail was back at her desk writing them letters. She had learned to live without her husband, but felt the deep maternal twinge at seeing her two boys set off for foreign places. Thaxter had his special place in her affections, and she would tease him about Parisian women as she did about the belles in Philadelphia, trying to break down what he described as his "cold, phlegmatic" attitude toward them. But first, she thought of little Charles, whose happy personality endeared him to everyone. "You was a favorite in the neighborhood, all of whom wonder how Mamma could part with you," but young as he was, he got the family admonition to make himself "useful to society." Then to John Quincy magnificent lines, reminding him that life was a gift of God and not to be spent "to gratify an idle curiosity"—that such a gift carried an obligation to his Creator and "in particular to your country." He must pursue with diligence the goal of the ancient Greek philosophers, "the knowledge and study of yourself." He was privileged to live in a time of greatness, and that demanded greatness of him. "You, my dear son, are formed with a constitution feelingly alive. Your passions are strong and impetuous. Yet though I have sometimes seen them hurry you into escapades, yet with pleasure I have observed a frankness and generosity accompanying your efforts to govern and subdue yourself."

Few twelve-year-olds were more aware of duty than John Quincy. He had become so proficient in French that he had served as John's secretary on the first trip across, and was given rough drafts of his father's letters to copy in finished style. Poignantly he had written letters of advice to his younger brothers, urging them to measure their own time carefully, and not to fritter it away. The Adamses had every reason to be proud of their four handsome children, and Nabby, the eldest and only surviving daughter, was a particular joy. Blonde and beautiful at fifteen, her education was as scrupulously attended to as her brothers' and she was in school at Boston.

Lovell, with John safely out of the way, kept Abigail apprised of Congressional activities and continued his siege:

> How *do* you do, lovely Portia, these very cold days? Mistake me not willfully: I said *days*.

His room in Philadelphia was chilly, but he managed not to covet his roommate's blanket:

> But really I doubt whether I shall be able to keep myself void of all covetousness. I suspect I shall covet to be in the arms of Portia

The page ended and continued on the back:

> 's friend and admirer—the wife of my bosom . . . There was not
> room to write *turn over*. I hope, however, that you did not stop
> long without doing so, madam, because a quick turnover alone
> could save the tenth commandment entire; and you must see now
> plainly that I had not the smallest suspicion of my being driven
> by my present sufferings to make a frantic breach there.

He referred her to Ecclesiastes 4:11, and knew she would pick up
her Bible to read:

> Again, if two lie together, then they have heat; but how can
> one be warm alone?

With Adams reminding her of her mature age, and Lovell
appealing to her charms, the thirty-six-year-old Abigail was not
about to cut off the correspondence. There were risks in trying to
match his type of wit. The wonder of it all is that he did not show
up in person, and that would inevitably be the course he would
take if she dropped her guard. She called him "a wicked man" but
attributed it to the assumption that he had been leading a monas-
tic life in Philadelphia, and his admiration of Sterne's *Tristram
Shandy*, which he repeatedly suggested she read and she repeatedly refused because it was "too vile." Or so she said, although
she was able to tell him she thought Sterne's bawdiness was

> intermixed with a rich stream of benevolence flowing like milk
> and honey . . . Possessed of an exquisite sensibility, a universal
> philanthropy—what a perverse genius must he have to hazard
> those fine powers and talents for a wicked wit.

She did not wait for him to see himself in that mirror of morality,
but put his reflection right into the frame:

> I have charity enough for the writer to believe that his asso-
> ciates have been wholly of his own sex for three years past, or he
> could not have so offended.

She promised that she had burned his letters, and pleaded he do the same with hers. Fortunately, neither did so.

Lovell professed his usual innocence. How could this "lovely moralist" interpret his remarks "about the keen air of the days" and his longing for "the comfort of my domestic fireside" as anything but a lamentation for his "separation from my own faithful mate?"

She could hardly go into detail. Letters were always being read by curious postmen and quite often appeared in the newspapers before they reached the addressees. So she could only grin at his impertinence, and continue to brighten his life as he did hers.

Abigail never made the mistake mature women frequently do, that of underestimating their appeal. Adams might jokingly say at fifty he was too old to be attractive to American women who made a fetish of youth, and too young to appeal to French women who preferred elderly men like Franklin. Abigail was attractive to younger and older men alike, and more important, she knew it; so there was never any feeling of despair.

Like John, she had a wide range of interests, and gave them —however prosaic—added definition by her extensive knowledge of the classics, literature, and poetry. Exulting over a spring morning, she could intone: "To feel the present Deity, and taste / The joy of God, to see a happy world" and wrap it in lines from Milton. Where Adams sometimes became pedantic, she never pontificated, making ethical observations pithy and pointed, and not dwelling interminably upon them.

Both she and her husband had the capacity to grow. On his first voyage to France, Adams had made it his business to learn as much as possible about ship-handling, along with learning enough of the French language to get about. Their conversations enriched each other and she, more than he, had the knack of enriching the lives of others. Flirtations, with their invariable tributes to her femininity, never made her lose sight of her horizons—and Adams's face, which Peale described as soft, gentle, and compassionate, and which its fussy proprietor thought was growing flaccid and weak, was her never-setting sun. "Two years, my dearest friend," she wrote in December 1781, "have passed since you left your native land. Will you not return ere the close of another year?"

She was adept at business, selling the trinkets and laces and things he purchased abroad, to keep abreast of the inflated prices; she managed the farm and bought some added acreage, along with a tract in Vermont she knew he wanted. If she was alert to any shortcomings in her children, she objectively measured them against her own. As a woman she had singular pride in her daughter, describing her to the affectionate father as one who would not "make an ungraceful appearance at the head of your table" if he invited her to Holland. "She has a stateliness in her manners which some misconstrue into pride and haughtiness, but which rather results from a too great reserve . . . she wants more affability . . . Her manners rather forbid all kinds of intimacy." On the other hand Abigail looked back on her own youth and thought herself too sensuous "to be very prudent" as Adams might recall from their courtship days.

When Royall Tyler, fresh from Harvard, came to call upon Nabby he was so captivated by Abigail he was hard put to ascertain whether mother or daughter was magnetizing him. A wild, wealthy, good-looking young man, he delighted Abigail with his sparkling, sometimes brilliant, conversation; and Nabby admired the manner in which he blended his untamed spirit with an uncommon degree of learning. With Abigail he shared a love of poetry and brought some of his own to read to her, and the talk moved easily into Shakespeare, Milton, Dryden, playwrights and novelists, and such old literary friends and ancient philosophers long cherished by Abigail. Tyler became a suitor for Nabby's hand, and resolved to settle down and study law. He had Abigail fairly well convinced he had forsaken his wanton ways. She broached the courtship to John with some hesitation:

> His patrimony . . . has been his bane—for with a disposition naturally volatile and gay, an easy address, an agreeable person, he became the favorite of the gay and fair.

Still, with "all these temptations and allurements to vice, the world accused him not of more than gaiety and volubility." He was, Abigail said, "exceedingly amiable."

"I confess," replied Adams, "I don't like the subject at all." He did not want Nabby, who he felt was too young to marry, "to be the prize, I hope, of any, even reformed, rake." A frivolous young man who had devoted his time to "gaieties . . . is not the youth for me, let his family, connections and taste for poetry be what they will." He wanted neither "a poet nor a professor of belle letters" for a son-in-law. "I positively forbid any connection between my daughter and any youth upon earth who does not totally eradicate every taste for gaiety and expense." Moreover

> I don't like this method of courting mothers. There is something too fantastical and affected in this business for me—it is not nature, modest, virtuous, noble nature . . . I would give the world to be with you tomorrow . . . I don't love to go home in a miff, pet or passion nor with an ill grace.

Then he wrote to Nabby, who so many said looked like him:

> "My image", my "superscription", my "princess," take care how you dispose of your heart. I hoped to be at home and to have chosen a partner for you—or at least to have given you some good advice before you should choose. . . . [Pick] a thinking being, and one who thinks for others' good and feels another's woe. It must be one who can ride five hundred miles upon a trotting horse and cross the Gulf Stream with a steady heart. One may dance or sing, play or ride, without being good for much.

Still not satisfied, he sent off another letter to Abigail:

> [He is] but a prodigal son, and though a penitent, has no right to your daughter, who deserves a character without a spot . . . You seem to me to have favored this affair far too much, and I wish it off . . . I cannot judge . . . I must submit to my daughter's destiny, to her own judgment and her own heart, with your advice and the advice of our parents and brothers and sisters and uncles and aunts, etc. . . . I had flattered myself with the hopes of

a few years of the society of this daughter at her father's house. But if it must be otherwise I must submit.

Abigail was not to be lectured:

> . . . you write so wise, like a minister of state . . . Life takes its complexion from inferior things. It is little attentions and assiduities that sweeten the bitter draft and smooth the rugged road.

As to Tyler and Nabby:

> I scarcely believe it in my power to prevent [it] without doing violence to hearts which I hope are honest and good.

Then inexplicably the young couple fell out. Nabby was crushed, and was sent off to Boston for the winter to mend her broken heart. A young French officer, attached to the fleet, helped to some extent to divert her mind, and when he sailed off he sent Abigail a note of gratitude for the company of Nabby and her:

> Shall I ever be so happy as that she should deign to awake in her mind a remembrance of him whose breast she has inspired with the most indelible sentiments!

but he did not identify the "she" who so inspired him.

Tyler came back, still avowing his love, but Nabby admitted him as a friend, rather than a suitor. Abigail reported to John:

> His temper and disposition appear to be good . . . He is regular in his living, keeps no company with gay companions, seeks no amusement but in the society of two or three families in town. Never goes to Boston but when business calls him there.

These alterations designed to please John and Abigail may have made him less alluring to Nabby, for when she ultimately married, the groom was not Royall Tyler.

Despite the fact that Harvard was Adams's alma mater, its reputation was fast being shaped along the original Tyler lines;

and Abigail worried about its suitability for her three sons, or at least for the elder two, who were fast approaching matriculation age. She thought the philosophy of Voltaire, Hume, and Mandeville too enticing to young minds, but could see Christianity, as it was taught, "gives not such pleasing latitude to the passions. It is too pure. It teaches moderation, humility and patience, which are incompatible with the high glow of health and the warm blood which riots in their veins."

Another wedding anniversary was spent alone:

> The family are all retired to rest; the busy scenes of the day are over; a day which I wished to have devoted in a particular manner to my dearest friend . . . Look to the date of this letter, and tell me what are the thoughts which arise in your mind. Do you recollect that eighteen years have run their circuit since we pledged our mutual faith to each other, and the hymeneal torch was lighted at the altar of Love? Yet, yet it burns with unabating fervor. Old Ocean has not quenched it, nor old Times mothered it in his bosom. It cheers me in the lonely hour; it comforts me even in the gloom which sometimes possesses my mind. . . .
>
> Life is too short to have its dearest enjoyments curtailed . . . Could we live to the age of the antediluvians, we might better support this separation; but when threescore years and ten circumscribe the life of man, how painful is the idea of that short space only a few years of social happiness are our allotted portion. Perhaps I make you unhappy. No. You will enter with a soothing tenderness into my feelings. I see in your eyes the emotions of your heart.

For Adams the absence was made more excruciating by the problems that beset his mission. Jealousies among American diplomats, the tedium of negotiations, the need to placate foreigners and a spate of illnesses—one of which almost carried him off— these were enough to make him long for Abigail and the simple life at Braintree.

But she no longer believed the plaintive cry. When Thaxter wrote of her John's oft-expressed wish to be home, she shook her head:

I have no reason to think that my friend would be permitted to retire from public life whilst his active powers can be of any service to his country. A state of inactivity was never meant for man; love and the desire of glory . . . [are] . . . the most delicate and rational passions.

The war was ended and independence established. Abigail believed:

. . . peace will ruin more merchants and traders than the war—many solemn faces you see in consequence of it. No such rapid fortunes to be acquired now. Taxes heavy, very heavy—trade stagnated, money scarce.

But among the blessings were items close to the hearts of women, and Abigail asked her husband for

two green silk umbrellas and two pieces of Irish linen; oh, dear Ireland, no linen like yours, so white, so strong.

Rumors were rampant that Adams was to be named ambassador to Great Britain. It worried her

to think of going to England in a public character and engaging at my time of life [thirty-eight] and John [forty-eight] in scenes quite new, attended with dissipation, parade and nonsense, I am sure I would make an awkward figure. The retired domestic circle, the feast of reason and the flow of soul are my ideas of happiness . . . My health is infirm. I am still subject to severe nervous pains in my head, and a fatigue of any kind will produce it. Mere American as I am, unacquainted with the etiquette of courts, taught to say the things I mean and to wear my heart in my countenance . . .

On the other hand

. . . strip royalty of its pomp and power, and what are its votaries more than their fellow worms? I have so little of the ape about me that I have refused every public invitation to figure in the gay world, and I have sometimes smiled upon recollecting that I had the honor of being allied to an ambassador.

Adams wanted her and Nabby to come to Europe, although he feared taking them to Paris because

> you will get into your female imaginations fantastical ideas that will never wear out, and will spoil you both

but it would get Nabby away from Tyler and

> . . . if the parties reserve their regard until they meet again and continue to behave as they ought they will still be young enough. Lawyers should never marry early . . . Knowledge of the law comes not by inspiration, and without painful and obstinate study no man will ever have it.

Adams had relented toward Tyler, offering him the use of his law office and library if Nabby came with her mother, and gave a blessing that was never to be used:

> . . . you and the young lady have my consent to arrange your plans according to your own judgments, and I pray God to bless and prosper you both whether together or asunder.

So, after a tearful farewell Nabby joined Abigail and boarded the *Active* in June 1784. Jefferson raced from Philadelphia to Boston to ask Abigail to change her plans and sail with him out of New York in July. It was quite a tribute to the lovely lady, and undoubtedly the sea voyage with him as a companion would have been stimulating. She had to beg off, for Adams had been expecting them for weeks.

The crossing was rough. The cow she brought to keep them in fresh milk and cream was so bruised by the heavy seas by the time they reached Newfoundland she had to be killed. But Abigail weathered bouts of seasickness, the bad food, and the dirty quarters by thinking of "the joyful day of meeting my long absent partner" and the "unutterable happiness which love alone bestows . . . on a favored few."

Aboard the *Active* on July 4, 1784, she spoke of her other love. The bright, clear weather seemed appropriate for "the an-

niversary of our Glorious Independence," and she jotted in her
journal a prayer and some thoughts:

> Whilst the nations of Europe are enveloped in luxury and dissi-
> pation and a universal venality prevails throughout Britain, may
> the new empire, Gracious Heaven, become the guardian and
> protector of religion and liberty, of universal benevolence and
> philanthropy. May those virtues which are banished from the
> land of our nativity find a safe asylum with the inhabitants of
> this new world.
>
> As our country becomes more populous we shall be daily
> making new discoveries and vie in some future day with the most
> celebrated European nation; for as yet, we may say, with the
> Queen of Sheba, the one half has not been told. We are but in
> the infancy of science, and have but just begun to form societies
> for the propagation and encouragement of the fine arts.

As the *Active* approached England, she wrote excitedly:

> Am I so near the land of my forefathers? And am I, Gracious
> Heaven, there to meet the dear long absent partner of my heart?
> How many, how various, how complicated my sensations.

And then, with a resolute air of independence she added,

> Be it unto me according to *my* wishes.

Best of Wives—Best of Women

Elizabeth Schuyler Hamilton

Twenty-two-year-old Alexander Hamilton had definite ideas about what he wanted in a wife. From Morristown, New Jersey, where the army was in winter quarters in December 1779, he wrote facetiously to John Laurens:

> I empower and command you to get me one in Carolina . . . She must be young, handsome (I lay most stress upon a good shape), sensible (a little learning will do) well bred . . . chaste, and tender (I am an enthusiast in my notions of fidelity and fondness), of some good nature, a great deal of generosity (she must neither love money nor scolding, for I dislike equally a termagant and an economist) . . . As to religion a moderate stock will satisfy me. She must believe in God and hate a saint.

Then he paused and asked:

> Do I want a wife? No, I have plagues enough without desiring to add to the number that greatest of them all.

Like most letters it was a soliloquy. The mind that produced it, however, was precision-honed. When Hamilton, within a few months, became engaged to Elizabeth Schuyler, of Albany, she met every specification of his blueprint. The second daughter of the autocratic, baronial General Philip Schuyler, she was seven months younger than Hamilton. They made an attractive couple. Her quiet charm complemented his polished grace, and people were captivated by her kindly brown eyes just as they were often transfixed by his deep-set violet-blue eyes. She was a brunette and his hair was auburn. Meticulously tailored, he carried his five-foot, seven-inch slenderness erect, and his bearing communicated his exquisite sense of integrity. Yet beneath his cool composure he was a mixture of "fire and logic."

Some thought there was more logic than fire in Hamilton's choice. Colonel Fleury, viewing it through French eyes, congratulated his friend on the "conquest" through which "you will get all that family's interest, & . . . a man of your abilities wants a Little influence to do good to his country . . . you will be in a very easy situation, & happiness is not to be found without a large Estate."

Hamilton did not underestimate the advantage of a rich alliance. He had admonished Laurens to "pay special attention" to it in lining up a prospective bride. "You know my temper and circumstances. . . ." Still it was an afterthought. He was too independent and ambitious to want apathetic affluence, and too proud to be subservient to another's wealth. Exacting to the penny in discharging any office of trust, throughout his life he was generously indifferent with his own money, leaving the tedium of domestic budgeting to his wife.

There were other considerations. Hamilton had no family, and the Schuyler household, with four fascinating daughters (one of whom was too young for any suitors, but still delightful company), was like an oasis to American officers, and even the British, who were hosted by General Schuyler after Burgoyne's defeat at Saratoga. Anthony Wayne, although he regarded their father as a "caitiff," let neither his feelings nor his marriage interfere with visits when he was in the vicinity.

> The General's daughters are accomplished, fine, sweet girls and very handsome. Had I been single, perhaps I might have made some impression, but as that was not the case, it would have been cruel to endeavor to win the affections of an innocent, good girl. I therefore studiously endeavored to keep out of the way of temptation, but was, notwithstanding, necessitated to pass four or five evenings out of six (being the time I was in Albany) in their company.

Translated, this means Wayne either did not think it wise because of Schuyler's connections to get involved, or could not. Angelica, the eldest, was the most beautiful and vivacious. Educated at a fashionable academy in New Rochelle, she acquired a cosmopolitan approach that would have shocked her patroon forebears as much as her elopement with a John Barker stunned her parents. Since they placed considerable emphasis upon the lineage of any suitor, and had no knowledge of Barker's background, the swift marriage without their blessing, consent, or awareness troubled them. It had a happy ending, for the groom's name was really John Barker Church, an English gentleman of substance who fled his homeland to avoid some complications in the aftermath of a duel, supported the patriot cause, and subsequently returned with Angelica to England and a seat in Parliament.

Hamilton had only seen Angelica through portraits during his courtship of Betsy. Something in them must have suggested to him if he needed fire in his marriage, Angelica could supply it. His perceptiveness was the more remarkable since Angelica only knew of him through table talk. He wrote her a letter under the pretext of getting her assistance in his suit, which was idle gallantry since Betsy had long since surrendered.

> I have not the happiness of a personal acquaintance with you. I have had the good fortune to see several very pretty pictures of your person and mind which have inspired me with a more than common partiality for both. Among others, your sister carries a beautiful copy constantly about her elegantly drawn by herself,

of which she has two or three times favoured me with a sight. You will no doubt admit it as a full proof of my frankness and good opinion of you, that I with so little ceremony introduce myself to your acquaintance and at the first step make you my confident.

Then followed long, lavish paragraphs in praise of Betsy.

I should never have done, were I to attempt to give you a cata- logue . . . of all the hearts she has vanquished—of all the heads she has turned—of all the philosophers she has unmade . . . It is essential to the safety of the state and to the tranquility of the army—that one of two things take place, either that she be im- mediately removed from our neighborhood, or that some other nymph qualified to maintain an equal sway come into it. By dividing her empire it will be weakened and she will be much less dangerous when she has a rival equal in charms to dispute the prize with her. I solicit your aid.

Much as Angelica admired her sister, she was realistic enough to dismiss the courtly, saccharine sentences and sense the mean- ing of the message. When they finally met, a strong bond of affec- tion developed that was to last through all Hamilton's life. Nine- teen years later, from Philadelphia Harrison Gray Otis wrote this item to his wife:

Tuesday Dined at Breck's, with Mrs. Church, Miss Schuyler, Genl. Hamilton . . . &c &c. Mrs. C. the mirror of affectation, but as she affects to be extremely affable and free from ceremony, this foible is rather amusing than offensive. Miss [Peggy] Schuy- ler a young wild flirt from Albany, full of glee & apparently desirous of matrimony. After Dinner Mrs. C. dropped her shoe bow. Miss S___ picked it up and put it in Hamiltons buttonhole saying "there brother I have made you a Knight." "But of what order" (says Madam C) "he can't be a Knight of the garter in this country." "True sister" replied Miss S___ "but *he would be if you would let him!*"

But the retiring, lovely Betsy was not to be underestimated. Before she was aware Hamilton was seriously interested in her, she met a young Philadelphia woman at Morristown who was quite confident he intended to marry her. When Tench Tilghman heard of the engagement he wrote to his brother: "Alas, poor Polly! Hamilton is a gone man." Polly returned to Pennsylvania thinking "she need not be jealous of the little Saint" and had "no other impressions than those of regard for a very pretty good tempered Girl."

If Betsy contemplated making any changes in Hamilton once they were married, she left no record of such a notion. He, on the other hand, was obviously a bit troubled she had not followed Angelica's lead in furthering her education.

> I entreat you, my charmer, not to neglect the charges I gave you, particularly that of taking care of yourself and that of employing all your leisure in reading. Nature has been very kind to you, do not neglect to cultivate her gifts and to enable yourself to make the distinguished figure in all respects to which you are entitled to aspire. You excel most of your sex in all the amiable qualities, endeavor to excel them equally in the splendid ones. You can do it if you please, and I shall take pride in it.—It will be a fund too to diversify our enjoyment and amusements and fill all our moments to advantage.

Like most such campaigns this was ineffective. Betsy preferred the domestic arts. She had her own personal magnetism, however, and scores of unanswered letters from various friends all invariably pleaded for a reply. Even her fiancé gently rebuked her for being a poor correspondent. Hamilton was to need her solid devotion more than her scholarship. He could sparkle in salons while she, presumably without objection, was content to care for him, the children, and their home. One genius in a family is usually enough. Hamilton, sufficiently complex and capable to intrigue generations of biographers and admirers, along with critics, was lucky to have a woman who made him her life study. Whatever face he presented to the world, Hamilton was idolized by his wife, children, and in-laws. Angelica's passion for him was to increase in intensity; his father-in-law, whose brusque manner alienated many, beamed with unflagging admiration.

It is unlikely that Hamilton mentioned his illegitimacy in any premarital discussions. John Adams was to cruelly describe him at a future date as "the bastard brat of a Scotch pedlar." By then it was common knowledge, and he was too famous to be tripped by such a trifle. Yet he always felt the sting, and it became a spur. Born in the semitropical West Indies, he might easily have fallen into the languid lethargy with which the warm sun, sea, and air ensnared many inhabitants. Yet almost symbolically his future was shaped by a hurricane. In the autumn of 1769 when he was twelve he got a job as an apprentice clerk in the trading house of a wealthy merchant in St. Croix. He showed so much promise that within a few months he was a bookkeeper in charge of a branch store. Shortly afterward, the merchant had to go to New York for treatment of a serious illness, and on October 15, 1771, the day he sailed, he designated the youthful Alexander, fourteen, manager of his entire operations.

It was an extensive business, involving the buying and selling of numerous commodities, but Hamilton handled it with the skill of a veteran, sending copies of letters received and his replies to the ailing owner, and turning back to him in March 1772 a prosperous and thriving enterprise. The appreciative employer made him chief assistant and dispatched him to various islands to analyze the markets. As he returned to St. Croix a violent hurricane swept through, devastating the place and killing a number of people. Hamilton wrote a letter and sent it off to a newspaper. It would now be judged amateurishly theatric, larded with religious messages in a shaky Shakespearean tone. Read against the death and destruction, however, it was regarded as a masterpiece, and it was decided that such talent should be nurtured. In a week's time Hamilton was on a Boston-bound ship, equipped with letters from his minister to friends at Princeton and a small purse collected to get the lad to college.

The ship, after battling a fire in mid-voyage, finally put into Boston in late October, and Hamilton took the first stage out, but found Princeton's classes well underway and the faculty adamant that he must wait until the next term. Undaunted, Alexander matriculated at King's College, later Columbia.

Through his adolescence he had often expressed the wish there were a war to free him from the specter of "groveling mediocrity." Almost as if he had commanded a genie, events began to unfold in swift succession during his college years. He defended the Colonies' position against Britain in debating societies, and then, realizing the limitations of his forum, once more turned to the press. His business experience in the West Indies had shown him the paralyzing effects of English mercantilism, and he brought to his pamphlets not the histrionics of the hurricane incident, but tightly reasoned economic arguments. *Holt's Journal* published his letters, and they attracted the attention of leaders like John Jay. Through all of the excitement Hamilton never permitted himself to be distracted from his studies.

A provincial commission as captain of New York artillery on March 14, 1776 held the prospect for the drama Hamilton desperately wanted; he rejected disdainfully an invitation to serve as brigade major on the staff of the quixotic William Alexander, who insisted on being called "Lord Stirling." Stirling had been named commander of the Continental forces in New York. Hamilton, determined to prove himself with the sword rather than the pen, chose the hard road of raising a company, drilling and disciplining indifferent militiamen, and bearing much of the cost from the monies sent to him by hard-pressed relatives for his own subsistence. He felt a measure of relief and satisfaction when his unit was absorbed into the Continental Army upon news of Howe's impending attack on New York.

During the ensuing battle, Hamilton saw (probably for the first time) Aaron Burr, a major of the staff attached to General Putnam. There were great similarities. Burr, not quite a year older than Hamilton, and at five feet six inches just a shade shorter, had penetrating black eyes and brown hair. Both were slightly built and comported themselves with self-conscious dignity. They were brilliant, excellent conversationalists, and attractive to—and attracted by—women they found interesting. On this occasion, Burr, cut off from his own unit, stumbled upon the untenable position in Brooklyn Heights to which Washington had assigned elements including Hamilton's artillery. Hamilton brashly sent an unsigned note to Washington protesting the strategy. Burr, reaching the same conclusion, sent off a caustic communique to Putnam, and then, in a brazen step, superseded Colonel Knox, and asked the soldiers if they wanted to follow him to safety or "be sacrificed like cowards?" While Knox was baffled, Burr led the Americans to a point where they could be regrouped for the battle of Harlem Heights. The hasty retreat, with the attendant confusion, cost Hamilton all of his baggage and one of his precious cannons.

Hamilton saw action at White Plains, but Washington's campaign in New York was a dismal failure and by November the battered Continental troops were picking their weary way through New Jersey to the comparative safety of Bucks County in Pennsylvania. Amid all the disillusionment of defeat Hamilton's artillery company was noteworthy for its well-ordered ranks and its disciplined marching; a spectator saw "a youth, a mere stripling, small, slender, almost delicate in frame beside a piece of artillery, with a cocked hat pulled down over his eyes, apparently lost in thought, with his hand resting on a cannon, and every now and then patting it, as if it were a favorite horse or a pet plaything." When Washington crossed the Delaware and launched his surprise attack on the Hessians at Trenton, Hamilton's artillery was there as a reserve unit, but he pressed his cannon into action to shell Von Lossberg's regiment as it emerged from Church Alley. During the subsequent Battle of Princeton he posted his guns outside Nassau Hall and demanded the surrender of British forces within. When they refused to comply, he sent a shot crashing through the chapel and knocked down the portrait of George II; and a second shot, better placed, brought the reluctant redcoats out with their hands in the air.

In the bleak winter months of early 1777 at Morristown the now triumphant Washington wrote to Joseph Reed in Pennsylvania:

my time is so much taken up at my desk, that I am obliged to neglect many other essential parts of my duty; it is absolutely necessary, therefore, for me to have persons that can think for me, as well as execute orders.

Hamilton's name, earlier offered by Greene for his gallantry, now came before Washington as a young man who could fill the requirements. So Washington summoned him and offered him the post of an aide-de-camp, with a Continental commission as lieutenant colonel. To the general's amazement, the young artillery captain hesitated, but after much deliberation, agreed; on March 1, 1777, the twenty-year-old Hamilton reluctantly left his beloved guns for a billet he felt certain would deprive him of glory. The strange, compelling need to prove the worth of his life at the risk of death—almost psychotic in its proportions—persisted until Burr, as much a victim as a victor, ended it in a senseless duel.

It was in November 1777 that Hamilton saw Elizabeth Schuyler for the first time. They were married in December of 1780.

His boon companion, James McHenry, attended the ceremonies in the First Reformed Church of Albany on December 14, and the large reception that followed in the Schuyler mansion. An erstwhile poet, he composed that evening an ode to the couple. In an appreciative note, Hamilton wrote:

> I thank you Dear Mac for your poetry and your confidence. The piece is a good one—your best. It has wit, which you know is a rare thing. I see by perserverence all ladies may be won. The Muses begin to be civil to you, in spite of Apollo and my prognosis.
>
> You know I have often told you, you wrote prose well but had no genius for poetry. I retract. Adieu.
>
> A. HAMILTON

Whether he felt Hamilton's susceptibility to good-looking women needed a cautionary note, or whether he was simply generalizing the postnuptial postulates, McHenry offered this advice:

Know then, dear *Ham*, a truth confest
Soon beauty fades, and love's a guest.
Love has not settled place on earth;
A very wan'rer from his birth;
And yet who happiness would prove
Like you must build his hopes on love,
When love his choicest gifts has giv'n
He flies to make another heav'n;
But as he wheels his rapid flight
Calm joys succeed and pure delight.
Faith adds to all; for works we're told
Is Love's alloy, and faith the gold.
. . . .
All these attendants *Ham* are thine,
Be't yours to treat them as divine;
To cherish what keeps love alive;
What makes us young at sixty-five.
What lends the eye its earliest fires;
What rightly managed still inspires.

Eliza, as he called his bride, must have been aware from the outset that Hamilton's pursuit of glory would be her chief rival. He felt Washington was depriving him of wider opportunities. In rapid succession he was seemingly denied appointment to a mission to France, the post of adjutant general, and a field command because of the general's desire to keep him on the staff. Only in the last instance was he right for the wrong reason. Washington, beset by quarrels among his officers over rank and promotions, could hardly jump a lieutenant colonel in his early twenties over men his senior in age, experience, and grade. "The pen of our army was held by Hamilton," a contemporary observed, "and for dignity of manner, pith of matter, and elegance of style, General Washington's letters are unrivaled in military annals."

Such accolades were not enough for Hamilton. "I explained to you candidly my feelings in respect to military reputation," he reminded Washington, "and how much it was my object to act a conspicuous part in some enterprise that might perhaps raise my character as a soldier above mediocrity." When the opportunity arose for such a demonstration, it came after Hamilton resigned as aide, and as owing more to Lafayette than Washington. But it was to be a brief excursion, for the scene was Yorktown, and the diminutive Hamilton, sword in hand, led the right wing against the beleaguered British only to find their white flag at the end of his charge. He left the service within a short time and went to Albany to study law.

On November 3, 1782 he wrote Lafayette:

> I have been employed for the last ten months in rocking the cradle and studying the art of fleecing my neighbors. I am now a grave counsellor-at-law, and shall soon be a grave member of Congress. The Legislature, at their last session, took it into their heads to name me, pretty unanimously, as one of their delegates.
>
> I am going to throw away a few months more in public life, and then retire a simple citizen and good *paterfamilias*. I set out for Philadelphia in a few days. You see the disposition I am in. You are condemned to run the race of ambition all your life. I am already tired of the career, and dare to leave it.

It was a mood of the moment. As with most lawyers his professional beginnings were filled with routine suits for various forms of debt and a scattering of criminal cases—one of which involved the defense of one Murphy in New York City on a charge of assaulting "with Swords and Stones and Knives . . . Margaret Russell, with intent . . . to Ravish and Deflour." The matter was further complicated by the fact that Margaret was a minor. Despite the pettiness of most of the litigation he was meticulous in trial preparation, the acknowledged key to success for trial lawyers. If the factual stuff was dull, the theories of federal supremacy he advanced had overtones of the broader reaches of his political thought—a philosophy he would carry into the Constitutional Convention of 1787, of which he was to be the principal architect.

Betsy was well bedded. The first of their eight children was born January 22, 1782, and Hamilton took singular pride in the boy, Philip. In March, congratulating Richard K. Meade on the birth of a daughter, he wrote: "I can well conceive your happiness . . . the sensations of a tender father of the child of a beloved mother can only be conceived by those who have experienced them . . . You cannot imagine how entirely domestic I am growing . . . I lose all taste for the pursuits of ambition. I sigh for nothing but the Company of my wife and baby. The ties of duty alone, or imagined duty, Keep me from renouncing public life altogether. Betsy is so fond of your family that she proposes to form a match between her boy and your girl, provided you will engage to make the latter as amiable as her mother." The Hamiltons had a daughter on September 25, 1784, and christened her Angelica. Between May 16, 1786 and August 4, 1797 four sons —Alexander, James Alexander, John Church, and William Stephen—were born, and on November 20, 1799 Eliza arrived. Angelica, bearing her lovely aunt's name, developed into a beautiful girl, and both the original Angelica and Hamilton mapped a course to ensure she would be an accomplished young woman. A portrait of Philip shows how closely he resembled his father in appearance, and Hamilton's frequent letters to the lad as he went through school show the deep affection between the two. One, from Philadelphia on December 5, 1791, when the youngster was nine and in school, is illustrative:

> I received with great pleasure, my dear Philip, the letter which you wrote me last week. Your mama and myself were very happy to learn that you are pleased with your situation . . . We hope and believe that nothing will happen to alter this disposition. Your teacher also informs me that you recited a lesson the first day you began very much to his satisfaction. I expect every letter from him will give me a fresh proof of your progress, for I know you can do a great deal if you please, and I am sure you have too much spirit not to exert yourself, that you may make us every day more and more proud of you. You remember that I engaged to send for you next Saturday, and I will do it, unless you request me to put it off, for a promise must never be broken, and I will never make you one which I will not fill as far as I am able, but it has occurred to me that the Christmas holidays are near at hand, and I suppose your school will then break up for a few days and give you an opportunity of coming to stay with us for a longer time than if you should come on Saturday. Will it not be best, therefore, to put off your journey till the holidays?

But determine as you like best, and let me know what will be most pleasing to you. A good night to my darling son.

On April 21, 1797, when Philip was at Columbia, he sent a note to his father, then at Albany, which indicates something of the way in which he was trying to emulate his distinguished parent:

Dear Papa: I just now received the enclosed letter from Grandpa in answer to a letter I wrote to him, in which he has enclosed to me three receipts for shares in the Tontine Tavern, amounting to £100. I have given the receipts to Mama. I delivered my speech to Dr. Johnson to examine. He has no objection to my speaking; but he has blotted out that sentence which appears to be the best and most animated in it; which is, you may recollect it—"Americans, you have fought the battles of mankind; you have enkindled that sacred fire of freedom which is now," and so forth.

Dear Papa, will you be so good as to give my thanks to Grandpapa for the present he made me, but above all for the good advice his letter contains—which I am very sensible of its being extremely necessary for me to pay particular attention to, in order to be a good man. I remain your most affectionate son.

From London Angelica Church beamed to Betsy:

I have received with inexpressible pleasure your long letter, and thank my Eliza for the agreeable details respecting your children. Philip inherits his father's talents. What flattering prospects for a mother! You are, my dear sister, very happy with such a Husband and such promise in a son.

The ordeal of marriage to a public man offers some compensation in the glamor it provides the wife. Betsy Hamilton, however, shunned the numerous parties in Philadelphia when her husband was secretary of the Treasury, partially because of preference and partially because of pregnancies. The magnetism of power, coupled with strong personal appeal, made Hamilton a willing subject for women, whether sincere or designing. While he drank little, he had occasional tendencies to become "liquorish" and often irritated husbands by too ardent attention to their wives. Otis, the indefatigable gossip, smirked to his wife that Christopher G. Champlin, a congressman from Rhode Island, complained "that Hamilton (who cast some liquorish looks at his cara sposa, the day we were at Breck's) appears to him very trifling in his conversation with ladies and that his wife said she did not like him at all. He was evidently *satisfied* with this intimation."

The wariness of husbands was heightened by the publicity given Hamilton's affair with Maria Reynolds.

On December 15, 1792, two congressmen (Muhlenberg from Pennsylvania and Venable from Virginia) along with Senator James Monroe came to Hamilton's Treasury office. All three were Jefferson men. They said they had reports of some questionable financial transactions between the secretary and one James Reynolds. Hamilton masked his rage and said he would be happy to discuss the matter. On a summer's day in 1791 a Mrs. Reynolds came to his home. His wife and children were there at the time. Maria Reynolds tearfully told him her husband had deserted her, and she needed money to get to New York. "I replied," Hamilton said, "that her situation was a very interesting one—that I was disposed to afford her assistance to convey her to her friends, but this at the time not being convenient to me (which was the fact) I must request the place of her residence, to which I should bring or send a small supply of money." The same evening he went to Maria's cheap lodgings, and Maria led him into her bedroom. Hamilton said he produced a banknote at once "but it was quickly apparent that other than pecuniary consolation would be acceptable."

However Hamilton handled the situation in the next few hours, there was no more talk of Maria going to New York. "After that I had frequent meetings with her at my own house, Mrs. Hamilton and her children being absent on a visit to her father." Hamilton said he tried to break the affair off, but Maria professed to be violently in love with him. Then she told him her husband wanted a reconciliation. "I advised to it and was soon after informed by her that it had taken place."

Their liaison continued nevertheless. Maria casually let slip that her husband was speculating in public securities and knew something about a Treasury leak. James Reynolds applied for a job in Hamilton's office, but the secretary's distaste for employees who traded on confidential data brought a brisk and quick refusal. Then an urgent note came from Maria.

> I have not tim to tell you the cause of my present troubles, only that Mr. has rote you this morning and I know not wether you have got the letter or not and he has swore that If you do not answer It or If he dose not se or hear from you to day he will write Mrs. Hamilton he has just Gone oute and I am a Lone I think you had better come here one moment that you May know the Cause then you will the better know how to act Oh my God I feel more for you than myself and wish I had never been born to give you so mutch unhappiness do not rite to him no not a Line but come here soon do not send or leave any thing in his power.

Reynolds's letter reached Hamilton before he had time to act on Maria's plea. It said he found her writing a note—a bit too ardent—and the repentant wife had confessed everything. Reynolds claimed to be heartbroken but was determined to have satisfaction: "It shant be onely one family thats miserable."

Hamilton decided to submit to the blackmail. First and foremost was his concern for Betsy and the children. Washington and Adams, he thought, would probably turn from him, if the incident came to light, and he would be the butt of jokes in social circles. There were plenty of stories already abroad about his supposed philandering, but "there is a wide difference between vague rumors and suspicions and the evidence of a positive fact." Reynolds asked for $1,000 as "plaister for his wounded honor." Once received, he would leave town and "leve her to Yourself to do for her as you think proper." Hamilton told the committee he had a hard time scraping up the money, and paid it in two installments.

Muhlenberg and Venable, obviously embarrassed, said they were satisfied and got up to leave. But Hamilton insisted they hear the rest of the story. Two weeks later, he said, Reynolds wrote:

I have not the Least Objections to your Calling, as a friend to Boath of us, and must rely intirely on your and her honnor . . . So dont fail in Calling as Soon as you Can make it Conveneant. and I rely on your befriending me if there should anything Offer that would be to my advantage.

The invitation was scarcely one the sophisticated Hamilton would accept. It took several letters from Maria, "ready to Burst with Greef" and hardly able to "rise from My pillow which your Neglect has filled with the shorpest thorns," to convince him "I shal be misarable till I se you." The plaintive appeal that brought him again to her had a certain boudoir eloquence:

alas my friend what can [I] ask for but peace wich you alone can restore to my tortured bosom and do My dear Col hamilton on my kneese Let me Intreate you to reade my Letter and Comply with my request tell the bearer of this or give her a line you need not be the least affraid let me not die with fear have pity on me my freend for I deserve it I would not solicit this favor but I am sure It cannot injure you and will be all the happiness I Ever Expect to have But oh I am distressed more than I can tell My Heart is ready to burst and my tears wich once could flow with Ease are now denied me.

He went off to assuage Maria's "Greef," and circumspectly entered through the back door. This prompted Reynolds to demand, "Am I a person of such a Bad carecter that you would not wish to be seen Coming to my house in the front way?"

Each visit cost Hamilton $30 to $50 in "loans" to Reynolds— a price which put Maria much above the "frail women," as Philadelphia prostitutes were affectionately called by their sailor-patrons. It was also more than Hamilton could afford for very long.

One day Wolcott, his comptroller, advised him that Reynolds and a former Treasury employee, Clingman, had been arrested for attempting to defraud the government. They had perjured themselves to get letters of administration for the estate of a man who had a claim against the United States, but they had neglected to wait until he became a decedent. In jail Reynolds comforted

Clingman with assurances of an early release because a word from him could "hang the Secretary of the Treasury." Hamilton had no problem with this. He might be willing to pay blackmail for personal indiscretions, but no one could blackmail him in his official capacity. He directed Wolcott to proceed with the prosecution. The culprits agreed to make restitution and turn state's evidence against the Treasury clerk who had been their accomplice. On this basis they were released—without Hamilton's knowledge or consent. Clingman, however, confided to Muhlenberg, for whom he had once worked, that the secretary had used Reynolds in secret speculations based on official information.

Muhlenberg consulted with Venable and Senator Monroe, and their impulse was to go to Washington. But they decided to confront Hamilton, who said he was "ready to meet fair inquiry with frank communication."

The unreliable Reynolds skipped the city the minute he was out of jail, leaving Maria to Clingman, who apparently had been sharing her bed, with her husband's approval, on nights when Hamilton was otherwise occupied. Reflecting on the episode, Hamilton said admiringly: "The variety of shapes which this woman could assume were endless." From a master of expository English this statement suggests several possible interpretations. But then again, it may have said everything.

When the tale was told, all three legislators said they were satisfied and would keep secret the documents given them by Clingman. In 1797, to Hamilton's astonishment and anger, they suddenly burst into print. James Callender, a free-lance writer who sometimes did political pieces at Jefferson's behest, included them in his *History of the United States for the Year 1796*. Hamilton dispatched bristling letters to Muhlenberg, Venable, and Monroe, demanding to know why they breached their word. The first two replied promptly, voicing their dismay and denying the papers were ever in their possession. Only Monroe remained silent. Hamilton, accompanied by his brother-in-law, John Church, recently arrived in Philadelphia, called on Monroe. He heatedly told Hamilton he had sent the material "to his Friend in Virginia" and "had no intention of publishing them & declared upon his honor that he knew nothing of their publication until he arrived at Philada from Europe." The incensed Hamilton called him a liar, and a duel was arranged; but Aaron Burr mollified the two and the pistols were laid aside. Hamilton then published a pamphlet giving the details of his affair with Maria and describing, with documentation, the blackmail plot and his refusal to allow his personal problem to violate his public trust.

Hamilton's courage in the matter is often applauded, but what of Betsy's? A lesser woman could have exploded with righteous indignation and fled with her family to the sanctuary of her father's mansion in Albany. Yet her firm loyalty to her husband amid the "slings and arrows" prevented incalculable damage to his career at a time when he sorely needed precisely that kind of support. Nor was her loyalty merely a political expedient. It was an abiding faith which Betsy throughout her long life proclaimed in a husband whose strength she valued above his weaknesses.

The disclosure did nothing to dampen General Schuyler's admiration for his son-in-law, and probably enhanced his stature in the eyes of the adoring Angelica. Urbane, cosmopolitan Angelica, who, in her London home, heightened Hamilton's fame by constantly extolling him to British and French statesmen, had written Elizabeth in 1794:

> You and my dear Hamilton will never cross the Atlantic, I shall never leave this Island, and as to meeting in heaven—there will be no pleasure in that.

Shortly afterward, she described Hamilton as her "Amiable" in another letter to Betsy:

> by my Amiable, you know I mean your Husband, for I love him very much and if you were as generous as the old Romans, you would lend him to me for a little while, but do not be jealous, my dear Eliza, since I am more solicitous to promote his laudable ambition, than any person in the world; and there is no summit of true glory which I do not desire he may attain; provided always that he pleases to give me a little chit-chat, and some-

times to say, I wish our dear Angelica was here. Ah, Bess! You were a lucky girl to get so clever and so good a companion.

He wrote to Angelica on December 8, 1794,

> You say I am a politician, and good for nothing. What will you say when you learn that after January next, I shall cease to be a politician at all? So is the fact. I have formally and definitely announced my intention to resign, and have ordered a house to be taken for me at New York. My dear Eliza has been lately very ill. Thank God, she is now quite recovered, except that she continues somewhat weak.
>
> My absence on a certain expedition [suppression of the Whiskey Rebellion in western Pennsylvania] was the cause.
>
> You will see, notwithstanding your disparagement of me, I am still of consequence to her . . . Having contributed to place . . . the Nation on a good footing, I go to take a little care of my own; which need my care not a little.

Again on March 6, 1795, he wrote, this time from Albany:

> To indulge in my domestic happiness the more freely, was with me a principal motive for relinquishing an office in which 'tis said I have gained some glory . . . Eliza and our children are with me here at your father's house, who is himself at New York attending the Legislature. We remain here till June, when we become stationary at New York, where I resume the practice of the law. For, my dear sister, I tell you without regret what I hope you anticipate, that I am poorer than when I went into office.

Angelica was exuberant.

> I sincerely congratulate you my dear Eliza on the resignation of our dear Hamilton & on your return to New York where I hope to pass with you the remainder of my days, that is if you will be so obliging as to permit my *Brother* to give me his society, for you know how much I love & admire him.

Church's investments in American enterprises brought the couple to America in May 1797. Eliza had been in Albany during part of the Churches' stay in Philadelphia; so Angelica spent as much time as Hamilton could spare from his duties in his company. The visit seemed to increase her ardor for him, and now the prospect of permanent residence close to Hamilton had her quite elated.

The reunion occurred during the furor of the Reynolds affair. Hamilton, who might have been expected to be somewhat sheepish towards Betsy during the trying time, gave her something else to think about. Angelica's unabashed declarations for him in her letters to Betsy had generally been answered by Hamilton with warmth, but also with a measured degree of caution. Angelica accompanied her sister to Albany, and Hamilton wrote this rather interesting note to his wife, addressing her briefly in the third person:

> I need not tell her how happy I shall be to return to her embrace and to the company of our beloved Anglica. I am very anxious about you both, you for an obvious reason, and her because Mr. Church mentioned in a letter to me, that she complained of a *sore throat*—Let me charge you and her to be well and happy, for you comprize all my felicity.

Precisely how Betsy felt about the equal recognition Hamilton accorded Angelica, she kept locked within herself. The next year, 1798, when she was away from him once more, he wrote:

> I always feel how necessary you are to me—But when you are absent I become still more sensible of it, and look around in vain for that satisfaction which you alone can bestow. I dined with Angelica today—Margaret was with her.

Then, possibly to banish any fears that news might precipitate, he added reassuringly:

> You are my good genius; of that kind which the ancient philosophers called a *familiar*

but the classical allusion was underscored by a poem which ended:

Adieu, best of wives and best of mothers
Heaven ever bless you & me in you.

New York and Philadelphia society lost little time in linking Angelica and Alexander. Betsy, with her brood, which now included two sons—one five years old and another just one, and destined to become pregnant again in February 1799—was secure enough in her love that she let the two have their fling. The inevitable gossip, punctuated by such incidents as the shoe bow, gave rise to rumors that troubled Hamilton's close friends. Angelica gave dazzling dinner parties and balls, as much to furnish her "amiable" with a splendid setting as to satisfy herself. Hamilton, now inspector general of the Army, as America girded herself against a possible war with France, had resigned his "extensive & lucrative" law practice. As second in command to Washington, who indicated his willingness to again take the field should actual hostilities break out, he was, for all practical purposes, in charge of all military matters. "Though not yet in the field of Mars," his friend Robert Troup wrote, "he maintains an unequalled reputation for *gallantry*—such at least is the opinion entertained of him by the ladies. When I have more leisure, I will give you the history of the Ghost of Baron [Ciominie?] & Mrs. Church as published by our Gallant General." The acid remark was inspired by Troup's feeling that Angelica, whom he disliked, was putting Hamilton in an untenable position, especially in view of the publicity about the Maria Reynolds episode. Hamilton was so enchanted by Angelica, who at forty-two was a few months older than him, that Maria was almost a dim memory.

It is almost impossible not to believe these two highly charged individuals were lovers. Angelica rarely mentioned her husband in her correspondence. Church was preoccupied with his insurance business in New York, where if Troup is to be given credence, he was quick to collect premiums, but slow in paying claims. He was active, too, in the Bank of the Manhattan Company, which Hamilton's arch rival, Burr, had founded against all the political and financial pressure Hamilton could mount against

it. "Church is said to be much pushed for money," Troup confided to a friend, "and indeed family affairs are in a train which in
my opinion will by & by cause an explosion which will spread
general ruin around it—I mean the ruin of almost the whole
connexion. I consider it unfortunate that he ever removed with
his family to this country." Troup indicated in a subsequent letter
that he "had ventured, at every risk, to communicate with a certain friend of ours on a certain subject. I fear notwithstanding
that things continue in the same course. You can hardly [word
illegible] how ruinous are the consequences of the general belief."

But Hamilton's personal world of happiness got a crushing
blow in 1801. His pride and joy, twenty-year-old Philip, was killed
in a duel on the same ground near North Bergen, New Jersey,
where Hamilton would be mortally wounded three years later. It
was, as always, a trivial matter which cost his life. Young Hamilton, recently graduated from Columbia and destined for the bar,
was at the theater with a friend named Price. They occupied a
box adjoining one occupied by George Eacker, a lawyer and political opponent of Hamilton. The two young men made satirical
remarks about a speech Eacker delivered on July 4, 1801, in
which he attacked Hamilton's theories. Eacker could not help but
overhear, and invited them into the lobby. In the course of the
argument that ensued, he called either Hamilton or Price a
"damned rascal." Challenges followed, and on Sunday, November 22, Eacker and Price fired two fruitless shots at each other,
and their seconds intervened and called the match off. The next
day Eacker met Philip, who fell with a shot through his side,
without even discharging his pistol. He was carried off to a house.
"Never did I see a man so completely overwhelmed with grief as
Hamilton has been," Troup noted. "I was present . . . when Mrs.
Hamilton came to see her son on his deathbed and when she met
her husband & son in one room [the scene] beggars all description!" Angelica sent word to her brother in Albany: "His [Hamil-
ton's] conduct was extraordinary during this trial. I cannot reach
particulars now, my sister is a little composed, and the corpse will
be removed from my house within an hour."

The tragedy precipitated still another, for the Hamiltons' talented and beautiful seventeen-year-old daughter, Angelica, became mentally unbalanced and lived for another fifty-six years in a gentle haze, spending hours at the piano her Aunt Angelica had brought her from London in brighter days and playing music her father had chosen for her which linked her to the memory of her "dear brother."

Betsy, pregnant again at the time of Philip's death, gave birth to another son on June 2, 1802. He was given the name of his late brother, and called "Little Phil" by the family.

Depressed by his personal misfortunes, Hamilton's mood was made darker by the fact that his bitter rivals, Jefferson and Burr, were now occupying the offices of president and vice-president. His inflexibility made it hard for him to adjust to Jefferson's Republicanism, and after an unsuccessful attempt to form a "Christian Constitutional Society" designed to support Christianity and the Constitution and promote "the election of *fit* men," he concentrated on his law practice and his new home. "A garden, you know," he wrote to Charles Cotesworth Pinckney on December 20, 1802, "is a very usual refuge of a disappointed politician. Accordingly I have purchased a few acres about nine miles from town, have built a house, and am cultivating a garden." The tract he chose roughly corresponds to that between St. Nicholas and Tenth avenues, and 141st and 145th streets in New York City, except that its western reaches fronted on the Hudson River. Throughout the planning and construction, old General Schuyler offered valuable, practical suggestions, including the following:

> I shall . . . go up and contract for the timber and purchase the boards and planks, and if possible I will cause the boards and planks to be put into water for two months and then piled up with decks between them that they may be seasoned before they are worked up.
>
> It will save very considerable expense if the clap boards and boards for the floors were sawed the proper breadth and thickness at the saw mills, I therefore wish you to send me how many of each Mr. _____ thinks will be wanted, their breadth and thickness.

Two years later, he wrote to his daughter Betsy, on August 22, 1802:

> I am anxious to visit you and to participate in the pleasure of your country retreat which I am informed is fast reaching perfection. Embrace my dear Hamilton and the children. He and they participate with you in your mother's and my warmest affections. May health and happiness be the portion of all. God bless you my dearly beloved child.
>   I am ever, most tenderly and affectionately, yours,
>
>   PH. SCHUYLER

However historians may measure Schuyler's role during the Revolution, his constant concern and love for the circle of his family is a thing of beauty. After Philip's death in the duel he wrote moving letters to Betsy, "My dearly beloved and Amiable Child"; and when she gave birth to "young Phil," his opening sentence was: "How your endearing attentions rivet you continually to my heart. May the loss of one be compensated by another Philip. May his virtues emulate those which graced his brother, and may he be a comfort to parents so tender and who have endeared themselves to theirs."

On April 23, 1803:

> DEAR CHILD: This morning Genr. Ten Broeck informed me that your horses which went from hence were drowned, and that you had lost paint, oil, &c to a considerable amount—Supposing this account to have been truly stated to the General, I send you by Toney my waggon horses of which I make you present.
>   I intended to have your house painted If you cannot recover the paint, purchase no more as I will have the house painted.

Designed by John McComb, whose best-known structure is New York's City Hall, the house was impressive in its solidity, but not pretentious. Its interior featured two "octagon" rooms with four fireplaces, with "two setts of Italian Marble . . . such as General Hamilton may chose" along with a drawing room, and the usual run of bedrooms on the second floor. It had the plainness of a late seventeenth-century English country house, relieved by porches and a more ornate "Piazza."

Hamilton's reference to finding refuge in his garden was not an idle rhetorical flourish. Like many other leading figures of his age, he had an interest in horticulture. He collected cuttings and bulbs, and a note to his architect carries a rough sketch of a circular flower garden as a centerpiece for the larger garden: "If it can be done in Time," he scribbled, "I should be glad a Space could be prepared in the center of the flower garden for planting a few tulips, lilies, hyacinths and ———. The Space should be a circle of which the diameter is Eighteen feet; and there should be nine of each sort of flowers; but the gardener will do well to consult as to the season. They may be arranged thus: Wild roses around the outside of the flower garden with laurel at foot. If practicable in time I should be glad some laurel should be planted along the edge of the shrubbery and round the clump of trees near the house; also sweet briars and ———. A few dogwood trees not large, scattered along the margin of the grove would be very pleasant."

Judge James Kent, planning with Hamilton to head off Burr's aspirations to be governor of New York, stayed at the new house on April 21, 1804. "There was a furious and dreadful storm on Saturday night," he wrote his wife. "It blew almost a hurricane. His house stands high and was very much exposed, and I am certain that in the second story, where I slept, it rocked like a cradle."

Burr's decision to run for governor was prompted by the political realities of his untenable position as vice-president. Under the Constitution as it then read, the second highest candidate in electoral votes became the vice-president. Burr, a Federalist, had deadlocked with Jefferson, each with seventy-three votes; John Adams, the incumbent, was out of the race with sixty-five; Charles Pinckney had sixty-four, and John Jay one.

For Hamilton the presidential election of November 1800 was a national disaster. Even though Burr was nominally of his party, the intense dislike with which both men regarded each other made Hamilton personally indifferent as to how Burr fared when the deadlock was thrown into the House of Representatives. It took thirty-six ballots there before Jefferson was chosen. Burr, with the second highest number, became vice-president. But Jefferson was determined as soon as he was inaugurated to undercut Burr at every opportunity so that if the two ran against each other in 1804, Burr would look weak and ineffective. Burr, a skilled politician, saw the handwriting on the wall, and thus looked to New York as a temporary shelter where as governor he could recoup his strength for a presidential drive in 1808.

But the Clintons and Livingstons who controlled the Democratic Party in the state had different ideas. To checkmate their candidate, Burr set out to form a coalition of independent Democrats and the badly splintered Federalists. Hamilton, who nursed the hope that he would one day bring the Federalists together, now saw Burr as a direct threat to his future plans. Were he to be elected, he could establish such a strong base Hamilton could never dislodge him. So Hamilton and Judge Kent busied themselves with pleas to their fellow Federalists to withdraw their support from Burr, even if it meant letting the Democrats win by default. As the campaign grew warmer, Hamilton became more expansive in his attack on Burr, only to find many Federalists turning a deaf ear.

The amazing similarities between Burr and Hamilton, in height, their demonstrated courage during the Revolution, their appearance and bearing, coupled with their recognized abilities as lawyers, their devotion to their wives and families, and their predilections to flirtations on the side, had one small difference. Burr was warm and gracious to "little people," while Hamilton was usually reserved, sometimes haughty, and occasionally imperious. So despite Hamilton's frantic efforts to turn the Federalists against Burr, the latter had strong appeal.

At a small, private dinner party in Albany, Hamilton denounced Burr unreservedly. Precisely what he said among his friends has never been fully recorded, but one of the guests, in a letter dated April 12, 1804, said: "Gen. Hamilton . . . spoke of him as a dangerous man and ought not to be trusted." The same correspondent wrote to Schuyler on April 23 "I could detail to you a still more despicable opinion which General Hamilton had expressed of Mr. Burr." Like hundreds of ostensibly private communications in the eighteenth century both letters found their way into the newspapers. Burr could hardly let the expressions go unchallenged. He won Federalist backing but lost the election. On June 18 he sent Hamilton a cold communication, asking him to affirm or deny the statements as his.

Hamilton agonized over the answer for two days. He pointed out no specific words were attributed to him, and therefore he was in no position to affirm or deny. "I stand ready to avow or disavow promptly and explicitly any precise or definite opinion which I may be charged with having declared of any gentleman . . . I trust, on more reflection, you will see the matter in the same light with me." The tenor of his general remarks he dismissed as the "animadversions of political opponents upon each other." If Burr was not satisfied, "I can only regret the circumstance, and must abide the consequence." These closing words put him at the mercy of Burr's whim. Thus the able lawyer and master of the language was deserted by his talents when he needed them most.

Burr replied: "Political opposition can never absolve gentlemen from the necessity of a rigid adherence to the laws of honour and the rules of decorum. I neither claim such privilege nor indulge it in others."

The puzzling features of the incident are, not that it occurred, but that Burr waited so long, and chose such relatively placid words to trigger it. As a consummate politician he had a private intelligence system perhaps second to only Jefferson's. Letters Hamilton wrote in 1801 to other Federalists were vitriolic to a degree almost hysterical. Burr could hardly have missed learning that Hamilton ripped his character to shreds—and any one of the letters, with Hamilton's signature affixed, was specific beyond any possible palliating explanation.

Hamilton certainly did not mention the duel to Betsy, for obvious reasons. Burr had suggested it be held promptly, but

Hamilton asked that it be deferred until the close of the Circuit Court since he had cases scheduled for trial. Burr acquiesced, and the delay put the date beyond July 4. Both men attended the Society of Cincinnati banquet that evening, and Hamilton, as its president, was exuberant—leading the singing, and, at one point, standing on the banquet table to coax the assembly to render a familiar military song with more gusto. Burr was said to have watched him intently with a gloomy countenance. Few in the room were aware that a duel was impending between the two. When the festivities were over, Hamilton returned to the oppressive silence to compose a final letter to Betsy:

> This letter, my very dear Eliza, will not be delivered to you unless I shall first have terminated my earthly career, to begin, as I humbly hope, from redeeming grace and divine mercy, a happy immorality.
>
> If it had been possible for me to have avoided the interview, my love for you and my precious children would have been alone a decisive motive. But it was not possible, without sacrifices which would have rendered me unworthy of your esteem. I need not tell you of the pangs I feel from the idea of quitting you, and exposing you to the anguish which I know you would feel. Nor could I dwell on the topic lest it should unman me.
>
> The consolations of Religion, my Beloved, can alone support you; and these you have a right to enjoy. Fly to the bosom of your God and be comforted.
>
> With my last idea I shall cherish the sweet hope of meeting you in a better world.
>
> Adieu best of wives—best of women.
>
> Embrace all my darling children for me.
>
> > Ever yours
> > A.H.
>
> July 4, 1804
> Mrs. Hamilton

The duel was arranged for the morning of July 11. The night before, he wrote another letter for Betsy, asking her to look after his aged aunt, Mrs. Mitchell, who "is the person in the world to whom as a friend I am under the greatest obligations. I have not hitherto done my duty to her." He indicated that he did not intend to fire at Burr. "The scruples of a Christian have determined me to expose my own life to any extent rather than subject myself to the guilt of taking the life of another. This much increases my hazards, and redoubles my pangs for you. But you had rather I should die innocent than live guilty. Heaven can preserve me, and I humbly hope will; but in the contrary event I charge you to remember that you are a Christian. God's will be done! The will of a merciful God must be good. Once more, Adieu, my darling, darling wife."

In his later years Hamilton had come to see the senselessness of duelling. His decision not to defend himself has led to all sorts of conjectures, apart from the Christian principles he now understandably asserted with such vigor. He had told Philip to avoid firing at Eacker, possibly on the basis that Eacker and Price had been unable to hit each other with two shots apiece, and further, a death caused by duelling subjected the victor to prosecution for, at least, manslaughter. Another theory is that he knew himself to be in the wrong. One of his final letters makes this clear—and, had it been sent as a reply to Burr's initial letter, might have avoided the whole tragic affair:

> it is not to be denied that my animadversions on the political character, and views of Colonel Burr have been extremely severe; and, on different occasions, I, in common with many others, have made very unfavorable criticisms on particular instances of the private conduct of this gentleman . . . because it is possible that I may have injured Colonel Burr, however convinced myself that my opinions and declarations have been well founded, as from my general principles and temper in relation to similar affairs, I have resolved to . . . reserve and throw away my first fire, and I have thoughts even of reserving my second fire, and thus giving a double opportunity to Colonel Burr to pause and reflect.

Burr's first shot struck Hamilton in the side and penetrated the liver and diaphragm and "lodged in the first or second lumbar vertebra." Burr immediately came toward his fallen foe, looked at

him with an expression of regret, and was hurried off by his seconds in the customary effort to avoid identification. Hamilton's
friend Dr. Hosack, who had come along as his surgeon, raced to
him, and "found him half sitting on the ground, supported in the
arms of Mr. Pendleton. His countenance of death I shall never
forget. 'This is a mortal wound, Doctor;' when he sunk away, and
became to all appearance lifeless." They carried him to his barge
and pushed off toward the New York shore—the doctor mean-
while struggling to revive a man in whom he could feel no pulse and
no heartbeat. "When we had got, as I should judge, about 50
yards from the shore, some imperfect efforts to breathe were for
the first time manifest; . . . He breathed; his eyes, hardly opened,
wandered, without fixing on any objects; to our great joy he at
length spoke: 'My vision is indistinct,' were his first words. His
pulse became more perceptible; his respiration more regular; his
sight returned . . . He asked me once or twice, how I found his
pulse; and he informed me that his lower extremities had lost all
feeling; manifesting to me that he entertained no hopes that he
should long survive . . . Perceiving that we approached the shore,
he said, 'Let Mrs. Hamilton be immediately sent for—let the
event be gradually broken to her; but give her hopes. . . .' His
sufferings, during the whole of the day, [were] almost intolerable
. . . During the night he had some imperfect sleep, but the suc-
ceeding morning his symptoms were aggravated, attended however with a diminution of pain. His mind retained all its usual
strength and composure. The great source of his anxiety seemed
to be in his sympathy with his half-distracted wife and children.
He spoke to her frequently of them. 'My beloved wife and children'
were always his expressions . . . As a proof of his extraordinary
composure of mind, let me add, that he alone could calm the
frantic grief of their mother, 'Remember, my Eliza, you are a
Christian,' were the expressions with which he frequently, with a
firm voice, but in a pathetic and impressive manner, addressed
her . . . At about two o'clock, as the public well know, he ex-
pired. . . ."

Hamilton died in the house of his friend William Bayard, once situated at 80-82 Jane Street. Betsy and the children were quickly joined at his bedside by Angelica, who sent a message posthaste to her brother:

> At Mr. Bayard's, Greenwich
> Wednesday Morning
>
> My Dear Brother: I have the painful task to inform you that Gen. Hamilton was this morning wounded by that wretch Burr, but we have every reason to hope that he will recover. May I advise that you repair immediately to my father, as perhaps he may wish to come down.
> My dear sister bears with saintlike fortitude this affliction. The town is in consternation, and there exists only the expression of grief and indignation.
> Adieu, my dear brother
>
> Ever yours,
> A. Church

Oliver Wolcott, one of Hamilton's closest friends, wrote to his wife:

> I have just returned from Mr. Wm. Bayards—where Hamilton is—I did not see him—he suffers great pain—which he endures like a Hero—Mrs. Hamilton is with him, but she is ignorant of the cause of his Illness, which she supposes to be spasms—no one dare tell her the truth—it is feared she would become frantic.

The pistols used in the duel belonged to John Barker Church, and had figured in an earlier duel between him and Burr, as well as the fatal duel involving Philip, which paradoxically took place at the same site.

Philip Schuyler, on Monday, July 13, wrote to Betsy:

> My Dear, Dearly Beloved and Affectionate Child:
>
> This morning Mr. Church's letter has announced to me the severe affliction which it has pleased the Supreme being to inflict

on you on me and on all dear to us. If aught under heaven could aggravate the affliction I experience, it is that incapable of moving or being removed I cannot fly to you to pour the balm of comfort into your afflicted bosom, to water it with my tears, to solace yours and mine in this depressing situation . . . I entreat you my beloved Child to come home as soon as you possibly can with my dear Grandchildren. Your sisters will accompany you. May Almighty God bless and protect you and pour the balm of consolation into your distressed soul is and will always be the prayer of

Your affectionate and distressed parent.
Ph. Schuyler

But within a few months Schuyler died.

Burr immediately became the villain of the piece, forced to flee to avoid prosecution in both New York and New Jersey. His political enemies made the most of the sad event, but more objective people like Judge Peters of Pennsylvania, an intimate friend of Hamilton, admitted that "as an old military man Colonel Burr could not have acted otherwise than he did. I never knew Colonel Burr speak ill of any man, and he had a right to expect a different treatment from what he experienced." Even Gouverneur Morris, who had been chosen to deliver the funeral oration—a role he abhorred since he was strongly opposed to the custom which dictated eminent men be buried with long homilies reminiscent of the ancient Romans—was forced to declare: "I cannot thoroughly excuse him [Hamilton] without criminating Colonel Burr, which must be wrong . . . Colonel Burr ought to be considered in the same light with any other man who has killed another in a duel." The irrepressible Morris, so strongly affected by the sight of the dying Hamilton, had written: "The scene is too powerful for me so that I am obliged to walk in the garden to take breath. After having composed myself I return and sit by his side till he expires." Morris even attended the autopsy, but not this melancholy sight nor any other aspect interfered with Morris's determination to give a balanced encomium. He ticked off in his mind the several things that could and could not be mentioned. He had to "pass over handsomely" Hamilton's illegitimacy and ignore the fact that he was often "indiscreet, vain and opinionated." Nor should reference be made to his partiality toward monarchy rather than republicanism, and the fact that he "foolishly published the avowal of conjugal infidelity" in the Reynolds matter would make any reference to his devotion as a father and husband a bit much. On the other hand, it might "excite public pity for his family, which he has left in indigent circumstances." It all mattered little, for the crowds about Trinity Church were so great on July 14, 1804, his voice carried only to those in the front. Never a moralist and himself an accomplished lover, Morris would have been the last person in New York to sit in judgment on Hamilton's romances. Under no circumstances would he be hypocritical about conduct he thoroughly approved. His puckishness, even in somber settings, led him to speculate afterward: "How easy would it have been to make them [the crowd], for a moment, absolutely mad!" With British and French warships in port on friendly calls, and formally dressed in mourning—with the city almost wholly saddened in belated recognition of the fallen Hamilton—the mood was tense enough to be tinder if Morris was inclined to apply on oratorical match. But he was too much a gentleman to play on emotions, and too much a lawyer to set off something needlessly. Besides, where—at what point— would he do his igniting? It was better, he told himself, that he spoke prosaically and allayed any mob passions.

He was in the forefront in raising funds to ease the burden on poor Betsy. But he wisely rejected Archibald Gracie's suggestion that "twenty intimate friends whose circumstances will permit them to do what their hearts might prompt" could agree to pay off Hamilton's debts of some $100,000. The amount was closer to $50,000, Morris found when he examined the books; but most certainly it would be an affront to the pride of Hamilton's widow and children. A subscription, which eventually raised $39,700, was undertaken, secured to some extent by the huge tract of land in the New York wilderness Hamilton had bought for speculation. The trustees paid off the mortgage on The Grange, as the Hamilton country seat was called, and it was presented free and clear to the family. By 1808, when a final tabulation was taken, it was estimated about $20,000 would be left for the benefit of the Hamiltons.

Hamilton's fame naturally obscured the greatness of his wife. She struggled to maintain The Grange in the first years after his death, directing the workmen and managing the estate with the care she always manifested in her household budgets. Baron von Steuben had once said that Hamilton, the secretary of the Treasury, handled his money matters, and that Mrs. Hamilton was Hamilton's secretary of the treasury. When the funds left by her father became depleted, she personally went to Washington in 1810 to see if her late husband was entitled to anything for his long services. "If anything is to be done," Angelica Church asserted, "your presence is better than twenty agents and I sincerely hope that for your case and for the honor of my native country, a liberal allowance will be made." In 1816 Congress finally passed a law giving her $3,600 for "five years' full pay for the services of her husband as lieutenant-colonel in the Revolutionary War, being the commutation of his half-pay for life" and interest on the sum from November 16, 1783, which amounted to $7,009.64 or $10,609.64 in all.

This enabled her to see that her older sons were properly educated. But Angelica persuaded her to leave The Grange in due course, and move into the city. She was restive there, however, and Angelica had no easy time keeping her away from the place. Despite the vicious criticisms levied at her husband during his lifetime, Eliza never wavered in her love and devotion, and The Grange became for her a symbol of the happiness of her marriage. She made trips back to it. "I rode up in the carriage that was formerly mine," she wrote to her daughter, shortly after locating in New York City, "and you know very easy it was. The boat did not arrive until late in the evening. I am now in the full tide of occupation, four men to attend to, fine morning with the place looking lovely. A carriage dearest and yourself, with the house in order, would be delightful to have." But later, when she was back in town, Angelica wrote:

> Your brother deems it the most prudent that you remain where you are, as it is utterly impossible for you to be at the Grange without horses, and their expense will pay your house rent. He thinks the Grange might be let. If you please early on Saturday morning—say at seven o'clock—I will be ready to attend you to the Grange.

Gradually the economic realities forced her to relinquish it.

As to the children, she moved quickly to find a situation for young Alexander, who had just turned eighteen before his father's death. Two months after she became a widow, she wrote from Albany to her husband's friends trying to find the son a position in some "counting house." "He is young," she wrote to General Clarkson,

> and . . . your goodness I trust will Excuse the request I make that you will have an Eye upon him, and could you permit him some times to accompany you, in your walks, that he might hear from you those just sentiments of Religion, as well as those on Other subjects that have always marked your Character, for to the Greivous Affliction I am under will be aded the trembling Mothers Anxiety for her fatherless Child lest he should fall in to Error.

Clarkson acquiesced gently and suggested that the boy go to Boston, where a job in a firm there awaited him. But Eliza had misgivings about Boston. New England Federalists, champions of John Adams, had not been overly friendly toward Hamilton's memory, and she had thought of Bostonians as tight-fisted, money-mad people. So she declined with thanks. "The present day has Evils of every sort," she wrote Clarkson, "assailing a young mind, that has just steped from the studys of a college class."

Alexander had graduated from Columbia in 1804, and became a lawyer. He went to join the Duke of Wellington's army in

Portugal, but came home just before the War of 1812 to take a commission as captain of infantry. In 1822 he became United States attorney for New York and a land commissioner, and led a comparatively undistinguished life.

The next son, James Alexander, graduated from Columbia in 1805, served as an officer in the War of 1812, and was appointed interim secretary of state by Andrew Jackson in 1829. He, too, became a United States attorney for the southern district of New York, but apart from some diplomatic work, made no lasting mark.

John Church Hamilton, the fourth son, graduated from Columbia in 1809, studied law, and served in the War of 1812. It was he who worked with his mother to prepare Hamilton's papers for publication.

The fifth son, William Stephen, went to West Point, served in the Black Hawk War, and went to California, where he ultimately died a bachelor. His trek to the Far West was a gradual one, and he made occasional trips back east to see his mother and the family. In 1837 when she was eighty, the redoubtable Eliza made a long journey all the way to Wisconsin to visit him, sending letters back to "Little Phil," who also had become a lawyer, describing her trip. "Pittsburgh is a considerable town on the junction of three rivers, no beauty but good Buildings, gloomy from the use of coal. I shall write to you from Cincinnati where I shall be today. Adieu! write to me and let me know how Angelica is." Two months later on the Mississippi she wrote, May 23, 1837:

> My Dear Son: I have passed the Ohio, the river is very spacious, but very difficult of navigation, the shores beautiful and the vessel approaching the shore at the distance of one dozen feet; no wharf, the water is so mixed with clay that it is not drinkable without wine. This evening we shall be at St. Louis . . . Our passage will be tedious as we go against the stream. Let me hear from you, particularly respecting Angelica and all the family.
>
> > Your affectionate mother,
> > ELIZABETH HAMILTON.

Always foremost in her mind was the memory of her husband. In 1839, she wrote again to Philip:

> I thank you My Dear Son for yours of the fifteenth. I hope you may have leisure and the opportunity to have the Speach of your beloved Father copied. Solicit it most anxiously, and if that won't do request it as a favour for me. Hire a person to copy it and let me be at the expense. How desirous must you be to see all given to the publisher that your father has done for our country.

She was writing from New York, and was anxious about a land allotment for military service which Hamilton never bothered to pick up. "I wish you to make inquiry where the location is to be made and when this is the last of your father's services of the grant of land."

"Young Phil" had no college education, having come to adolescence when his mother was almost impoverished. He studied law with one of his brothers, and was known for his gentle ways and kind disposition. His major achievement as a lawyer was securing the conviction when he was assistant United States attorney under his brother James of the pirate Gibbs, who was hanged on Bedloe's Island. But he inherited more his mother's placidity than his father's aggressiveness, and his unending struggle against poverty was not made easier by the fact that most of his clients were poor.

Angelica Hamilton, until her death at seventy-three, was under medical care. Eliza, who was just four and one-half when Hamilton died, appears to have most closely resembled her mother, with the reservoir of inner strength so characteristic of Betsy.

Tireless in her determination to see that the nation would never overlook the worth of her husband, Betsy made repeated appeals to the United States government to publish his manuscripts—and neither the calendar nor the climate hampered her. Because Hamilton's theories of a strong central government were to be out of fashion until the twentieth century, and a number of his contemporaries regarded him as a controversial figure, she had a difficult time. But the quiet young wife whose husband had to chide and cajole her to write letters to him when he was away from the family circle turned into a somewhat prolific writer as a widow. She sent word to men like Rufus King, asking for copies of correspondence Hamilton had with them, only to find they frequently thought it might be impolitic to put them into print. In nothing was she more adamant than her insistence that Hamilton was the architect of Washington's Farewell Address. At eighty-two she penned a lengthy memorandum for posterity:

> Desirous that my children should be fully acquainted with the services rendered by their Father to our country, and the assistance given by him to General Washington during his administration, for the one great object, the Independence and Stability of the Government of the United States, there is one thing in addition to the numerous proofs which I leave them and which I feel myself in duty bound to State; which is; that a short time previous to General Washington's retiring from the Presidency in the year 1796 General Hamilton suggested to him the idea of delivering a farewell address to the people on his withdrawal from public life, with which idea General Washington was well pleased, and in his answer to General Hamilton's suggestion gave him the heads of the subjects on which he would wish to remark, with a request that Mr. Hamilton would prepare an address for him; Mr. Hamilton did so, and the address was written, principally at such times as his office was seldom frequented by his clients and visitors, and during the absence of his students to avoid interruption; at which times he was in the habit of calling me to sit with him, that he might read to me as he wrote, in order, as he said, to discover how it sounded upon the ear, and making the remark, "My dear Eliza, you must be to me what Moliere's old nurse was to him."
>
> The whole or nearly all the "address" was read to me by him as he wrote it and a greater part if not all was written by him in my presence. The original was forwarded to Gen. Washington who approved of it with the exception of one paragraph, of, I think, about four or five lines, which if I mistake not was on the Subject of public schools, which was stricken out. It was afterwards returned to Mr. Hamilton who made the desired Altera-

tion, and was afterwards delivered by General Washington, and published in that form, and has ever since been Known as "General Washington's Farewell Address." Shortly after the publication of the address, my husband and myself were walking in Broadway, when an old soldier accosted him, with a request of him to purchase General Washington's Farewell Address, which he did and turning to me Said, "That man does not know he has asked me to purchase my own work."

The whole circumstances are at this moment, so perfectly in my remembrance, that I can call to mind his bringing General Washington's letter to me (In the hall of the house where we then resided in Liberty Street, near Broadway) which returned the "address" and remarking on the only alteration which he (General Washington) had requested to be made.

New York, Aug. 7th, 1840   ELIZ^th HAMILTON

Witness
    as

J. A. WASHINGTON
J. A. MACDONALD

In 1849 the government purchased the Hamilton manuscripts, seventeen years after Eliza confided to her daughter and namesake:

> I have my fears I shall not obtain my object. Most of the contemporaries of your father have also passed away. I have since you left this, seen Mr. S. Kane, he is doing all he can, as is Mr. Clymer.

This remarkable woman had another ambition which she realized. The loss of her eldest son and the tragedy of her daughter Angelica, accentuated by her own widowhood and fatherless children, sparked her compassionate nature into helping orphans. Despite her own shaky economic condition, she took much of the property which her brothers and sisters generously gave her from their shares of General Schuyler's estate, and sold it piece by piece to help provide shelter and food for them, and the poor and friendless. A contemporary wrote:

> To Mrs. Hamilton is directly owing the first orphan asylum of New York. On its fiftieth anniversary a memorial service was held in the Church of the Epiphany [in Washington where she was visiting] and the work and its greatly extended good were gone over. The seed had become a tree with mighty branches. Mrs. Hamilton was feeble and could not sit through the whole service, but came only for a part; always to the communion service. This Sunday she came in toward the close. Our minds and hearts were filled with the good work of this gentle lady when she entered—a very small, upright little figure in deep black, never altered from the time her dark hair was framed in by the widow's cap, until now the hair was as white as the cap.
>
> As she moved slowly forward, supported by her daughter, Mrs. Holly, one common feeling made the congregation rise and remain standing until she was seated in her pew at the front.

If Eliza appeared "feeble" on that occasion, there is ample evidence that she had astonishing vigor at ninety-five. She converses, a friend marveled, "with much of that ease and brilliancy which lent so peculiar a charm to her younger days. And then, after passing the compliments and congratulations of the day, insists upon her visitors taking a merry glass from General Washington's punch bowl, which, with other portions of his table set, remains in her possession." To match the vigor of her mind, she demonstrated her physical fitness by walking from her house in H Street in Washington to visit Judge Cranch three miles away.

James Monroe came to call upon her, to patch up the differences that existed since the Reynolds affair. A nephew describes the scene:

> I had been sent to call upon my Aunt Hamilton one afternoon. I found her in her garden and was there with her talking, when her maid servant came from the house with a card. It was the card of James Monroe. She read the name, and stood holding the card, much perturbed. Her voice sank, and she spoke very low, as she always did when she was angry. "What has that man come to see

me for?" escaped from her. "Why, Aunt Hamilton," said I, "don't you know, it's Mr. Monroe, and he's been President, and he is visiting here now in the neighborhood, and has been very much made of, and invited everywhere, and so—I suppose he has come to call and pay his respects to you." After a moment's hesitation, "I will see him," she said.

The maid went back to the house, my aunt followed, walking rapidly, I after her. As she entered the parlor Monroe rose. She stood in the middle of the room facing him. She did not ask him to sit down. He bowed, and addressing her formally, made her rather a set speech—that it was many years since they had met, that the lapse of time brought its softening influences, that they were both nearing the grave, when past differences could be forgiven and forgotten—in short, from his point of view, a very nice, conciliatory, well-turned little speech. She answered, still standing, and looking at him, "Mr. Monroe, if you have come to tell me that you repent, that you are sorry, *very* sorry, for the misrepresentations and the slanders, and the stories you circulated against my dear husband, if you have come to say this I understand it. But otherwise, no lapse of time, no nearness to the grave, makes any difference." She stopped speaking, Monroe turned, took up his hat and left the room.

Elizabeth Schuyler Hamilton died in 1854, aged ninety-seven, after a brief illness that did not becloud her senses until a few days before her passing. They found a tiny bag around her neck and in it a sonnet written upon a yellowed, worn piece of paper, mended here and there with sewing thread. Hamilton had written it for her when they were courting:

ANSWER TO THE INQUIRY WHY I SIGHED

Before no mortal ever knew
A love like mine so tender—true—
Completely wretched—you away—
And but half blessed e'en while you stay.

If present love [illegible] face
Deny you to my fond embrace
No joy unmixed my bosom warms
But when my angel's in my arms.

My Dear Child

The Unsung Deborah Franklin

For most Americans, Deborah Read Franklin will always be the young girl smiling at seventeen-year-old Benjamin Franklin on an October Sunday morning in 1723, as the new arrival from Boston wandered through Philadelphia. "I was in my working dress," he recalled, "my best clothes being come round by sea. I was dirty from my journey; my pockets were stuffed with shirts and stockings." He had "three great puffy rolls"—one "under each arm, and eating the other. Thus I went up Market Street as far as Fourth Street, passing by the door of Mr. Read, my future wife's father; when she, standing in the door, saw me, and thought I made, as I certainly did, a most awkward, ridiculous appearance."

Within a short time he was lodging at the Read house, and the two teen-agers got to know each other. Deborah was strongly built—more handsome, perhaps, than beautiful, if a later portrait furnishes a key—with a high-colored complexion and cool blue eyes. "I had a great respect and affection for her, and had some reason to believe she had the same for me," and a year later he asked her to marry him. Mrs. Read, recently widowed, suggested they wait until Franklin returned from a trip to London, and both of them agreed without argument.

But the long sojourn in England changed his perspective. He sent only one letter to Deborah and that hinted he might remain abroad indefinitely. When he did get back to Philadelphia in 1726, he discovered that she had married Rogers, a potter; but their brief, unhappy marriage came to an end, for all practical purposes, when she learned Rogers had another wife. She had no positive proof, and Rogers skipped off to the West Indies, leaving a trail of debt. So young Mrs. Rogers the second was understandably frustrated. Franklin was suitably sympathetic, but with the sophistication he had acquired in Great Britain, through "low women that fell in my way" he found that marriage was not essential to relieve his strong sexual drive. Not that he was against marriage or pleased with the alternatives, for they had "been attended with some expense and great inconvenience, besides a continual risk to my health by a distemper which of all things I dreaded, though by great good luck I escaped it." Like Saint Augustine he prayed at dawn to be kept chaste, and in the evening added "but not yet," hurrying off to liaisons with an assortment of Philadelphia women. Late in 1730 or early in 1731 one of his ladies bore him a son, but Franklin veiled her identity so well that neither the scandal-mongers of his day or the seekers after truth today have been able to ascertain it. Deborah Read Rogers has been suggested as the mother, but her intense dislike of the boy, William, discounts this theory. In Franklin's subsequent career, his political enemies tried to block William's appointment as governor of New Jersey on the ground of illegitimacy, and may have succeeded in embarrassing the Franklins but not in resolving the question of maternity.

The immediate impact of the event was to make him decide to marry. "A single man," he observed, "resembles the odd half of a pair of scissors." Not being in love, he could view his mission with a certain detachment. Mrs. Godfrey, who with her husband Thomas and family, rented rooms in his house,

> projected a match for me with a relation's daughter, [and] took opportunities of bringing us often together, till a serious courtship on my part ensued, the girl being in herself very deserving. The old folks encouraged me by continual invitations to supper, and by leaving us together, till at length it was time to explain. Mrs. Godfrey managed our little treaty. I let her know that I expected as much money with their daughter as would pay off my remaining debt for the printing-house, which I believe was not then above a hundred pounds. She brought me word they had not such sum to spare. I said they might mortgage their house in the loan office. The answer to this, after some days, was they did not approve the match; that, on inquiry of Bradford, they had been informed the business was not a profitable one . . . and, therefore, I was forbidden the house and the daughter shut up.

He suspected the parents thought he might elope with their daughter and thus relieve them of the need to provide any dowry. When he made no effort in this direction,

> Mrs. Godfrey brought me . . . some more favourable account of their disposition, and would have drawn me on again; but I declared absolutely my resolution to have nothing more to do with that family. This was resented by the Godfreys; we differed, and they removed, leaving me the whole house, and I resolved to take no more inmates.

His survey continued:

> I looked round me and made overtures of acquaintance in other places; but soon found that, the business of a printer being generally thought a poor one, I was not to expect money with a wife, unless with such a one as I should not otherwise think agreeable. . . . A friendly correspondence as neighbours and old acquaintances had continued between me and Mrs. Read's family, who all had a regard for me from the time of my first lodging in their house. I was often invited there and consulted in their affairs, wherein I sometimes was of service. I pitied poor Miss Read's

unfortunate situation, who was generally dejected, seldom cheerful, and avoided company. I considered my giddiness and inconstancy when in London as in a great degree the cause of her unhappiness, though the mother was good enough to think the fault more her own than mine, as she had prevented our marrying before I went thither, and persuaded the other match in my absence. Our mutual affection was revived, but there were now great objections to our union. The match was indeed looked upon as invalid, a preceding wife being said to be living in England; but this could not be easily proved, because of the distance; and though there was a report of his death it was not certain. Then, though it should be true, he had left many debts, which his successor might be called upon to pay. We ventured, however, over all these difficulties, and I took her to wife September 1st, 1730.

Franklin brushes past the other "difficulties." Although Deborah was a devout member of Christ Church, a ceremony there or anywhere else was out of the question. Pennsylvania law, following the Quaker distaste for clergymen, made private marriages valid, even if a couple never thereafter lived together as husband and wife. But Deborah's uncertain status made her ineligible even for this, and it is most likely they simply agreed to an arrangement. Although Franklin was fifty before he engaged in his "flirtations," at twenty-four he was well aware of his propensities; and it may have occurred to him that he had an escape hatch if Deborah proved impossible to live with or he met someone with whom he fell deeply and uncontrollably in love. Divorce was next to impossible in 1730; so he was ideally situated. If his wife was not accomplished and beautiful, she was physically attractive and practical. With all the comforts of domesticity Franklin could concentrate on his many interests with the calm required by a young talented philosopher. So on September 1 Deborah and her mother moved into his home, and she assumed the title of "Mrs. Franklin." When the illegitimate William was born, he became a part of the family circle.

Deborah had little interest in her partner's inventions, writings, or contemplations. She helped occasionally in his printing shop, not as an apprentice, but as a saleslady, since he carried a wide variety of items along with books and stationery, including sack, lampblack, chocolate, linseed oil, coffee, patent medicines, powdered mustard, palm oil, spectacles, and the like. He gave space in the *Gazette* to notify the public that "The Widow Read, removed from the upper End of Highstreet to the New Printing-Office near the Market, continues to make and sell her well-known Ointment for the ITCH with which she has cured abundance of People in and about this City for many Years past."

If Deborah was indifferent to much of his activity, she managed to learn the rudiments of bookkeeping. In 1733 he gave her power of attorney to collect, in his name, all debts owing him. Native intelligence, coupled with his teaching, brought her to a point where she was fairly capable of handling his affairs—an ability that was of immense assistance to him when he began to make extensive trips in America and to take long sojourns abroad.

Seldom did the couple entertain at home, preferring to take friends to dinner at a tavern. The Franklin house always had surplus people. In addition to Deborah's mother, his nephew came down from Boston, an apprentice or two probably lodged there, and in 1732 Francis Folger Franklin was born there. Philadelphians of prominence, attracted by Franklin's abilities, virtually ignored Deborah. She was never included in their invitations. Yet it is equally likely that she wanted no part of the social world, being content to live in one of her own choosing.

Still she was no placid lump of dough. Spirited in her own right, in 1753 she astonished an Englishman, Daniel Fisher, who had come from Virginia looking for work. When he called at the house, he found Deborah sitting on the next door steps, protesting that "all the world claimed a privilege of troubling her Pappy (so she usually calls Mr. Franklin) with their calamaties and distresses." When Fisher became Franklin's clerk, and he and Deborah were on more friendly terms, he described her coldness toward William Franklin. The two seldom spoke to each other, and one day as he passed, she turned to Fisher and said: " 'Mr. Fisher,

there goes the greatest villain upon earth!' This greatly con-
founded and perplexed me, but did not hinder her from pursuing
her invectives in the foulest terms I ever heard from a gentlewoman."

With the ebullient Franklin she seems to have had a happy, if
often a lonely life. At one of his frequent nights-out with friends
about 1742, someone jokingly said instead of singing songs in
praise of their mistresses, maybe they occasionally should offer
one in toast to their wives. This probably inspired Franklin's
hymn to Deborah in the guise of "plain Country Joan":

Of their Chloes and Phillises Poets may prate
    I sing my plain Country Joan
Now twelve years my Wife, still the Joy of my Life
    Blest Day that I made her my own
                                        My dear Friends
    Blest Day that I made her my own.

2

Not a Word of her Face, her Shape, or her Eyes
    Of Flames or of Darts shall you hear;
Tho' I beauty admire, 'tis Virtue I prize,
    That fades not in seventy Years
                                        My dear Friends

3

In Health a Companion delightfull and dear,
    Still easy, engaging, and Free
In Sickness no less than the faithfullest Nurse
    As tender as tender can be,
                                        My dear Friends

4

In Peace and good Order, my Household she keeps
    Right Careful to save what I gain
Yet chearfully spends, and smiles on the Friends
    I've the Pleasures to entertain
                                        My dear Friends

5

She defends my good Name ever where I'm to blame,
    Friend firmer was ne'er to Man giv'n,
Her compassionate Breast, feels for all the Distrest,
    Which draws down the Blessing from Heav'n,
                                My dear Friends

6

Am I laden with Care, she takes off a large Share,
    That the Burthen ne'er makes me to reel
Does good Fortune arrive, the Joy of my Wife
    Quite doubles the Pleasures I feel
                                My dear Friends

7

In Raptures the giddy Rake talks of his Fair
    Enjoyment shall make him Despise
I speak my cool sence, that long Experience
    And Enjoyment have chang'd in no wise
                                My dear Friends

(Some Faults we have all, and so may my Joan,
    But then they're exceedingly small;
And now I'm us'd to 'em, they're just like my own,
    I scarcely can see 'em at all
                                My dear Friends
    I scarcely can see them at all.)

8

Were the fairest young Princess, with Million in Purse
    To be had in Exchange for my Joan
She could not be a better Wife, mought be a Worse
    So I'd stick to my Joggy alone
                                My dear Friends
    I'd cling to my lovely ould Joan.

If Deborah recognized herself in these verses she did not get sentimental over the fact, for on the back of one sheet she jotted some charges to a customer. In her "Shop Book" she refers to Poor Richard's Almanacks as "Poor Dicks."

Their son, "Little Franky," as his father affectionately called him, died in 1736 of smallpox. Throughout his long life Franklin would recall that sad moment with "a sigh"—and it was not until seven years later, in September 1743, that Deborah had another child, Sarah, baptized in Christ Church on October 5 and destined to be the delight of her parents.

Franklin told young women who wrote to him, and in the course of their letters apologized for poor spelling, that he regarded it as "the best in the world, for every letter of it stands for something." Presumably he was as indulgent with Deborah's, which was purely phonetic. On Christmas eve, 1751 she wrote Margaret Strahan in England:

> I am ordored by my master to write for sum books for Salley Franklin. I am in hopes shee will be abel to write her selfe by the Spring. . . .
> My Dafter Gives her Duty to Mr. Strayhon and his Lady and her Compleyments to Master Billey and all his Brothers and Sisters. My Son is Gon to Boston on a Visit to his friends. I suppose Mr. Franklin will write him Selfe. Mr. and Mis Hall air verey well. They have lost thair other Child. She lays in this winter. My Compleyments to Mr. Strayhon and all your Dear little Famely. I am Dear Madam your Humbel Sarvant
>
> DEBORAH FRANKLIN

By contemporary standards, Deborah's spelling was not all that bad. It stands out more starkly because of her intimate connection with a man who was not only the best writer in America, but one of the best in the world.

Strahan, a London printer, had been one of Franklin's first European friends, and after Sally's birth the two half-jokingly, half-seriously wrote of hopefully uniting their families through her marriage to Strahan's son. Franklin, a devoted father, was anxious for his children to have the broadest education. Deborah was annoyed at the attention given William, whom Franklin was pushing in influential places. Among the few criticisms she levied at her husband was her feeling that he was favoring the boy over the girl. This belief, coupled with the smug conceit William displayed, accounted for her ever increasing annoyance with him. There was, of course, no imbalance in Franklin's attentions to Sally. "My Daughter," he wrote Strahan in 1754, "is now 11 years old, grows finely, an honest good Girl, as dutiful and sweet-temper'd as one could wish. I promise myself much Comfort in her when I grow old, if we should live. But these things will be as God pleases." In 1760 when Franklin was visiting Strahan in London, he wrote Deborah, enclosing a written proposal that Strahan made for the marriage of Sally with his son:

> He was very urgent with me to stay in England and prevail with you to remove hither with Sally. He propos'd several advantageous Schemes . . . I gave him, however, two Reasons why I could not think of removing hither. One, my Affection to Pensilvania, and long established Friendships and other Connections there; The other, your invincible Aversion to crossing the Seas. And without removing hither, I could not think of parting with my Daughter to such a Distance. I thank'd him for the Regard shown us in the Proposal; but gave him no Expectation that I should forward the Letters. So you are at Liberty to answer or not, as you think proper. Let me however, know your Sentiments. You need not deliver the Letter to Sally, if you do not think it proper.

There is no record of any reply by Deborah to the suggestion.

While one of Poor Richard's maxims warned "The first mistake in public business is the going into it," Franklin got deeply involved. When he received the appointment from the Crown as deputy postmaster for America, Deborah was able to share some of the work and interest. Even when his civic conscience led him into plans for a hospital, college, and other local improvements in Philadelphia, she was within the perimeter. But gradually his fame grew, and his scientific experiments and observations were commanding attention in Europe as well as throughout the Colonies. He received honorary degrees, joking that he achieved academic recognition without having had to go to college—and he was active in politics, principally in Pennsylvania, but with a breadth of vision that in 1754 led him at Albany to recommend a colonial union. Thus when he passed his fiftieth birthday, Franklin, through his self-made sophistication, drew not only the plaudits of the famous, but developed a magnetism that attracted younger women.

The first to fall under his spell was attractive twenty-three-year-old Catherine Ray of Rhode Island, whom he met in Boston late in 1754. The vivacious girl parried his wit, teased him as being a "conjurer," and gently rebuffed him when he got too amorous—an attempt he admitted was "an erratum." They were together for a while, and he accompanied her back to the point where she took "a very little Skiff" across to home on Block Island. "I thought too much was hazarded, when I saw you put off to Sea . . . tossed by every Wave . . . I stood on the Shore and look'd after you, till I could no longer distinguish you, even with my Glass." Back in "the Arms of my good old Wife and Children," he answered a letter from her in March 1755—one she had written on January 20 "just come to hand." "I write this during a N. East Storm of Snow," he told her, "But since you promis'd to send me Kisses in that Wind . . . 'tis the gayest Wind that blows, and gives me the best Spirits . . . Your Favours come mix'd with the Snowy Fleeces which are pure as your Virgin Innocence, white as your lovely Bosom—and as cold—But let it warm towards some worthy young Man, and may Heaven bless you both with every kind of Happiness." He did not answer her next several letters, and on June 28, 1755, received the following:

Dear, Dear Sir,

Excues my writeing when I tell you it is the great regard I have for you will not let me be Silent, for Absence rather increasis than lesens my affections then, my not receiveing one line from you in answer to 3 of my last letters . . . gives me a Vast deal of uneasiness and occation'd many tears, for Suerly I have wrote too much and you are affronted with me . . . I'll only beg the favor of one line . . . Tel me you are well and forgive me and love me one thousandth Part So well as I do you. . . .

My proper Respects to Mrs. Franklin and Daugter

Pray take care of your health and except the Sugar Plums they are every one Sweetn'd as you used to like.

She had worried about what happened to her letters, probably because she had been impetuous or too expansive in her declaration of love and was concerned they might have been intercepted in his absence by Deborah. In September he set her mind at ease with a response that began: "Begone, Business, for an Hour, at least, and let me chat a little with my Katy." He explained he received her March 3 letter "just before I set out on a long Journey and the others while I was on that Journey, which held me near Six Weeks," after which "publick Affairs of various kinds . . . render'd it impracticable" to respond earlier.

I long to hear whether you have continu'd ever since in that Monastery; or have broke into the World again, doing pretty Mischief . . . I commend your prudent Resolutions in the Article of granting Favours to Lovers; But if I were courting you, I could not heartily approve such Conduct . . . You have spun a Long Thread, 5022 Yards! It will reach almost from Block Island thither. I wish I had hold of one End of it, to pull you to me: But you would break it rather than come. . . .

. . . The Cheeses . . . were excellent: All our Friends have tasted it, and all agree that it exceeds any English Cheese they ever tasted. Mrs. Franklin was very proud, that a young Lady should have so much Regard for her old Husband, as to send him such a Present. We talk of you every Time it comes to Table; She is sure you are a sensible Girl, and a notable Housewife; and talks of bequeathing me to you as a Legacy; But I ought to wish you a better, and hope she will live these 100 years; for we are grown old together, and if she has any faults, I am so us'd to 'em that I don't perceive 'em, as the Song says. . . .

Indeed I begin to think she has none, as I think of you. And since she is willing I should love you as much as you are willing to be lov'd by me; let us join in wishing the old Lady a long Life and a happy.

Whether Deborah was as congenial about all this as Franklin made her out to be, she and Catherine became friends, but when the young woman eventually married and brought her husband to Philadelphia in 1776—having been wed in 1758—Deborah was no longer alive. Franklin only saw Catherine three other times before this last visit but remained a correspondent until his own death.

The heady draught of a young woman's affection did not up- set his perspective. He valued Deborah, and his letters to her and his purchase of presents for her show his deep attachment. They usually addressed each other as "My dear Child," as if the phrase was a magic elixir which made them forever young in each other's eyes. During 1755 while Catherine was agonizing over her unan- swered letters, he found time to write to a friend in London "to request you would send my Wife Sattin sufficient for a Gown, somewhat darker than the enclos'd Pattern." In November 1756 while at Easton, Pennsylvania, he gently chided her:

My Dear Child,

I wrote to you a few days since, by a special messenger, and inclosed letters, for all our wives and sweethearts, expecting to hear from you by his return . . . but he is just now returned without a scrap for poor us. So I had a good mind not to write to you by this opportunity; but I never can be ill-natured enough, even when there is the most occasion. The messenger, says he left the letters at your house, and saw you afterwards at Mr. Dentie's and told you when he would go, and that he lodged at Honey's, next door to you, and yet you did not write; so let Goody Smith give one more just judgment, and say what should be done to you; I think I wont tell you that we are well, nor that we expect to return about the middle of the week, nor will I send you a word of news; that's poz. My duty to mother, love to the children, and to Miss Betsey and Gracey, &c. &c. I am, Your *loving* husband,

B. FRANKLIN

P.S. I have *scratched out the loving words*, being writ in haste by mistake, when *I forgot I was angry.*

In the spring of 1757 he set off for London on provincial business, taking William with him. Before leaving he gave Deborah an account book in which he asked her to carefully record all her expenditures. The entries were started just prior to his departure so she would have an idea of what he wanted, but once on her own, she found it tedious and there are blank spaces and empty pages between notations. Some she did set down give us a glimpse of how the money was spent:

	£	s	d
paid the womon that Irons for us	£1	–	–
paid the poor tax 15 and fier Componey 1-6	–	16	6
laid ought fullishley	–	10	
and Generousley	–	10	
paid for a pair of purpill shoes for Salley	–	7	6
a pound of anchovise	–	3	6
my Cash did not quite hold ought this month			
Salleys french master	–	10	–
a bras dogs and fier Shoefil fier and tong	7	15	–
for splittin sume large wood and Clering the Seller	–	9	–
paid out tacks	8	8	–

There is a note of resignation in her final entry:

September took for famely expenses in Cash £6-0-0 as I am not abell to set down every penney. I think to doe this way.

Although Franklin arrived in New York on April 8, four days

after starting from Philadelphia, the shipping arrangements, always subject to a variety of things, delayed his sailing until June 5. The interval, part of which was relieved by visits from Deborah and Sally at Woodbridge, New Jersey, gave him time to think of additional things for Deborah to do, and, like most conscientious travelers, to draw a new will. The concluding paragraph expressed gratitude to God for giving him a "life so happily, so free from Sickness, Pain and Trouble, and with such a Competency of this World's Goods as might make a reasonable Mind easy; that he was pleased to give me such a Mind, with moderate Passions . . . ; That he gave me to live so long in a Land of Liberty, with a People that I love, and rais'd me, tho' a Stranger, so many Friends among them; bestowing on me, moreover, a loving and prudent Wife and dutiful Children."

From New York on April 29 he asked Deborah to

> Send me the Indian Sealskin Hussiff [housewife—a pocket case for needles, pins, scissors, etc.] with all the Things that were in it . . . In the right hand little Drawer under my Desk, is some of the Indian Lady's Gut Cambrick; roll it up as you would a Ribband; wrap it in Paper, and put it into the Houseiff with the other Things.
>
> Among my Books on the Shelves, there are two or three little Pieces on the Game of Chess; One in French bound in Leather, 8vo. One in a blue Paper Cover, English; two others in Manuscript; one of them thin in brown Paper Cover, the other in loose Leaves not bound. If you can find them yourself, send them: But do not set anybody else to look for them.

Still land-locked on May 27, he dispatched another letter:

> I am making up a Bundle of Papers to send you. Put them in my Room. . . .
>
> In my Room, on the Folio Shelf, between the Clock and our Bed Chamber, and not far from the Clock, stands a Folio call'd the Gardener's Dictionary, by P. Miller.
>
> And on the same side of the Room on the lowest Shelf, or lowest but one, near the Middle, and by the Side of a little Partition, you will find standing or rather lying on its fore Edge,

a Quarto Pamphlet, cover'd with blue Paper call'd a Treatise of Cyder-making.

Deliver those two Books to Mr. Parker.

Finally the ship sailed and from Falmouth on July 17, 1757, he wrote to her:

> The bell ringing for church, we went thither immediately, and with hearts full of gratitude, returned sincere thanks to God for the mercies we had received; were I a Roman Catholic, perhaps I should on this occasion vow to build a chapel to some saint; but as I am not, if I were to vow at all, it should be to build a *lighthouse.*

Deborah at first was a dutiful correspondent, writing to him regularly every two weeks. One letter enclosed a letter Sally had composed in French for her father. "I had no desire of her larning that Language," Mrs. Franklin said, "but shee desired it her self." Franklin had undoubtedly helped in the planning, and asked his daughter to write occasionally in French. He told Deborah:

> I should have read Sally's French Letter with more Pleasure, but that I thought the French rather too good to be all her own Composing. I suppose her Master must have corrected it. But I am glad she is improving in that and her Music. I send her a French Pamela.

This French version of Richardson's popular novel was a challenging bit for a fourteen-year-old girl who had just been studying the tongue for four weeks; but Franklin, who had taught himself Latin, French, Greek, and other languages, wisely felt a full-fledged story would spur her ambitions more than routine exercises.

Strahan, highly impressed with Franklin and his son, now set out to get Deborah and Sally to join them, wagering with Franklin that a letter he wrote on December 13, 1757, would convince her. He used every argument, including a passage that Deborah might not have found amusing:

For my own part, I never saw a man who was, in every respect so perfectly agreeable to me. Some are amiable in one view; some in another, he in all. Now madam as I know the ladies here consider him in exactly the same light I do, upon my word I think you should come over, with all convenient speed to look after your interest; not but that I think him as faithful to his Joan, as any man breathing; but who knows what repeated and strong temptation, may in time, and while he is at so great a distance from you, accomplish.

Franklin was confident Deborah's fear of the sea and love for Philadelphia were too strong, and realized how uncomfortable she would be in the high places he was now frequently visiting. For him it was all very satisfactory, reveling as he did in the company of new-found women friends. On January 14, 1758, after recovering from a siege of sickness the previous fall, he told her he refused to accept Strahan's bet. "I tell him I will not pick his pocket; for I am sure there is no inducement strong enough to prevail with you to cross the seas. I would be glad if I could tell you when I expected to be at home, but that is still in the dark." Less than two weeks later, he hastily wrote a note: "I begin to think I shall hardly be able to return before this time twelve months. I am for doing effectually what I came about; and I find it requires both time and patience. You may think perhaps that I can find many amusements here to pass the time agreeable. T'is true, the regard and friendship I meet with from persons of worth, and the conversation of ingenious men, give me no small pleasure; but at this time of life, domestic comforts afford the most solid satisfaction, and my uneasiness at being absent from my family, and longing desire to be with them, make me often sigh in the midst of cheerful company. My love to my dear Sally. I confide in you the care of her and her education; I promise myself the pleasure of finding her much improved at my return."

Deborah was solicitous about his health, giving him detailed advice, and in February he wrote her:

My Shirts are always well air'd as you directed. Mrs. Stevenson takes Care of that. I am much more tender than I us'd to be, and sleep in a short Callico Bedgown with close Sleeves, and Flannel close-footed Trowsers; for without them I get no Warmth all Night, so it seems I grow older apace. But otherwise at present I am pretty well.

Give my Thanks to Dr. Bond for the Care he takes of you.

His thoughts during this time were of home, for he tells her of a long list of things he is shipping: china, pottery, "one old true China Bason mended . . . Six coarse diaper Breakfast Cloths; they are to spread on the Tea Table, for no body breakfasts here on the named Table, but on the Cloth set a large Tea Board with the Cups," blankets, "2 fine Damask Table Cloths and Napkins," silver ladles, "56 Yards of Cotton printed curiously from Copper Plates, a new Invention, to make Bed and Window Curtains . . . Also 7 Yards of printed Cotton, blue Ground, to make you a Gown; bought it by Candlelight, and lik'd it then, but not so well afterwards; if you do not fancy it, send it as a Present from me to Sister Jenny. There is a better Gown for you of flower'd Tissue . . . there was no more of the Sort, or you should have had enough for a Negligee or Suit . . . I also forgot, among the China to mention a large fine Jugg for Beer, to stand in the Cooler. I fell in Love with it at first Sight; for I thought it look'd like a fat jolly Dame, clean and tidy, with a neat blue and white Calico Gown on, good natur'd and lovely, and put me in mind of _____ Somebody."

Deborah's temper flared at British interference with the mails which "Mr. Franklin had at a considerable expence" set up for twice weekly service between Philadelphia and New York. She complained to Lord Loudon that she had been "insulted in my Own House" by one of his officers. Loudon replied that there was no intent "to offend anyone much less Mrs. Franklin," but he demanded she direct postmasters recognize the franking "Priviledges of a Peer" or he would be forced "to disagreable Measures."

While she exercised a careful eye over postal affairs, she stayed aloof from the political squabbles in Pennsylvania. Franklin commended her in June 1758: "You are very prudent not to engage in Party Disputes. Women should never meddle with them except in Endeavours to reconcile their Husbands, Brothers and Friends who happen to be of contrary Sides. If your Sex can keep cool, you may be a means of cooling ours the sooner, and restoring more speedily that social Harmony among Fellow Citizens that is so desirable after long and bitter Dissensions." Then he added:

> I have no Prospect of Returning till next Spring, so you will not expect me. But pray remember to make me as happy as you can, by sending some Pippins for my self and Friends, some of your small Hams, and some Cranberries. . . . I am glad you like the Cloak I sent you. The black silk was sent by our Friend Mr. Collinson. I never saw it.
>
> Your Answer to Mr. Strahan was just what it should be; I was much pleas'd with it. He fanc'd his Rhetoric and Art would certainly bring you over.
>
> I have order'd two large print Common Prayer Books to be bound on purpose for you and Goodey Smith; and that the largeness of the Print may not make them too bulkey, the Christnings, Matrimonies, and every thing else that you and she have not immediate and constant Occasion for, are to be omitted. So you will both of you be repriev'd from the Use of Spectacles in Church, a little longer.

She was frightened at night by the bells he had rigged on the lightning rod atop their house to signal when it was charged with electricity. He told her to "tie a Piece of Wire from one Bell to the other, and that will conduct the lightning without ringing or snapping, but silently. Tho' I think it best the Bells should be at Liberty to ring, that you may know when the Wire is electrify'd, and, if you are afraid, may keep at a Distance."

His friend John Hughes reported that his family was in good health, and "I Continue to visit frequently in your Absence," looking for "an Oppertunity to Serve You or Yours, but Mrs. Franklin's Good Oeconomy Renders friends I think almost Unnecessary however I believe we Shall keep up a friendly Correspondence Untill Your Return."

While neither Deborah nor Franklin sought to impress people with their comfortable wealth, she could hardly have helped enjoying a measure of status. The snubs she endured at the time she went to live with Franklin were erased by the scarlet cloak and other attire made of imported materials, and the attendance of her slaves. Franklin, out of affection and a bit of vanity, saw that she and Sally had the latest fashions. For Sally there were books and sheets of music, some of them sent by her brother. But the boxes included such things as "A Candle Screen to save Debby's Eyes" and a "Reading Glass . . . set in Silver and Tortoise Shell."

Deborah, active in church work, reported in August that she "went to hear the Negro Children catechised . . . There were 17 that answered very prettily indeed, and 5 or 6 that were too little, but all behaved very decently. Mr. Sturgeon exhorted them before and after the Catechising. It gave me a great deal of pleasure, and I shall send Othello to the School." Othello was either the child of Franklin's "Negro Man Peter, and his Wife Jemima" or the "Negrow boy" for whom Deborah paid £41 10s. in 1757. A school for black children had been opened in 1758, and they were taken to Christ Church on Wednesdays and Fridays for religious instruction. The idea generated much enthusiasm in London's Anglican circles, and the excerpt from Deborah's letter was printed with appropriate credit to her. Franklin expressed surprise at this, and at a meeting he attended found himself elected chairman of the movement "for the current year." He gave her an account of the proceedings, and while congratulating himself that she "will not complain this Year as you did the last, of being so long without a Letter" since "I have wrote to you very frequently," said in a postscript, "I . . . forgot to purchase the Eider Down and Corn Plaster you wrote for." He promised to remedy the oversight. She sent him dried venison and he pronounced it "very acceptable, and I thank you for it. We have had it continually shav'd to eat with our Bread and Butter for Breakfast, and this Week saw the last of it. The Bacon still holds out; for we are choice of it. Some Rashers of it, yesterday relish'd a Dish of Green Pease . . . The smok'd Beef was also excellent."

Since 1756 the Franklins had been living in a house rented from John Wister on Market Street, and while they had been gradually buying parcels of property to eventually build their own, Franklin's absence had delayed the plans. Deborah was getting restive, and in August 1760 her husband wrote, "I am concern'd you should be so perplex'd about a House, and hope you are settled before this time." His allusion was to still another temporary residence, which Deborah did not find until April 1761 at the present 326 Market Street.

She sustained a shock in December, 1761, when her mother "in a fit fell in the fire" and was burned to death. Franklin did not learn of this tragedy until March 1762, and wrote he was "extreamly sensible of the Distress and Affliction it must have thrown you into" but added philosophically, "The Circumstances attending her Death were indeed unhappy in some Respects; but something must bring us all to our End, and few of us shall see her Length of Days." His wife's grief was subsequently tempered by word that he was finally coming home, and she got out the neglected account book in May and scrawled: "I begin agen to keep an a Counte of expenses," listing such diverse items as "goodeys for my pappey 2 jars," "Sallit and greens," "Salley a Blew necklis," "a Jet Necklase for my Selef," "Shues for Salley," "for Billey fier Companey," "for the Liberrey for papey and Mr. Grase," and other items.

Franklin "got home well the first of November," he informed Strahan, "and had the Happiness to find my little Family perfectly well; and that Dr. Smith's Reports of the Diminution of My Friends were all false. My House has been full of a Succession of them from Morning to Night ever since my Arrival, congratulating me on my Return with the utmost Cordiality and Affection." But the atmospheric change from England's adulation to Philadelphia's bitter political fights made him wistful for Great Britain. "In two Years at farthest," he wrote in another letter to Strahan, "I hope to settle all my Affairs in such a Manner, as that

I may then conveniently remove to England, provided we can persuade the good Woman to cross the Seas. That will be the great Difficulty; but you can help me a little in removing it."

Deborah saw him only intermittently during 1763. He was occupied with a hundred different things. The postal service had to be extended to Canada now that it belonged to Britain, and he went to Virginia in April and spent nearly a month. Back in Philadelphia briefly in May, he wrote his sister Jane in Boston that he was setting out for New England in the beginning of June, "but have no Expectation of bringing my Dame to undertake such a Journey; and have not yet ask'd her Opinion of Sally's going." Sally, now twenty, joined him in New York, and en route together through Rhode Island he was thrown from a horse and virtually into the arms of Catherine Ray Greene. Now a housewife and mother, Catherine insisted Franklin and his daughter stay until he was fully recovered, but within a few days he was ready to press on. His thank-you note written from Boston August 1, 1763, contemplated being read by a wider audience than her, as the concluding line suggests: "With perfect Esteem and Regard, I am, Dear Katy (I can't yet alter my Stile to Madam) Your affectionate Friend. . . ."

Franklin was in Philadelphia for a sufficient length of time in 1764 to get his new house started, and Deborah thus had something to keep her fully occupied. Then, after the usual vitriolic squabbles of Pennsylvania politics, he was chosen once more to represent the province in England and on November 7 set sail from Chester, accompanied to the dock by 300 friends on horseback. He had wanted Sally to go along with him but Deborah was adamant. From the Isle of Wight on December 9 he sent word to "Debby" that the ship "this moment" had "come to an Anchor here . . . we have had terrible Weather, and I have often been thankful that our dear Sally was not with me. Tell our Friends that din'd with us on the Turtle that the kind Prayer they then put up for thirty Days fair Wind for me, was favourably heard and answered, we being just 30 Days from Land to Land."

If Deborah Franklin had done nothing more than write

letters, she would deserve a niche in history. Unfettered by grammar and spelling, she gives us delightful vignettes of what she sees and thinks. Sally has just returned from visiting her brother William, now the royal governor of New Jersey; and Deborah has just sent "Naney," a servant, off to Burlington, New Jersey, to spend Christmas. Thus Debby's letter to Franklin:

Philadelphia Jan the 8 1765

My Dear Child

I donte think the Packit will sail at the time but I write lest it shold and I shold be found wanting in my Duty and you be displesd.

In the firste plase Salley is Come home Shee traveled the coldest day I ever felte or that I ever remember and staid at the ferry [?] house till the next day then walked over one halef of the river and then in the bote the other halef but Shee is att home Safe now and we air all blocked up Could. I donte think we have had so much Snow this thirty years one Can hardly see the Topes of the postes now it is two deep to go a Slaying I am told the river is inhabeyted with Taverens but I have not seen it. Jamey Allin fell in but as mony pepel was on he had presente helpe. I did not hear that he got Cold. Poor Naney is quite fritened. She ses they hante such snowing wather in London and what makes it the more terrabel we hante Cole to burne which shee is sorry for but their was an opertunity and Shee desired to go and keep Christmas att Burlinton. So I wraped her in a dubel gound after She was drest and gave her sum good advise to keep her self warme and she wente a way while it snowed faste. I hope shee got thair safe but I have not heard. The marbel fireplaces is come safe but be Kind eneuef to tell our worthey friend Mr. Collinson that thair was not one Case in ither of the Boxes. I sente for our Cusin Wilkison to take the marbel ought and Stueby to take Care of the bundel of Levess but it was not thair. The Mantel is quite Curis indeed, but I donte remember wather you sed in what room the beste [?] shold be put. Yisterday I Spook to Nabor Headock but he ses thair is no such Thing as painting till next March with ought the wather shold olter verey much so I must indever to make my self as esey as I Can but I did raly think I shold a bin allmoste ready to a mouefed as soon as this wather has brook up. . . .

. . . God bless you my dear Child. I am your afeckshenit wife

D. FRANKLIN

I long to know hough your Arm is and wather John [a servant] was of aney Sarvis to you I hope you did not meet with any hurt in the passag.

And this on February 10, 1765:

I am set down to Confab a littel with my dear child as it Semes a Sorte of a hollow day for we have an ox arosteing on the river and moste pepel semes plesd with the a fair but as I partake of none of the divershons I stay at home and flatter myselef that the next packit will bring me a letter from you.

By the laste packit thair was a letter from mr. Jackson to you the poste Came in laite att night I did not know hough to ackte as you had not sed aney thing to me a bought what I shold due with the letters. . . .

We have nothing stiring amoungst us but phamlits [pamphlets] and Scurrilitey but I have never sed or dun aney thing or aney of our famely you may depend on it nor shall we. All our good friends Cole on us as yousall and we have bin asked ought but I have not gon but Salley has within this mounth but Shee was att Billeys all moste seven weeks.

This day the man is a puting up the fier plases that Came from London the darke one is in the parler. I am in hopes the harthes will be laid the wather will begin to be wormer and the Sun Stronger. The plasterer is a finishing the lathing of the stair Cases and I am a geting the lore parte of the house clened ought readey for the laying the kitching flore all this a bought the house.

Now a littel of what hapens Dr Whit of Jermanton deyed this week. Mr. Plumsted in comin from N York had liked to be drounde he fell in seven times he gave a man ten pounds to pul him over the river on a bord leyin flat doune. He was in that Condishun for two owers but got home well and not aney Cold as I hear of. Now for a verey good pees of news our Governer gave in money for the poor ten pounds and fortey Cord of wood

which is worth Sixtey pounds and more as it is sold now you
donte know hough everey bodey loves him and we think our
Governer is a kingbird. Salley is well and will write this time.

Feb. 17

Sens I wrote the above our Cusin Antoney Willkison deyed
verey sudenly. I had not herd that he was unwell tell his man
Came for me he was dead he sed I have not seen my Cusin sense
as the wather is verey sever and slepey. On Freyday I got a man
to helpe Gorge to Cute and Clear a way the Ise att the street dore
and a bout the pump and guter. It was near three feet thick. I
never knew such a winter in my time but I am in hopes the
worste of the wather is over. For severel day Gorge and my self
have bin att the New house a geting the roomes readey for the
painter as Mr. Hadock ses he hopes he shall get to worke in
march. I shall get the harthes Laid and if verey Cold wather is
then we Can make a fier to prevent the painte reseveing aney
dommaig. I only wish I was remouefed then I hope to be more
relieved but I have not one ower my one att this time as a
reporte is got aboute that you air arived in London and our
friends all Come to know for them selves.

Franklin on February 14 forwarded "blue Mohair Stuff . . .
for the Curtains of the Blue Chamber. The Fashion is to make
one Curtain only for each Window. Hooks are sent to fix the Rails
by at Top, so that they may be taken down on Occasion. I almost
Wish I had left Directions not to paint the House till my Return.
But I suppose tis done before this time." Appreciative of her
determination not to be drawn into the arguments stirred by the
violent broadsides being published against him in Philadelphia,
which cast up the illegitimacy of William, he added: "I am glad
their Pamphlets give you so little Concern. I make no other Answer to them at present than what appears in the Seal of this
Letter." The Franklin family arms bore the legend, *exemplum
adest ipse homo* (the example presents the man himself). He tells
her:

Let no one make you uneasy with their idle or malicious Stories or Scribblings, but enjoy yourself and Friends, and the Comforts of Life that God has bestow'd on you, with a chearful Heart. Let Sally divert you with her Music. Put her on Practising on the Armonica. Mr. Brenmer with his Violin may assist and improve her there as well as on the Harpsichord. A few Months, I hope, will finish Affairs here to my Wish, and bring me to that Retirement and Repose with my little Family, so suitable to my Years, and which I have so long set my Heart upon.

Deborah wrote in April:

Aprill 7 this day is Cumpleet 5 munthes sense you lefte your one House. I did reseve a letter from the Capes senes that not one line. I due supose that you did write by the Jan packit but that is not arived as yit. Miss Wikeof Came and told me that you was arived and was well that her Brother had wrote her he had seen you mr. Neet has wrote that you was well and miss Graham has wrote all so that shee had the pleshuer of a visit from you and several have wrote that you was well all thes a Countes air as plesing as such things Can be but a letter wold tell me hough your poor armes was and hough you was on your voiag and hough you air and everey thing is with you which I wante verey much to know. Mr. Foxcrofte Came to town this day weeke and is to returne agen in a bought a week and as I had got sume of our things in the new house and beads in the uper roomes he lodges in the room fasing the market street and has his writeing thair all so yisterday sume of the Sashes was hung and if I wold alow my self I Cold find falte but I donte and so we go on but it has bin such bad wather.

This is freyday morning Aprill the 12. Yisterday I reseved yours Desember 10 and 27 Jan 12 all by the packit which was given up for loste but thank God is now safe arived.

As I have but a verey lettel time to write as the rodes is so verey bad, shall only desier to Joyne with you in Senser thanks to god for your preservervashon and safe arivel and what reson have you and I to be thankful for maney mersey we have reseved.

Billey and his wife is in town thay Came to the rases lodge at Mr. Galloway but Spente yisterday at our house as did Mr. Williams Brother. We was att diner. I sed I had not aney thing but vitels for I Cold not get aneything for a deserte but who knows but I may treet you with sum thing from Ingland and as we wor at tabel Mr. Sumain Came and sed the poste had gon by with the letters that the packit had brought so I had the pleshuer of treeting quite grand-indead, and our littel Companey as cherful and hapey as aney in the world none excepted o my dear hough hapey am I to hear that you air safe and well. Hough dus your armes doe was John of servis to you is your Cold quite gon o I long to know. The post is hear I muste levef of. Salley not up as Shee was at the Assembly last night with her Sister [in-law] and I have spook to more than twenty sense I wrote the a bove. . . .

. . . Adue my Dear child and take Caire of youre self for maneys sake as well as your one. I am your a feckshonet wife

D. FRANKLIN

Franklin wrote from London June 4, 1765:

My dear Child

I have now before me your Favours of April 13, 15, 17, 23, May 14, 18, 20. not so many Letters as Dates, some of them having two or three. . . .

I could have wished to have been present at the Finishing of the Kitchen, as it is a mere Machine, and being new to you, I think you will scarce know how to work it. The several Contrivances to carry off Steam and Smell and Smoke not being fully explain'd to you. The Oven I suppose was put by the written Directions in my former Letter. You mention nothing of the Furnace. If that Iron One is not set, let it alone till my Return, when I shall bring a more convenient copper one. . . .

I cannot but complain in my Mind of Mr. Smith, that the House is so long unfit for you to get into, the Fences not put up, nor the other necessary Articles got ready. The Well I expected would have been dug in the Winter, or early in the Spring; but I hear nothing of it. You should have garden'd long before the Date of your last, but it seems the Rubbish was not removed.

I am much oblig'd to my good old Friends that did me the Honour to remember me in the unfinish'd Kitchin. I hope soon to drink with them in the Parlour. . . .

It rejoices me to learn that you are freer than you us'd to be from the Head Ach and that Pain in your Side. I am likewise in perfect Health. God is very good to us both in many Respects. Let us enjoy his Favours with a thankful and chearful Heart; and, as we can make no direct Return to him, show our Sense of his Goodness to us, by continuing to do Good to our Fellow Creatures, without Regarding the Returns they make us, whether Good or Bad. For they are all his Children, tho' they may sometimes be our Enemies. The Friendships of this World are changeable, uncertain transitory Things; but his Favour, if we can secure it, is an Inheritance forever.

I am, my dear Debby, Your ever loving Husband,

B. FRANKLIN

The prospect of occupying the grand new house inspired Deborah to try her luck again with account-keeping; so she headed a sheet "July the 1 1765 Laid ought on all a Cashons in house keeping and other necesarees." But her good intentions disintegrated, and she frequently forgot to put dates and amounts. July gives way to "Auguste"; following some twenty entries "March the 20th 1766" suddenly looms up, and eleven lines later it is "October 1." While food is the principal theme ("for chickins and Eges," "3lb of Chocklet," and similar articles), there are "a pair of shues for my self," "Stays for Salley," "thred to knite and 2 ounse to sow," "hard sope," "Carpit at the vandue," "to poor man loste a leg," and "to poor woman."

She tells him in August "I think you will be verey pleased at the look" of the house "as it dos make a fine Squair and an equal spaise on each sid . . . and at this time yuur man Gorge is a leveling of it and it look much better than when I firste Come into it."

But the furor of the Stamp Act throughout the Colonies gave Franklin's foes new ammunition; they blamed him for not vigorously opposing its enactment. He had done all he could and, when it was inevitable, secured the appointment of his friend, John Hughes, as tax agent for Pennsylvania. Mobs in other colonies forced newly appointed agents to resign, but the doughty Hughes stood firm, and there were threats to pull down his house and

Franklin's. The danger was imminent and Deborah bustled Sally off to Burlington, New Jersey, but refused to seek safety for herself—steadfastly determined to protect her new house. Unaware of what was taking place, Franklin wrote her in August asking for dimensions so "that I may get a handsome Glass for the Parlour. I want also the Dimensions of the Sash Panes" and "the Windows for which you would have me bring Curtains, unless you chuse to have the Curtains made there." He asked whether she had "Carpets made, and do you want any more? . . . Have you mov'd every thing, and put all Papers and Books in my Room, and do you keep it lock't? Is the Passage out to the Top of the House fixed with Iron Rails from Chimney to Chimney? As to oiling the Floors, it may be omitted till I return; which will not be till next Spring. I need not tell you to take great Care of your Fires. What Room have you chose to sleep in? I wish you would give me a particular Account of every Room, who and what is in it, 'twould make me seem a little at home. What Colours are they painted?"

But Debby was primarily concerned with defending her household against mobs incensed by charges that Franklin had planned the Stamp Act and was trying to get the test act, which required individuals to swear their allegiance to the Crown, extended to the Colonies when she wrote on September 22:

My Dear Child

I have reseved yours by Capt. Friend and one which was to a Cume by N yorke and by the packit and yisterday by Capt. Cotin they all give me pleshuer indead and I love to hear from you I am so verey poor a writer that I donte undertake to say aney thing a bought the dis [order] in this porte of the world but to me it semes we air verey wicked and so is the pepel in London and other plases on your sid the watter I pray god mend us all.

You will se by the papers what worke has hapened in other plases and sumthing has bin sed relaiteing to raising a mob in this plase. I was for 9 day keep in one Contineued hurrey by pepel to removef and Salley was porswaided to go to burlinton for saiftey but on munday laste we had verey graite rejoysing on a Count of the Chang of the Ministrey and a preyperaition for binfiers att night and several houses thretened to be puled down. Cusin Davenporte Come and told me that more than twenty pepel had told him it was his Duty to be with me. I sed I was plesed to reseve Civility from aney bodey so he staid with me sum time to words night I sed he shold fetch a gun or two as we had none. I sente to aske my Brother to Cume and bring his gun all so we maid one room into a Magazin. I ordored sum sorte of defens up Stairs such as I Cold manaig my self. I sed when I was advised to remove that I was verey shuer you had dun nothing to hurte aney bodey nor I had not given aney ofense to aney person att all nor wold I be maid unesey by aney bodey nor wold I stir or show the leste uneseynis but if aney one Came to disturbe me I wold show a proper resentement and I shold be very much afrunted with aney bodey.

. . . It is paste three a clock I have only to tell you who was so good as to visit me on laste munday night Cusin Davenporte my Brother J Foxcrofte Mr. Whorton sener he Come paste 8 a Clocke on horse back his son Samey Mr. Banton Mr. S. Rodes thay ofred to Stay all night but I beged thay wold not leste they shold get Sick my three Cusins Lakockes and Mr. Hall nabor Shumakers sones nabor Whisters Son and more of the nabors young Dr. Tenent who Came home in Friend Came and ofred me all the asistens in his power. I thanked him. I shold not for get Mr. John Ross and Brother Swore it is Mr. Saml Smith that is a seting the pepel a-mading by teling them that it was you that had pland the Stampe ackte and that you air indivering to get the teste ackte brought over hear but as I donte go much to town I mabey shall be esey for a while after the eleckshon is over but tel that I muste be disturbed. I shal send your letter by friend god bles you and keep you is the prayer of yours forever.

D. FRANKLIN

In October she headed a letter:

This is an anser to your
qustons

When you wente from home Billey desired to take sume more of your Books then what you laid ought so I got him a trunke to

take them up in and as the shelveses looks prettey emtey I took
down the reste and dusted them and had the shelves taken down
and put up in the South Garrotes in the new house and Mis
Elmer and my self put them up I took all the dead letters and
papers that was in the Garrot and put them into boxes barrels
and bages as I did not know in what maner you wold have
shelves in your room. Now this I did for several resens one as it
did imploy my mind and keepe me verey busey and as the wather
was prittey good and I shold make room if Mrs. Franklin [Will-
iam's wife] shold Come to town to stay aney time I was ready to
reseve her. Now for the room we Cale yours thair is in it your
Deske the armonekey maid like a Deske a large Cheste with all
the writeings that was in your room down stairs the boxes of
glases for musick and for the Elicktresatecy and all your close
and the pickters as I donte drive nailes leste it shold not be write.
Salley has the Southroom two pairs of Stairs In it is a beed a
burow a tabel a glase and the pickter shee youst to have in her
room a trunke and books but thees you cante have aney noshon
of. The Northeroom Nanney took for her one and I Cante tell
much a bought it only it has a bead and Curtin and it is keep
locked. I never saw it but ones I thinke excepte when shee was
ill. The Blewroom has the Armoneyca and the Harpseycord in it
the Gilte Sconse a Carde tabel a seet of tee Chaney I bought sens
you wente from home the worked Chairs and Screen a verey
hansom mohoganey Stand for the tee kittel to stand on and the
orney metal Chaney but the room is not as yit finished for I think
the paper has loste much of the blume by paisteing of it up thair-
fore I thought beste to leve it tell you Cume home. The Curtins is
not maid nor did I pres for them as we had a very graite number
of fleys as it is observed thay air verey fond of new painte. The
Southeroome I sleep in with my Susanah [her maid] a bead with
ought Curtins a Cheste of Drowers a tabel a Glase and old black
wolnot chairs sum books in my Closet and sume of our famely
pickters. In the frunte room which I had desind for gests I had
the beed which you sente from Ingland a Chamber majogney
tabel and stand. In the rom down stairs is the sid bord that you
be spoke which is verey hansum and plain with two tabels maid
to suite it and a Doz of Chairs allso. I sold to mr. Foxcrofte the
tabeles we had as they did not sute the room by aneymeens. The
potterns of the Chairs air a plain Horshair and look as well as a
Paddozway everey bodey admiers them. The littel Southroom I
had papered as the wales was much soyled. In that is a pritey

Card tabel and our Chairs that yoused to stand in the parler and orney mental Chaney over the fierplase on the flower a Carpit I bought cheep for the goodnes. It is not quite new. The large Carpit is in the blewroom the fier not maid yit in the room for our friends. The Pickter of the Erel of Bute is hung up and a Glase. This is but a verey imperfeckte a counte. In the parlor thair is a Scotch Carpet which was found much Folte with and your time pees stands in one Corner which is all wrong I am told. So then I tell them we shall have all things as they shold be when you cume home. As to Curtins I leve it to you to due as you like your self or if as we tolked be fore you went. If you Cold meet with a turkey Carpet I shold like it but if not I shall be verey esey as all thees things air be cume quite indifrent to me att this time but sense you doe so kindly inquier what things I want I shall tell you that when mrs. Franklin Come to town and wente to the Aseembly Salley had nothin fitt to wair suteabe to waite on her and as I never shold a put on in your absens aney thing good I gave Salley my new robe as it wanted but very littel oltering. I shold be glad if you wold bring me a plain darke Sattin for a gound and if our Cusin wold make me a littel lase of a proper weedthe for a Cape or two I shold like it as it was their makeing and a light cloke such as you sente for Salley but it moste be biger than hers. I shold a had that but it was two small for me. In the Northroome we sett as it is not quite finished yit as the dores air not up. We have a tabel and chairs and the Smal Book case Brother John's Pickter and the King and Quens pickter and a small Scotch Carpet on the flower. I desier you to remember drinking Glases and a Large tabel clothe or two when you Cume but I shante wante them tell then. If you shold meet with a pair of Silver Conisters I shold like it but as you pleas everey thing I have menshioned. When I say dores it is the bofet dores. They air Glaised but it on know[n] to me. They air in your room. I shall Counte the paines and send to you. The Crain was put up this week and not before the railes not don as yit but promised soon to be dun. O my Child there is graite odes between a mans being at home and a broad as every bodey is a fraid thay shall doe wrong to everey thing is lefte undun. . . .

. . . I have Counted the paines in the dores thair is 8 in each dore be sides the spaces att tipe the largest Sise. I will get mr. Rhodes to take mashuer of the fierplaces and the pier for a Glase. All the Chimneys that I have yoused is verey good. I have baked in the oven and it is good. The . . . pente houses is not dun

nor the stepes as the loot is not setteld. I fair you have not
reseved all my letters . . . I due take all the Caire of the fiers in
my power and some sort beside—for the men keep fier in two
roomes while they worked and I did littel else but tend them
least any acksidente shold hapen.

Deborah kept a lonely vigil. Franklin hoped to come home in
1766 but Pennsylvania reappointed him agent for another year—
and so he stayed. She wrote him on January 12, 1766, telling him
it was so "verey Cold" she "did not go ought," and from visits to
the sick a few days before her "poor Chin" got "froste bit with the
Cold." A long list of sick and dying relatives, acquaintances, and
friends followed, but before that melancholy news she thanked
him for "the painted floor cloathe and . . . the set of Chaney"
which arrived "quite whole," "and if I live tell your Birthday I
think to fill it with punch and treet sum of your friends." Her
letter closed with reassurance of her "graitefull heart. I thanke
you for the fine tee Pot for the Carpetes and the verey fine brom.
It is verey handsome. For the Salte which is very excepeabel to
me for I like it verey much indeed. For the butyfull Candel stickes
and for the Shoefels and tonges which is Cureyous." Salley wrote
her father on March 23 to tell him Goodey Smith was dead and
"poor Mama" was "in great distress, it must be hard to lose a
Friend of 50 years standing." Then she shifted to a more cheerful
topic. "We have heard by a round about way that the stamp act is
repeal'd, the People seem ditermined to beleave it, tho it came
from Ireland to Maryland. The bells rang we had bonfires and
one house was illumanited, indeed I never heard so much noise in
all my life the very Children seem distracted." If the news was
premature when it left the British Isles, it was accurate when it
arrived. Repeal was approved March 18. On April 6 Franklin
wrote jubilantly to Deborah:

My dear Child,

As the Stamp Act is at length repeal'd, I am willing you
should have a new Gown, which you may suppose I did not send

sooner, as I knew you would not like to be finer than your Neighbours, unless in a Gown of your own Spinning. Had the Trade between the two Countries totally ceas'd, it was a Comfort to me to recollect that I had once been cloth'd from Head to Foot in Woolen and Linnen of my Wife's Manufacture, that I was never prouder of any Dress in my Life, and that she and her Daughter might do it again if it was necessary. I told the Parliament that it was my Opinion, before the old Cloaths of the Americans were worn out, they might have new ones of their own making. And indeed if they had all as many old Clothes as your old Man has, that would not be very unlikely; for I think you and George reckon'd when I was last at home, at least 20 pair of old Breeches. Joking apart, I have sent you a fine Piece of Pompador Sattin, 14 Yards cost 11s. per Yard. A Silk Negligee and Petticoat of brocaded Lutestring for my dear Sally, with 2 Doz. Gloves, 4 Bottles of Lavender Water, and two little Reels. The Reels are to screw on the Edge of a Table, when she would wind Silk or Thread, the Skein is to be put over them, and winds better than if held in two Hands. There is also an Ivory Knob to each, to which she may with a Bit of Silk Cord hang a Pinhook to fasten her plain Work to like the Hooks on her Weight. I send you also Lace for two Lappet Caps, 3 Ells of Cambrick (the Cambrick by Mr. Yates) 3 Damask Table Cloths, a Piece of Crimson Morin for Curtains, with Tassels, Line and Binding. A large true Turkey Carpet cost 10 Guineas, for the Dining Parlour. Some oil'd Silk; and a Gimcrack Corkscrew which you must get some Brother Gimcrack to show you the Use of. In the Chest is a Parcel of Books for my Friend Mr. Coleman . . . I send you also a Box with three fine Cheeses. Perhaps a Bit of them may be left when I come home. . . .

. . . There are some Droll Prints in the Box, which were given me by the Painter; and being sent when I was not at home, were pack'd up without my Knowledge. I think he was wrong to put in Lord Bute, who had nothing to do with the Stamp Act. But it is the Fashion here to abuse that Nobleman as the Author of all Mischief. I sent you a few Bush Beans, a new Sort for your Garden.

The year 1767 began with some uncertainties. "I have got the Clothes," Franklin wrote his wife in February, "and have worn them, but find them too tight for me, and must have the Waste-coat let out. I thank you for the Garters they are excellent. The Apples and Meal not come ashore yet." There were deeper worries. His printing partnership with David Hall in Philadelphia had been terminated the year before, and he was thus cut off from the comfortable 500 pounds it had given him each year. Deborah seemed more sentimental than ever when she began her April 2 letter with

> My Dear Child
>
> I did reseve your Dear littel letter by the packit it gave me much pleshuer to hear that your dear armes air so much better . . . On Sunday which was Esterday the poste Came in and brought me a letter and Salley one. You tell her to let you find that shee ades to the number of her friends. Before this dus reach you, you will be informd of the adishon of her friends I doute not but it will make you Sereious it makes me so in dead my menshoing agen that I wold let you know in what manner I ackte as I am obliged to be father and mother.

Sally, at twenty-four, was thinking about marrying Richard Bache, a thirty-year-old Englishman who had come to Philadelphia in 1766 and opened a drygoods store featuring "European and East-India" imports. He began the business on a shoestring, and its future was indefinite when he courted the popular Sally, who had the blond hair of her father and the robust handsomeness of her mother. Deborah confided to her husband:

> I treet him as a friend and shall while I am alone for I thinke he deserves it and was I to due other way I thinke it wold only drive her to see him sum wair eles which wold give me much uneseynes. I hope I ackte to your Satisfackshon. I due acordin to my beste Judgment.

In May she informed Franklin Sally had gone to Burlington to visit her brother, who had reportedly been challenged to a duel by William Hicks, a Philadelphia lawyer, over a political squabble.

I was the reder [readier] to let her go as shee is not verey well and looks verey paile so as to give me much uneseyness but she all way looks ill in summer and 2 or 3 day Changes her but I think shee has bin maid unesey a bought her Brother who was chalinged on Munday night. I shold not a sed one word to you but I thinke sumbudey will tell. The Chaling was sente by young Hickes brought by young Dr. Kersly verey much in drinke. Salley was verey much scaired and wold not let her Brother go withoute her. So you can see this dafter of ours is a mear Champin and thinks shee is to take Cair of us. Her Brother and shee is verey hapey togather indead but I long to see her back a gen as I Cold not live a bove another day with ought her as I am sir cum-stansed a mind flutered sum times glad then depresed and so on. O that you was att home but be ashuered that no littel famely ever had more hormoney in it than youres has and I truste will have.

. . . My old friend Debbey Norris has lefte us. She was one of my first play maites and I raly Loved her. I wente to the bureyal and I desire to visit Mrs. Norris soon . . . It is all moste night I muste bid you adue and am my Dear Benney your Afeckshonat wife.

D FRANKLIN

The duel never took place, and Sally, who rode out with her brother because she "was very much afraid Hicks would attack him on the Road," informed Bache, "He is safe and on that account my mind is easier."

Franklin told Deborah he received letters from both Sally and Bache, along with hers, and informed them "I left the Matter to you and her Brother, for at this Distance I could neither make any Enquiries into his Character and Circumstances, nor form any Judgment, And as I was in doubt whether I should be able to return this Summer, I would not occasion a Delay of her Happi-ness if you thought the Match a proper one . . . I sent Sally in a Box per Mr. Odell two Summer Hats." William Franklin sent word to his father that Bache was heavily in debt, and possibly "he is mere Fortune Hunter, who wants to better his Circum-stances [by] marrying into a Family that will support him."

On June 22 Franklin informed his wife:

It seems now as if I should stay here another Winter, and therefore I must leave to your Judgment to act in the Affair of your Daughter's Match as shall seem best. If you think it a suitable one, I suppose the sooner it is compleated, the better. In that case, I would only advise that you do not make an expensive feasting Wedding, but conduct every thing with Frugality and Oeconomy, which our Circumstances really now require to be observed in all our Expences; For since my Partnership with Mr. Hall is expir'd, a great Source of our Income is cut off; and if I should lose the Post Office, which among the many Changes here is far from being unlikely, we should be reduc'd to our Rent and Interest of Money for a Subsistence, which will by no means afford the chargeable Housekeeping and Entertainments we have been used to; for my own Part I live here as frugally as possible not to be destitute of the Comforts of Life, making no Dinners for any body, and contenting my self with a single Dish when I dine at home, and yet such is the Dearness of Living here in every Article, that my Expences amaze me. I see too by the Sums you have received in my Absence, that yours are very great, and I am very sensible that your Situation naturally brings you a great many Visitors which occasion an Expence not easily to be avoided. . . .

I know very little of the Gentleman or his Character, nor can I at this Distance. I hope his Expectations are not great of any Fortune to be had with our Daughter before our Death. I can only say, that if he proves a good Husband to her, and a good Son to me, he shall find me as good a Father as I can be but at present I suppose you would agree with me that we cannot do more than fit her out handsomely in Cloaths and Furniture, not exceeding in the whole Five Hundred Pounds, of Value. For the rest, they must depend as you and I did, on their own Industry and Care; as what remains in our Hands will be barely sufficient for our Support, and not enough for them when it comes to be divided at our Decease.

. . . I suppose the blue Room is too blue, the Wood being of the same Colour with the Paper, and so looks too dark. I would have you finish it as soon as you can, thus. Paint the Wainscot a dead white; Paper the Walls blue, and tack the gilt Border round just above the Surbase and under the Cornish. If the Paper is not equal Coloured when pasted on, let it be brush'd over again with the same Colour; and let the Papier machee musical Figures be

tack'd to the middle of the Cieling; when this is done, I think it
will look very well.

    . . . I am glad to hear that Sally keeps up and increases the
Number of her Friends. The best Wishes of a fond Father for her
Happiness always attend her. I am, my dear Debby, Your affec-
tionate Husband

B. FRANKLIN

When Deborah wrote on July 4, 1767 she was worried.

I was in hopes that this poste wold a brought the Packit letters
but it has not. Varis [Various] air the Conjeckters of our nabors
sum say you will Cume home this somer others say not. I Cante
say aney thing as I am in the darke and my life of old age is one
Continewd State of suspens. I must indever to be Contente.

Franklin closed his next letter,

I long to see you and be with you, being as ever, my dear Debby,
Your affectionate Husband . . .

    Deborah echoed the hope that he would return in almost
every letter. Sally had married in October 1767, and with her new
husband took up residence in the Franklin home. In 1769 she
gave birth to a son, and he was christened Benjamin Franklin
Bache. Remembering her own lost boy, Deborah idolized the
child, and he gave new dimension to her life. Franklin, lionized
by women in England and France and toasted by prominent men
in both countries, seemed in no hurry to return, despite his expectations in letters to her. He was resolved to make his later years "a
bright point" filled with more accomplishments and honors, and
while sympathetic and concerned for his "Debby," the repeated
expressions of her "febel" health and the melancholy catalogue of
the dead and dying—news that it was—could hardly serve as an
inducement to rush back to Philadelphia. He had, of course,
ample and legitimate excuses since he was serving now as repre-

sentative for several other colonies beside Pennsylvania. On September 10, 1774 he wrote:

> It is now nine long Months since I received a Line from my dear Debby. I have supposed it owing to your continual Expectation of my Return; I have feared that some Indisposition has rendered you unable to write; I have imagined any Thing rather than admit a Supposition that your kind Attention towards me was abated. And yet when so many other Old Friends have dropt a Line to me now & then at a Venture, taking the Chance of finding me here or not as it might happen, why might I not have expected the same Comfort from you, who used to be so diligent and faithful a Correspondent, as to omit scarce any Opportunity?
>
> This will serve to acquaint you that I continue well, Thanks to God—It would be a great pleasure to me to hear that you are so. My Love to our Children, and believe me ever
>
>   Your affectionate Husband

It is not known whether she ever got the letter. She suffered a stroke on December 14, 1774 and died five days later. Franklin finally returned to Philadelphia on May 5, 1775. But he was back in France December 4, 1776, as one of a three-man commission to negotiate a treaty of alliance, and Philadelphia was not to see him again until September 14, 1785.

Among the French women he found enchanting, and who thought him equally so, was the wealthy and beautiful widow, Madame Helvetius, to whose salon philosophers, statesmen, and scholars flocked. She had the same sense of humor Franklin possessed and shocked Abigail Adams by the way she always greeted him—kisses on each cheek and arms about his neck. It is thought that she was the one who, protesting his neglect, provoked the bawdy reply that he was delaying his visits until the nights were longer. In any case he asked her to marry him—how seriously it is hard to say—and in return he got the stock answer with which she discouraged other suitors by saying she was pledged to the memory of her departed husband. Franklin, a few days later, sent her one of his "bagatelles" in which he claimed to have dreamed he had been transported to "the Elysian Fields" and there met her husband.

> He received me with much courtesy, having known me by repu- tation, he said, for some time. He asked me many things about the war and about the present state of religion, liberty and government in France. "You ask nothing then," I said to him "about your dear friend Madame Helvetius; and yet she still loves you to excess; I was with her less than an hour ago." "Ah!" he said, "you remind me of my former happiness. But we must forget if we are to be happy here. For several years at first I thought of nothing but her. At last I am consoled. I have taken another wife; the most like her I could find. She is not, it is true, altogether so beautiful, but she has as much good sense and plenty of wit, and she loves me infinitely. She studies continually to please me, and she has just now gone out to search for the best nectar and ambrosia to regale me with this evening. Stay with me and you will see her." "I perceive," I said, "that your former friend is more faithful than you; she has had several good offers and has refused them all. I confess to you that I have loved her, to madness; but she was cruel to me and absolutely rejected me for the love of you." "I pity you," he said, "in your misfortune; for she is indeed a good and beautiful woman, and very amiable."

Helvetius, he said, then gave him some advice on how to win the Madame. Then

> the new Madame Helvetius came in with the nectar; immediately I recognized her as Madame Franklin, my former friend. I claimed her again, but she said coldly: "I was a good wife to you for forty-nine years and four months, almost half a century. Be content with that. I have formed a new connexion here which will last for eternity."
>
> Indignant at this refusal from my Eurydice, I at once re- solved to quit those ungrateful shades, return to the good world and see again the sun and you. Here I am. Let us avenge our- selves.

The Traitor's Lady

Peggy Shippen Arnold

In 1778 when the British occupied Philadelphia, Captain John André sketched Margaret Shippen, youngest of Chief Justice Edward Shippen's four daughters. Although the blue-eyed blonde was not yet eighteen, one enthusiastic Englishman proclaimed her the most beautiful woman in America. André's pencil puts her in a less extravagant perspective, depicting her as attractive despite the imbalance accorded her piquant features by an elaborate hairdo that towers a foot and a half above her forehead. ·

Her birth on June 11, 1760 was announced somewhat chauvinistically by her father: "A fine baby which, though of the worst sex, is yet entirely welcome." Shippen had hoped for a boy, since only one of his three sons had survived infancy. The newest addition to his family, he said, deferred the day he could ride in his own coach, but "by the blessings of God" he would do his children "all tolerable justice." He had come to the Philadelphia bar after having studied law in London, and through the influence of his lineage and an affluent marriage, got a variety of governmental posts which provided him with substantial income to maintain a splendid home on South Second Street. Such sinecures reinforced his innate caution, and whatever the merits of the issues dividing the Colonies from England, Shippen resolved to steer a middle course. But caution turned to genuine fear when Pennsylvania politics began to get rough, and he abandoned his offices and fled with his family to a farm in New Jersey, where he set up a general store. Just as his luxury-loving wife and older daughters were reluctantly trimming their sails, New Jersey enacted a "Test Act" to smoke out, under oath, the allegiance of the inhabitants.

So it was back to Pennsylvania, which had not yet enacted such a statute. They took a house at the Falls of the Schuylkill, and Shippen managed his neutrality so well that he escaped recrimination when the family, during the British occupation, returned to the city to prevent their home from being appropriated for quartering British officers.

It was against this background of fear and flight that Peggy stepped into the mainstream of history, beginning innocuously enough with the giddy social whirl designed by André, as diversion from a dull winter quarters. Twenty miles away, on the cold slopes of Valley Forge, Washington and the main American army were immobilized by weather, sickness, and starvation.

The accomplished André, whose sparkling conversations on art, music, and travel enraptured the circle of young women in which she was included, did not, contrary to romanticists, fall in love with her; nor, so far as is known, did she with him. The twenty-seven-year-old bachelor who completely captivated her friend Peggy Chew gave Peggy Shippen a lock of his hair, but this was commonplace in the customs of the eighteenth century—a memento of friendship. But their minds moved on different planes.

As a child the "shy and timorous" girl, as many thought her, preferred to watch her father as he performed his various tasks. Neither his library nor his reproductions of old masters caught her fancy. The dry, arid world of figures and business management intrigued her, and not even the polite education permitted females of her caste diverted her. It is too easy to read into this pattern the driving ambition which moved her, and too convenient to indulge in a sanguine psychological analysis. That a knowledge of finances would be a useful weapon in a quest for position may or may not have occurred to her, but it provides a clue to her thoughts. Was her propensity to "hysteria"—as some have labeled it—more calculated than unwitting? The tool of a consummate actress rather than the refuge of a bewildered child? These are questions to ponder as we see the strength of her character unfold. That she loved luxury tells us nothing more than that she was human. That she seems to have regarded her mother as weak, and was almost studied in her indifference, is rather revealing. Yet she was able to read into her father's policies a quality of courage, assisted perhaps by her deep affection for him. Later in life when she skillfully managed an involved financial transaction, she wrote

> Few women could have affected what I have done. And to you, dear parent, I am indebted for the ability to perform what I have done, as you bestowed upon me the most useful and best education that America at that time afforded.

In 1778 that affection was put to a test. Like other teen-agers she was caught up in the excitement of the British revelry ("a dancing fury" Shippen called it). Because of her social standing she was invited to a number of events, including a dinner for 172 guests aboard H.M.S. *Roebuck*. The commanding officer, Captain A. S. Hammond, recalled, "We were all in love with her." Then as Sir William Howe was about to depart for England in June, André staged a lavish entertainment in his honor, with the guests transported down the Delaware on festooned barges to the accompaniment of bands aboard "musical barges." Fourteen young ladies, including Peggy, were selected "from the foremost in youth, beauty and fashion," as André put it, to cheer their "knights" in a mock tournament. André designed their costumes, which the Quakers thought shockingly flimsy. At the last minute, a deputation of their number called on Chief Justice Shippen and asked him to forbid Peggy's participation. Shippen acquiesced. It is not hard to picture the reaction of the high-spirited girl, who could not have helped resenting her father's capitulation. This was not just another ball. It still stands as the most spectacular pageant of its kind in eighteenth-century America. Her disappointment, coupled with the inevitable embarrassment, must have been traumatic.

Two weeks later the British began to evacuate the city, leaving it to be occupied by elements of the Continental Army. Thus did Benedict Arnold and Peggy Shippen enter each other's lives.

At thirty-seven the five-foot, nine-inch Arnold was a controversial figure. A man of extraordinary physical stamina, his ice-blue eyes and jet-black hair lent emphasis to his strong-featured face. He had distinguished himself, not only by his daring, but because he was a soldier's soldier—always in front of his troops and sharing their hardships. More than any other American officer, he was capable of welding the unpredictable militiamen into effective fighters. Once embarked on a mission, nothing could stop him. If the pursuit carried him to the water's edge he drew upon his experience as a sailor to improvise a flotilla, and not even the roughest river or the vastness of the Great Lakes blunted his determination. Washington was well aware of his worth, most recently demonstrated in the fall of 1777 when his valor led to the stunning defeat of "Gentleman Johnny" Burgoyne's army at Saratoga. It was this victory that convinced France to openly ally itself with America and changed the entire course of the war. Moreover, it blunted the impact of the dismal defeats Washington was simultaneously suffering at Brandywine and Germantown against Sir William Howe.

Arnold's right leg had been shattered by a bullet, and through long winter weeks he lay in a "fracture box," after cursing the doctors as charlatans and refusing to let them amputate. Congress expressed its thanks to generals Gates, Lincoln, and Arnold but gave a special honor to Gates by ordering a gold medal struck.

Small wonder Arnold became bitter. Gates had watched the battles from a safe vantage point while Arnold rallied and exhorted the troops and had a horse shot from under him before his own thigh was hit.

However adept he was as a military man, Arnold was not scrupulous about his accounts, and when pressed to make reports of expenditures countered with blasts that he was too busy fighting a war to pay attention to bookkeeping—and moreover, he inevitably added, much of his private funds were spent when public monies were not available for equipment. Yet this carelessness, whether by accident or design, made him frequently suspect as a profiteer—a charge he would find a vicious slur upon his honor, although frequently true. A junior officer, rankled over Arnold's refusal to promote him to major, perceptively wrote: "Money is this man's god, and to get enough of it he would sacrifice his country." Arnold had been able to obscure such allegations with fresh displays of courage, and in the spring of 1778, still suffering from excruciating pain, made his arduous way for several hundred miles to Valley Forge to seek a new command from Washington. This kind of dedication impressed the commander in chief, for he was constantly beset by mediocre officers bickering over rank. It was obvious that Arnold was unfit for the field; so he assigned him as military commander in Philadelphia, "to preserve tranquility and order in the city and give security to individuals of every class and description . . . till the restoration of civil government."

In light of subsequent events it was a mistake. But at the time, despite Arnold's lack of diplomacy, there was much to recommend it. He stood as a buffer between the radical faction in Pennsylvania and the loyalists and Quakers who had not forsaken their homes; while his tour of duty would be comparatively short, it offered the possibility of respite in which the thirst for vengeance might dissipate. Unfortunately it presented him with opportunities of making some private deals with goods supposedly seized for public use; and the extravagant manner in which he lived, far in excess of his salary, started a whole new train of rumors. "Patri-

ots" were irritated by his cordiality with Tories, who were invited
to his dinner parties and balls.

Although it is tempting to see in his actions a calculated move
toward his ultimate treason, it is more likely that he looked upon
the war as an investment in his personal future. It had lifted him
from anonymity to fame, but he was not content to leave it at
that. The outcome of the Revolution was still in doubt, and England might well be the victor. If that were the case, glory would
turn to ashes. A hedge against this possibility lay in marrying a
woman from a family acceptable to the British. The death of his
wife, and the need for a more permanent situation for his three
young sons, added to the urgency.

In September 1777, he began courting by mail "the heavenly
Miss Deblois" of Boston, whose Tory father had been forced to
flee to Halifax. His love letters were so stilted they could have
been lifted from a manual. Lucy Knox had introduced him to her,
and since her own Tory family disapproved of her marriage to
Henry Knox, parallels existed in case Betsy Deblois's parents took
the same position.

Betsy's father made his adverse sentiments known quickly,
and either because of this, or on her own, the girl gave him. no
encouragement. A sample of the kind of letter he penned may
furnish a sufficient reason:

> Twenty times have I taken my pen to write to you, and as often
> has my trembling hand refused to obey the dictates of my heart.
> A heart which has often been calm and serene amidst the clash-
> ing of arms and all the din and horrors of war trembles with
> diffidence and the fear of giving offence when it attempts to
> address you on a subject so important to its happiness. Long
> have I struggled to efface your heavenly image from it. Neither
> time, absence, misfortunes, nor your cruel indifference have been
> able to efface the deep impression your charms have made. And
> will you doom a heart so true, so faithful, to languish in despair?
> Shall I expect no returns to the most sincere, ardent, and disin-
> terested passion? Dear Betsy, suffer that heavenly bosom (which
> surely cannot know the cause of misfortune without a sympa-
> thetic pang) to expand with friendship at last and let me know

my fate. If a happy one, no man will strive more to deserve it; if on the contrary I am doomed to despair, my latest breath will be to implore the blessing of heaven on the idol and only wish of my soul.

When she apparently told him it was useless, he tried a different tack, just before setting out for Valley Forge:

A union of hearts, I acknowledge, is necessary to happiness; but give me leave to observe that true and permanent happiness is seldom the effect of an alliance formed on romantic passion where fancy governs more than judgment. Friendship and esteem, founded on the merit of the object, is the most certain basis to build a lasting happiness upon and when there is a tender and ardent passion on one side, and friendship and esteem on the other, the heart must be callous to every tender sentiment if the taper of love is not lighted up at the flame.

Heaven was on the side of Betsy, and in his new location Arnold surveyed the prospects in Philadelphia. Had he continued his suit Arnold might have succeeded, for her refusal was not so adamant as to induce her to return a ring with four diamonds, inscribed "E.D. from Benedict Arnold."

Arnold was not one to waste time. When he decided Peggy Shippen would admirably meet his qualifications, he took out copies of his ardent letters to Miss Deblois and, with only minor changes, expressed his undying love in the same language, many of the paragraphs being verbatim.

At first he made no headway. Peggy was obviously weighing the situation as carefully as he, and considering all alternatives. The departure of the English had left a void of potential suitors. Arnold was considerably older and limped badly, but he had stature and an aggressiveness that pleased her. He had endeared himself to Tory merchants in town, and whatever his humble background, would be acceptable to postwar Philadelphia society. Moreover, he offered a perfect balance for her own ambitions, however vague they were at the moment. If America made its independence stick, his fame was a virtual guarantee of success. If England prevailed, his "humanitarianism," coupled with her own sympathies, made a preferred status inevitable.

By December 1778 Chief Justice Shippen was writing to his father: "My youngest daughter is much solicited by a certain general . . . Whether this will take place or not depends upon certain circumstances" (which he did not disclose in the letter). By January 1779 members of the family and close friends were speculating on the probability of the marriage. Arnold had informed his future father-in-law that he expected no marriage settlement to come with Peggy, a fact certain to please the frugal Shippen, and hoped "Our difference in political sentiment will . . . be no bar to my happiness." He added his belief that the present conflict would soon be resolved and the country restored to normalcy. While he was not wealthy, he had "sufficient (not to depend upon my expectations) to make us both happy." Shippen, familiar with Arnold's high style of living, may have accepted this without challenge. Had he asked for a detailed financial statement he would have undoubtedly fared no better than Congress or others.

If Arnold's romance was moving along at a satisfactory pace, his relations with the Pennsylvania Executive Council were deteriorating rapidly. Joseph Reed, the president, led the attack and demanded that Congress look into Arnold's financial activities, charging that he was speculating and using public position and property for his own advantage. Congress asked for evidence, but the Council, fearful that such action on its part would be tacit recognition of the supremacy of the Congress—which it vehemently contested—dragged its feet. Arnold's speculations were far more extensive than even Reed and his cohorts suspected, but he assumed the mask of outraged innocence. He was a military man, he said; let him be judged by a military court which was knowledgeable about the steps a military commander had to take in the performance of his duties. While the charges and countercharges kept Philadelphians fascinated, Arnold married Peggy Shippen on April 8, 1779 in the parlor of her father's house. He was supported by an aide during the ceremony, and sat with his bad leg propped on a cushion during the reception. Only the family and a few close friends were present. A church ceremony —in light of the bitterness evinced in some quarters about Arnold —might have triggered some unpleasantness. More immediately, when one of Peggy's older sisters was married in the previous December, the wedding took place in the home with only a modest reception following. Shippen was cautious, in a time when exorbitant inflation was depriving hundreds of necessities, to avoid any ostentatious displays.

Arnold included in his "expectations" an extensive tract of land in upper New York which that appreciative state was contemplating as a gift for his Saratoga achievement. Not too anxious to encourage "democratic" settlers on its frontiers, its leaders felt established military heroes in such areas would be able to keep the lid on any citizen uprisings in the years ahead. It is probable that, before the marriage, Arnold suggested that as their domicile; but his purchase of Mount Pleasant, "the most elegant country seat in Pennsylvania," as a wedding present for Peggy, indicates her determination to remain in Philadelphia society.

That is as far as Peggy may have influenced any major decision by Arnold. When, within a month, he began the overtures to treason, she was certainly made aware of his objective, and concurred in his plans. But that she suggested it, or persuaded him, is beyond credibility. Arnold's strong will would brook no such interference. André's implication in the plot was, in the beginning, impersonal. As the newly named adjutant general to Sir Henry Clinton, and with promotion to the rank of major, he actively superintended a number of espionage schemes, of which, naturally, Arnold's was the most important. Intelligence, however, is a cold business, and no place for dramatics; André, for all his brilliance, was miscast in the role. There are traces of melodrama in virtually all of his operations, and his worst mistake would prove to be his last.

The long negotiations between the British and Arnold had been predicated upon his ability to get a command and then deliver the garrison. While haggling over place and price Arnold was absorbed in defending his Philadelphia activities before a court-martial, and unabashedly pressing Congress for back pay. He fixed his sights on West Point, since other Hudson River forts were included within its perimeter, and it was a logical assignment to seek in view of his damaged leg. Peggy importuned Congressman Robert Livingston of New York to suggest the idea to Washington, and Arnold's admirer, General Schuyler in Albany, enthusiastically endorsed it. Anxious to mitigate the mild reprimand he had felt obliged to issue Arnold since Congress had approved the court-martial findings of impropriety on two relatively minor counts, Washington offered Arnold command of the light horse, "a post of honour," and was surprised that the "brave and distinguished" officer looked crestfallen.

Peggy, attending a party at Robert Morris's in Philadelphia, learned the news when someone congratulated her. General Orders of August 1, 1780, had carried the appointment. "The information affected her so much as to produce hysteric fits," and it was immediately assumed the young wife and recent mother was concerned about the exposure to danger her husband would have to face. The nineteen-year-old girl had been under tension. Arnold's sister, Hannah, who had brought his sons by his first marriage to Philadelphia and lived with Peggy, had been scandalized by her constant companionship with Livingston. Not being privy to the reason, she coupled this with her jealousy of Peggy to create an unpleasant atmosphere at Mount Pleasant. Arnold, making it painfully evident that he could barely mount his horse, was relieved of the assignment two days later. The British, Washington discovered, were not going to attack Rhode Island after all, and the active role he anticipated for Arnold would not be materializing. So General Orders of August 3, 1780, assigned him to "command of the garrison at West Point."

Arnold moved quickly to establish himself in the vicinity, and Peggy, a recent mother, was left in Philadelphia with her sister-in-law, Hannah, and Arnold's youngest son. The two older boys were sent off to school in Baltimore. Jealous of Arnold's affection for his wife, the spinster Hannah set out to drive a wedge between them. The general was obviously annoyed at allusions to Peggy's infidelity and apparently rebuked his sister. She testily replied, "Ill nature I leave to you, as you have discovered yourself to be a perfect master of it . . . As you have neither purling streams nor sighing swains at West Point, 'tis no place for me; nor do I think Mrs. Arnold will be long pleased with it, though I expect it may be rendered dear to her for a few hours by the presence of a certain chancellor; who, by the by, is a dangerous companion for a particular lady in the absence of her husband." The thinly veiled reference to Livingston was underscored by the following shrewish innuendo: "I could say more than prudence will permit. I could tell you of frequent private assignations and of numberless billets doux, if I had an inclination to make mischief. But as I am of a very peaceable temper I'll not mention a syllable of the matter."

Just how far Peggy went in enlisting Livingston's innocent support for the West Point assignment is a matter of conjecture, but it is likely that she did not go beyond the bounds of many politically minded wives—using her physical charms to sustain Livingston's interest, but not to the point of adultery. Hannah, at best, was hardly an objective witness, and was obviously shocked as were many New Englanders at the easy manners of Philadelphians. Arnold's unpopularity in the city was bound to make Peggy a target, and she was forced to live under a cloud of bitter gossip. Even Hannah felt the coldness of some citizens.

Arnold was more solicitous than suspicious of Peggy. Even if Hannah's hints were justified he was not apt to be too disturbed on that score. Embarked as he was on a scheme to betray his country, he was willing to trust Peggy's discretion as to how far she had to go to solidify his situation. That he cared for her is evident in the detailed instructions he sent to her as she prepared to take the baby and join him at his quarters on the Hudson. He dispatched one of his aides, Major Franks, to accompany her; and Franks sent word they would leave Philadelphia on August 28. Arnold mapped the route for Peggy, urging her to bring her own sheets, noting where to stop, and stressing that above all else, she should consider the safety and comfort of herself and the child. The longest distance she should cover in a single day, if she felt up to it, was 26 miles; and he cautioned her to step out of the coach when being ferried across rivers. Peggy was not able to get things ready to depart on the twenty-eighth. Arnold, mentally tracing her journey on the basis of the original timetable, was worried enough to dispatch a dragoon as far as New Brunswick to search the roads for sight or news of her.

It was arranged that she should stay with Arnold at the home of Joshua Hett Smith near the village of Haverstraw, New York, close by King's Ferry on the Hudson. Arnold had satisfied himself that Smith would be sympathetic to any mission that would end the war, and Smith, whose ego was elated by Arnold's presence, "spread my table with cheerfulness" to receive the general and, in due course, Peggy.

Once she arrived, Arnold had other worries. Despite her dedication to his objective, Peggy's temperament was uncertain. What she might blurt out in the presence of his aides was anyone's guess. Franks, susceptible to the charms of all women, was a fop who would have dismissed any histrionics or casual remark as feminine foibles; but Arnold's other aide, Major Varick, a tough-minded young law student, would not. Already wary of Arnold's fraternization with suspected loyalists, he might fit pieces into a pattern. For the moment, however, he was inclined to attribute Arnold's irritable nature to the absence of Peggy, and now that she had come, he wrote, "Mrs. Arnold's presence here makes the family happy."

The impression was short-lived. Arnold was having difficulty making contact with the British: planned meetings went awry through mistakes, communications had to be trusted to unreliable couriers, and Smith's self-importance led him into several sharp clashes with Varick. Franks felt he received such "repeated insults and ill treatment" from the general, he was "resolved not to remain with him on any terms whatever." Varick, hearing this, confided to Franks his chagrin at a statement Smith made to him that "America might have made an honourable peace with Great

Britain when the commissioners came out in 1778." Franks then told Varick that Peggy, who was present during the argument which Varick gave Smith, remarked to him that Varick seemed to be a "warm and staunch Whig." Comparing notes, the two aides decided it would be wise to be careful around Peggy. They noticed that when she became unnerved, "she would give utterance to anything and everything on her mind . . . so much so as to cause us to be scrupulous of what we told her or said within her hearing."

Arnold and André finally got together on September 20, 1780, and André was captured three days later with the plans of West Point in his boot. He had expected to make his way back to the British *Vulture*, but to Arnold's consternation one of his batteries opened fire and forced the vessel away from its position. André, who despite Arnold's urgings had worn his officer's tunic under a civilian greatcoat, now, at Smith's suggestion, changed into one of Smith's suits to make his way overland to his own lines. Smith had been his guide, reveling in the mission Arnold entrusted to him, but wholly unaware of André's identity, and the fact that he was a British officer. When he had rowed out to get André aboard the *Vulture*, he was told he would bring a civilian, John Anderson, to Arnold, and assumed the tenor of the meeting was a deal involving property. André had a pass from Arnold, and Smith believed that André's uniform was simply an affectation of a man who loved military accouterments. Smith had escorted André almost to the British pickets before leaving him, and then returned to inform Arnold, giving the latter "apparently much satisfaction." Arnold, Peggy, and the two aides were at dinner. Peggy asked the servant for more butter, and when it turned out there was none in the house, Arnold remembered he had some oil he said he had bought in Philadelphia for $80. Smith, in a snide comment on the devalued Continental currency, said it was worth eighty pence.

This triggered another argument with Varick, and Franks joined in on Varick's side until Peggy asked "the dispute might be stopped because it gave her great pain." Arnold, seething at the scene, took Franks aside and told him "if he asked the devil to dine with him, the gentlemen of his family should be civil to him." Varick recalled Franks "went out of the room in a passion and to Newburgh on business. . . . The dispute between me and Arnold continued very high. I cursed Smith as a damned rascal, a scoundrel, and a spy." There is some bravado in the statement, made possible by the events then unfolding. Tough as Varick might be, Arnold was no man to brook words with a subordinate. He said "he was always willing to be advised by the gentlemen of his family, but, by God, would not be dictated to by them." Varick said Arnold later apologized and assured him "he would never go to Smith's house again or be seen with him but in company." Arnold may have been placated by Varick's assurance that his only concern was for the general's reputation, which Arnold repeatedly told him he was singularly solicitous about in New York. Varick's influential ties to powerful political figures in the state could have prompted Arnold's efforts to soothe his aide, upon whose help he might have to rely if things turned out wrong.

Wholly unaware of André's capture, Arnold and his wife planned to entertain Washington, Lafayette, Hamilton, and others of the commander in chief's party on September 25. Washington sent Hamilton and another aide ahead to make his apologies for a delay he encountered. They arrived about 9 A.M. While sitting around the breakfast table with Hamilton and some others, Arnold excused himself, went into an adjoining room, and there received the fateful letter from Colonel Jameson.

> I have sent Lieutenant Allen with a certain John Anderson taken going into New York. He had a passport signed in your name. He had a parcel of papers taken from under his stockings, which I think of a very dangerous tendency. The papers I have sent to General Washington.

Franks noted "soon after he received the letters" he "went up stairs to his lady . . . In about two minutes his Excellency General Washington's servant came to the door and informed me that his

Excellency was nigh at hand. I went immediately upstairs and informed Arnold of it. He came down in great confusion and, ordering a horse to be saddled, mounted him and told me to inform his Excellency that he was gone over to West Point and would return in about an hour."

Neither Franks nor any other officer present thought this "unusual"; and the courier, who had been ordered by Arnold not to disclose the fact of André's capture to anyone, shed no light. Even had he spoken there was nothing to link Arnold to the espionage except the pass; and as much as Franks and Varick might be angry with him over personal slights to them, neither imagined he could be involved in treason.

Varick, who had been sick, dressed to receive Washington, who as yet still had not received the drawings André had made under Arnold's direction, showing the fortifications at West Point. After eating some breakfast, Washington announced that he would ride over to West Point and see Arnold there. But Arnold was already safely aboard the *Vulture*, and Washington, anticipating nothing, set out. Varick went back to bed. "About an hour thereafter," he told his sister, "Mrs. Arnold (good woman) inquired how I was from the housekeeper and bid her go and see." Varick was impressed with the fact that Peggy had spent an hour with him on the previous day, "while I lay in a high fever, made tea for me, and paid me the utmost attention in my illness." Now she was

> mad to see him, with her hair dishevelled and flowing about her neck. Her morning-gown with few other clothes remained on her—too few to be seen even by gentlemen of the family, much less by many strangers.

Varick

> heard a shriek, ran upstairs, and there met the miserable lady, raving distracted. She seized me by the hand with this—to me—distressing address and a wild look: "Colonel Varick, have you ordered my child to be killed?" Judge you of my feelings at such

a question from this most amiable and distressed of her sex, whom I most valued. She fell on her knees at my feet with prayers and entreaties to spare her innocent babe. A scene too shocking for my feelings, in a state of body and nerves so weakened by indisposition and a burning fever. I attempted to raise her up, but in vain. Major Franks and Dr. Eustis soon arrived, and we carried her to her bed, raving mad.

Later, when he had a chance to review the chronology of events, Varick thought Peggy was putting on an act. She had managed to control herself quite admirably while Washington was in the house, and it is possible she spent that time destroying any correspondence she had received or sent. For the time being, however, he—like the rest of the household and guests—believed she was genuinely distraught. He continued:

When she seemed a little composed she burst again into pitiable tears and exclaimed to me, alone on her bed with her, that she had not a friend left here. I told her she had Franks and me, and General Arnold would soon be home from West Point with General Washington. She exclaimed; "No, General Arnold will never return; he is gone, he is gone forever; there, there, there, the spirits have carried [him] up there, and they have put hot irons in his head"—pointing that he was gone up to the ceiling. This alarmed me much. I felt apprehensive of something more than ordinary having occasioned her hysterics and utter frenzy.

When Washington came back to the house, she told Varick

there was a hot iron on her head and no one but General Washington could take it off, and wanted to see the general.

Dr. Eustis advised that Arnold must be sent for "or the woman would die." Varick repeated her curious phrase that Arnold would never return. Franks in the meantime had heard a rumor that a spy had been taken with a pass in his possession signed by Arnold, and Varick and he confided to the physician their fears that he was implicated. They were not ready to suggest this to Washington for fear that, if wrong, they would do irreparable damage to their superior. But Washington was now grimly aware of the treason, and had sent Hamilton off to try to intercept the traitor. Varick told Washington that Peggy asked to see him, and escorted the general to her bedroom. " 'No, that is not General Washington,' " Varick reported her saying, " 'that is the man who was a-going to assist Colonel Varick in killing my child.' She repeated the same sad story about General Arnold. Poor, unhappy, frantic, and miserable lady."

If Varick was convinced of her innocence, he was in distinguished company. Washington and Hamilton both had no doubt of it; and Hamilton, returning with a letter sent by Arnold from the *Vulture* to Washington under a flag of truce, thought it confirmed their judgment. Arnold had said:

> from the known humanity of your Excellency, I am induced to ask your protection for Mrs. Arnold from every insult and injury that a mistaken vengeance of my country may expose her to. It ought to fall only on me; she is as good and innocent as an angel, and is incapable of doing wrong. I beg she may be permitted to return to her friends in Philadelphia, or come to me, as she may choose . . . I have to request that the enclosed letter may be delivered to Mrs. Arnold, and she be permitted to write to me.

In a postscript he exonerated Franks, Varick, and Smith.

The twenty-three-year-old Hamilton told his fiancée, Elizabeth Schuyler:

> It was the most affecting scene I was ever witness to. One moment she raved, another she melted into tears. Sometimes she pressed her infant to her bosom and lamented its fate, occasioned by the imprudence of its father, in a manner that would have pierced insensibility itself. All the sweetness of beauty, all the loveliness of innocence, all the tenderness of a wife, and all the fondness of a mother showed themselves in her appearance and conduct. We have every reason to believe that she was entirely unacquainted with the plan, and that the first knowledge of it was when Arnold went to tell her he must banish himself from his country and from her forever.

The next day Varick said "she recovered a little and remembered nothing of what happened on the 25th." Hamilton was more explicit.

> This morning she is more composed. I paid her a visit, and endeavoured to soothe her by every method in my power, though you may imagine she is not easily to be consoled. Added to her other distresses, she is very apprehensive the resentment of the country will fall on her (who is unfortunate) for the guilt of her husband. I have tried to persuade her that her fears were ill-founded, but she will not be convinced. She received us in bed, with every circumstance that would interest our sympathy; and her sufferings were so eloquent that I wished myself her brother, to have a right to become her defender.

On the twenty-seventh she was even more composed and, with Major Franks as her escort, set out for Philadelphia, leaving behind a sympathetic Hamilton, Lafayette, and Varick, as well as a reflective but ostensibly convinced Washington.

News of the treason traveled fast. When they arrived at Kakiak on the twenty-eighth, Franks wrote Varick:

> Mr. Reed is the only man who would take us in at this place or give our horses anything to eat. . . .
> We got here, I very wet, Mrs. Arnold, thank God, in tolerable spirits; and I have hopes to get them home without any return of her distress in so violent a degree. She expresses her gratitude to you in lively terms and requests you make her acknowledgments to his Excellency, to the Marquis, and to Hamilton, and indeed to all the gentlemen for their great politeness and humanity. To the Marquis, Eustis, and Hamilton she will ever be warmly grateful.

The *Pennsylvania Packet* was less gullible if, indeed, it was equally unenlightened. It felt certain Peggy was involved, tracing the root of the evil to the time when "Colonel André, under the mask of friendship and former acquaintance at Mischianzas and balls, opens a correspondence in August 1779 with Mrs. Arnold which has doubtless been improved on his part." It took the occasion to lecture readers that "we should have despised and banished from social intercourse every character, whether male or female, which could be so lost to virtue, decency, and humanity as to revel with the murderers and plunderers of their countrymen." Since scores of Philadelphia belles who were patriots took part in the dances and banquets staged by the British during their occupation of the city, the sentences must have sent shivers up their spines.

Peggy's brother-in-law, Edward Burd, thought it impossible she was mixed up in the affair. "She keeps her room and is almost continually on the bed. Her peace of mind seems to me entirely destroyed. . . ." He felt that if she "should be sent off to her base husband, it will be a heart-breaking thing. . . ."

But the Supreme Executive Council of Pennsylvania, needing little encouragement from the crowds, who paraded an effigy of Arnold as the devil, acted swiftly on the twenty-seventh and ordered

> That the said Margaret Arnold depart this state within fourteen days from the date hereof, and that she do not return again during the continuance of the present war.

This October decree gave her precisely what she wanted: an excuse to rejoin her husband while seemingly being forced to do so. The New York *Royal Gazette* of November 18 announced:

> On Tuesday last [the fourteenth] arrived in town the lady and son of Brigadier General Arnold.

There were a number of Philadelphia expatriates in British-held New York City, and one of them noticed the strain on Peggy's face. She "is not so much admired here for her Beauty as she might have expected. All allow she has a great Sweetness in her Countenance, but wants Animation." The bland look soon disappeared as the young woman adjusted to her new surroundings, and the same correspondent saw her at a ball where she "appeared a star of the first magnitude, and had every attention paid her as if she had been Lady Clinton."

The Arnolds remained a year in the city, and Peggy gave birth to her second son. On December 15, 1781, they sailed for England, where they were well received in court circles. When Peggy was presented formally to the king and queen the following February, George III said she was "the most beautiful woman he had ever seen," and the queen ordered her ladies "to pay much attention to her." The good will was not universal, and the royal enthusiasm may have been inspired by the defection of an American general at a time when many Englishmen were heartily tired of the war. More than a few held Arnold in contempt for his treason, an attitude sharply underscored by the realization that a brave English officer had been sacrificed in the process. Edmund Burke showed how offensive Arnold's action was to the British sense of fair play when he expressed the hope the king would not put Arnold "at the head of a part of the British army" lest "the sentiments of true honor, which every British officer [holds] dearer than life, should be afflicted." There was a bit of rhetoric in this, for the British army had no compunctions in encouraging such betrayals, although they did not have to like the betrayers. Arnold was to feel this sting in 1784 when, with the war over, he tried to become affiliated with the East India Company and was coldly rejected.

Important as prestige was to Arnold's ego, money mattered more, and he drained every penny he could out of his transgression. He collected £10,000 for his treasonable action, drew the full pay of an English colonel until 1783, and then went on half-pay. Peggy was awarded a pension of £500 for life by the king, as much a tribute to her beauty as her complicity; and each child the couple had or would have was given an £80 pension. Arnold exacted commissions for his three sons in America, more in expectation of their increased value than any expectation of seeing them in the service, since the British Army was staffed mainly with men who bought their commissions from other officers. To the Loyalist Claims Commission he presented a bill for over £16,000 alleging that it represented the losses he sustained by his defection. Characteristically, he inflated the sum by such devices as putting in for the full value of Mount Pleasant even though he had only a small equity in it when his life estate was confiscated. Edward Shippen, one of his larger mortgagees, bought the property in at the public sale for Peggy's benefit. Still more brazenly, Arnold asserted had he remained in the American Army he would have been given command of the Southern Department of the Continental forces, which brought General Greene £20,000 worth of land from a grateful South Carolina and Georgia. This flimsy claim—since Washington had never offered him such a command—was too much even for Arnold to sustain, and he eventually withdrew it.

Whatever his intricate calculations, Arnold got enough to maintain his family in handsome style during their first years in London. With the war's end they gradually slipped out of the spotlight, and in 1785 a Philadelphian calling upon Peggy cautiously described her to his wife as "an amiable lady, and was her husband dead would be much noticed." Through this understatement one can read the fact that she was still beautiful. More by design than accident she kept away from the glittering London scene, concentrating her attention and affection on her growing family. In 1783 and 1784 she lost a baby boy and girl, and in 1785 gave birth to her dearly loved Sophia.

The restless Arnold decided to try his luck in the Canadian province of New Brunswick, and, reverting to his prewar experience as a merchant mariner, bought a brig and sailed off to St. John in 1785, after moving Peggy and the children into a less expensive home in London. He went into partnership with an American loyalist, and got some unknown woman pregnant. While the mother has slipped into anonymity, Arnold's fidelity to his children led him to include the boy in his will. Once he got his business established he returned to England, placed his sons by Peggy with private families there, and took Peggy and little Sophia back to St. John. He acquired a large home and brought Hannah and his other three boys to join his wife and him, and Peggy soon augmented the family with another infant son.

Arnold managed to make himself unpopular in his new setting, so that even the exiled loyalists who shared St. John with him
soon were denouncing him as a traitor. When his waterfront
warehouse burned to the ground in 1789, sentiment against him
was so strong that it was widely rumored he set fire to it to get the
insurance—despite the fact that he was not within several thousand miles, being absent on a far-flung trade mission, and that one
of his sons was almost trapped in the building. Peggy's aptitude as
a businesswoman, and her direct involvement in his financial
affairs, is evidenced by the fact that Arnold's partner sued them
both on charges they had cheated him out of £700; to add heat,
he openly accused Arnold of arson in the warehouse destruction.
Arnold sued for slander; his former partner's defense was that it
was impossible to injure the general's character since it was already "black as can be." Although Arnold won, the verdict gave
him small comfort, for the judgment awarded was two shillings
sixpence—a far cry from the £5,000 he sought.

Peggy, accompanied by a maid and her infant son, visited
Philadelphia late in 1789, but quickly discovered that outside the
warmth of her father's home and her own family, the atmosphere
was chilly and hostile. People paused on the street to glare with
disdain, and even the small circle of her friends wearied of descriptions she gave of London court life and her deferential references to "His Majesty" and "Her Majesty," which seemed both
stale and incongruous in a city newly named the capital of the
United States.

Her disappointment is reflected in a letter she wrote to her
sister when she returned to St. John:

> How difficult it is to know what will contribute to our happiness
> in this life. I had hoped that by paying my beloved friends a last
> visit, I should insure to myself some portion of it, but I find it far
> otherwise.

New Brunswick offered no sanctuary. In the spring of 1791
hatred for Arnold reached such proportions he was burned in
effigy as a "traitor," and at one point the mob threatened his

house until dispersed by troops. So on January 1, 1792, Peggy, her husband, and family sailed back to England, where a few months later he was the subject of an insult by the Earl of Lauderdale in the House of Lords. There followed the inevitable challenge to the duel by Arnold, and while arrangements dragged on, Peggy wrote her father the "situation . . . [is] a very unhappy one, till the Affair is settled; but I call my fortitude to my aid, to prevent my sinking under it, which would unman him and prevent his acting himself—I am perfectly silent on the subject; for weak Woman as I am, I would not wish to prevent what would be deemed necessary to preserve his honor." This admirable emotional control, achieved within the space of twelve years, lends credence to the belief that at West Point she had been an accomplished actress.

The duel ended before it began since the Earl, either out of respect for Arnold's marksmanship or in keeping with the British tradition of fair play, announced he would not fire since he had wronged his opponent. He thereupon apologized and Arnold's honor was satisfied. The incident was duly noted with approbation, and Arnold seized upon the favorable publicity to renew his application for active duty with the British Army. Despite letters of recommendation, including one from Sir Henry Clinton, his request engendered no interest. To bolster his sagging fortunes he took advantage in 1794 of the latest war between England and France—this precipitated by George III's determination to punish the French revolutionists for indiscriminately lopping off royal heads—and went back to sea as a privateer.

Arnold came dangerously close to hanging on an American gallows when he was captured by the French at the Guadeloupe port of Pointe-à-Pitre in 1794, but managed to escape from the ship to which he was confined by bribing the crew, and then swam to the safety of a British vessel. By one of the curious quirks with which history often amuses itself, when he was first apprehended he told the French authorities he was an American merchant, "John Anderson"—the pseudonym chosen by the ill-starred André.

This burst of good luck was brief. A year later his eldest son Benedict died of gangrene in Jamaica while serving with the British, and disputes over prize money with sailors under his command proved interminable. Peggy, his capable business manager, concluded in 1800 that the privateering brought more trouble than profit. Once more a mother, having borne Arnold a son in 1798, she now had to sustain still another shock when their little daughter Sophia suffered a paralytic stroke that left her a semi-invalid for life. A month later, in June 1800, her son Edward sailed for India as an army engineer. She was upset by this double blow at her little family. "His death," the anguished mother wrote her sister, "could scarcely be a more severe stroke."

It was to Edward in January 1801 she wrote a dolefully accurate letter that must have upset the young man considerably, since at such a long distance he was powerless to help or console. Arnold, she said, "is, at present, in the most harassed wretched state that I have ever seen him." Litigation over claims and the persistent demands of sailors for their money, "without the health or power of acting" had him in such a quandary, "he knows not which way to turn." By her estimate, she figured his captains had bilked him of "about £50,000."

Arnold's bad leg, always painful, now was matched by severe gout in the other, and a persistent cough he contracted in the tropics wracked his body. He aged quickly, able to move about only with the help of canes. His solicitous wife took him for a brief stay in the country in May, and he seemed a bit better, but on his return to London grew progressively worse, and he died on Sunday, June 14, 1801.

Peggy's friend, Ann Fitch, wrote Chief Justice Shippen:

> My sister & myself were with Mrs. Arnold when her husband expired, she evinces on this occasion—as you know she has done upon many trying ones before—that fortitude & resignation, which a superior & well regulated mind only is capable of exerting.

The message may have given her father momentary comfort, but he, her closest confidante, was too well aware of the strains she was under. This was confirmed by her next letter, in which she said she was in a "despairing state."

Her own health was tenuous. Along with the crushing burden of having to maintain a household and meeting Arnold's debts, she suffered severe abdominal pains, which in 1803 were finally diagnosed as cancer of the womb. At one point her depression seemed so unbearable she pondered suicide to spare her "excellent" sons and "dear, handsome Sophia" the agony of her wretchedness. But her faith and spirit were too strong for such a retreat. To her brother-in-law, Edward Burd, she wrote:

> my sufferings are not of the present moment only,—Years of unhappiness have past, I had cast my lot, complaints were unavailing, and you and my other friends, are ignorant of the many causes of uneasiness I have had.

But to her stepsons in Canada she proudly asserted:

> Although I have suffered, in my choice of evils, almost beyond human endurance, I now repent not at having made it.

She subsequently informed them:

> To you I have rendered an essential service; I have rescued your Father's memory from disrespect, by paying all his just debts; and his Children will now never have the mortification of being reproached with his own speculations having injured anybody beyond his own family . . . I have not even a tea-spoon, a towel, or a bottle of wine that I have not paid for.

To accomplish this Herculean feat of meeting £6,000 of her husband's identifiable obligations, Peggy vacated her expensive home, bought a "small but very neat house" from a servant, and sold her valuable furniture and everything that could bring in a few pounds. Her father helped from distant Philadelphia.

Occasionally she saw visitors from America. One of the last

was Robert Livingston, whose attentions to her had so scandalized Hannah. On July 15 she sent this letter to her father:

> sincere thanks for your very acceptable present, which came
> most opportunely, having been obliged to incur a great many
> unavoidable expenses . . . [I am] constantly under the effects of
> opium, to relieve a pain which would otherwise be intolerable . . .
> Mr. Livingston, your Minister to Paris, called upon me several
> times during his stay in London, where he was not well received.
> —He appears completely to have adopted French principles, and
> French ideas.—I have written this in great haste, and am always
> obliged to write while laying down, which is indeed almost
> wholly my position.—Pray remember me most tenderly to all the
> family, and believe me, my beloved Parent, most truly and affec-
> tionately
>
> Yours
M.A.

On August 24, 1804 she died.

History frequently leaves little postscripts. One took place in
1783 when Peter Van Shaack, an American exile in London,
took a walk through Westminster Abbey. He saw a couple standing before the recently built crypt which contained the body of
Major André. It proved to be Arnold and Peggy, and Van Shaack
said he turned from the scene "in disgust." More interesting than
Van Shaack's reaction would have been those of André's co-
conspirators who survived the plot.

Still another vestige, which came to light after both Arnolds
were dead, was the story that when Peggy was being escorted
back to Philadelphia after the treason was discovered, she spent
the night at Paramus, New Jersey, with Mrs. Theodosia Prevost.

> As soon as they were left alone, Mrs. Arnold became tran-
> quilized and assured Mrs. Prevost that she was heartily tired of
> the theatricals she was exhibiting . . . she had corresponded with
> the British commander, and . . . she was disgusted with the
> American cause and those who had the management of public
> affairs, and that through unceasing perseverance she had ulti-

mately brought the general into an arrangement to surrender West Point.

Mrs. Prevost later became the second wife of Aaron Burr, and recounted the incident to him. He, in turn, left it for his biographer.

When this tale was published, the Shippen family angrily refuted it by claiming Burr was at Paramus when Peggy arrived, made advances she repulsed, and concocted the story out of revenge. Historians in the nineteenth century discounted the account as fictional hearsay. Today leading authorities tend to believe it. As of now, at least, no one is ever likely to know.

Spinners of Myth and Legend

Annis Stockton and the Muses

The pulse of adventure—real or imagined, personal or national—provides rhythm for poets. Not even the dour Puritans of seventeenth-century New England tried to stifle the spate of collegiate odes to a variety of winsome lasses. "Look into your heart and write," the eminent Elizabethan Sir Philip Sidney had said, and his porcelain sonnets served as models for wistful amateurs. Awkward imitations they might be, but through them we still see the "bright eyes" of "the fayrest Fayre alive" with "colour fresh as damaske Rose" and "breath as Violet." Ardor may produce incongruities: "Her bodie white as Ivory, as smooth as polish'd Jet"; high moments of exultation occasionally get confused:

> As soft as Downe, and were she downe, Jove might come
>   downe and kiss
> A Love so fresh, so sweet, so white so smooth, so soft
>   as this.

If the veins of verse take curious turns, the blood still pounds.

Even the most precocious of Massachusetts men, however, could not match the energies of gentle Anne Bradstreet, who, while producing eight children, wrote some seven thousand lines. Brought as an eighteen-year-old bride from the warmth of the Earl of Lincoln's library to the bleak wilderness, she translated her musings and emotions into homespun poetry. When she trod the metered measure of English and European exemplars she faltered, but when she was Anne Bradstreet she was charming. Her enthusiastic brother-in-law had some of her work printed in London in 1650, proclaiming her "The Tenth Muse Lately sprung up in America"—but it was a heavy distillation of tedious thoughts. Left to her own design, she moved with easy confidence. Then when she grappled with the mysteries of faith, she saw the answers through the burnished splendor of a New England autumn:

> I wist not what to wish, yet sure thought I
> If so much excellence abide below;
> How excellent is He that dwells on high? . . .

None of the acrid smell of brimstone Michael Wigglesworth scorched into his "Day of Doom" blurred her vision of Heaven.

From such heights she could step to the private preserve of wife and mother, registering her thoughts "Upon her son Samuel's going to England" and "Upon her daughter's recovery from a Fever" or "In her solitary hours in her Husband's absence." As she viewed the burned ruins of their home she did not dramatize her feelings, or try to transform the happening into anything greater than her sense of loss:

> And here and there the places spy
> Where oft I sat, and long did lie.
>
> Here stood that trunk, and there that chest
> There lay that store I counted best; . . .

No such limitations bounded her devotion to her "dear and loving Husband"

> I prize thy love more than whole mines of gold
> Or all the riches that the East doth hold.

This patchwork poetry gives Anne Bradstreet no literary eminence in the judgment of sophisticated scholars. Such critiques are important only to other scholars, for she left in them a more valuable legacy: the portrait of a personality.

A century later scores of other women tried their hand with "rhyming," much as they embroidered samplers. Some had ambitions to share the fame of their idol, Alexander Pope, who rose above hardships and a physical handicap to become, by sheer dint of self-education, the acknowledged dictator of English literature by the time of his death in 1744. Pope's spiritual pull, manifest in couplets that easily converted into pious maxims, was a magnetic force for most aspiring American poets. The fact that he did not follow his own sanctimonious precepts was a source of considerable annoyance to the carefree Hogarth. Later, the political reformer and consummate rascal, John Wilkes, who must be laughing through eternity at the solemn perpetuation of his name in a Pennsylvania city, Wilkes-Barre, wrote an obscene parody on Pope's famous "Essay on Man," captioned it "Essay on Woman," and signed the Bishop of Gloucester's name—an event that plunged Parliament into turmoil, and put Wilkes in the Tower of London.

New Englanders who, at least in the eighteenth century, felt they were the repository of American intelligence, lost no time in hailing Mrs. Sarah Wentworth Morton as "The American Sappho" and praised her "warbling eloquence." Equally they were pleased with Mrs. Susanna Rowson and Abigail Adams's friend, Mrs. Mercy Warren. Far more dramatic, however, was the epic of Phillis Wheatley, a petite black woman.

Phillis was only eight years old when she was carried in slavery from Africa to Boston, where she was sold to a merchant,

James Wheatley, in 1761. She displayed astonishing precocity, learning English in less than sixteen months, and then tackling with considerable success the more formidable Latin and Greek. Happily the Wheatleys nurtured her genius, and by 1770, remarkably well-read, she published her first poem. Four years later she was something of an international celebrity, having been feted in London, where a volume of her poetry, dedicated to the Countess of Huntingdon, was published in 1773. Across the Channel Voltaire alluded to her "very good English verse," and her company and correspondence were eagerly sought. One of her admirers was the Earl of Dartmouth, to whom she dedicated a plaintive piece on liberty with this reminder:

> Should you, my lord, while you peruse my song,
> Wonder from whence my love of Freedom sprung,
> . . . .
>
> I, young in life, by seeming cruel fate
> Was snatch'd from Afric's fancy'd seat:
> . . . .
>
> Such, such my case. And can I then but pray
> Others may never feel tyrannic sway?

John Paul Jones, escaped from bleak Scotch beginnings beset by the "tyrannic sway" of oppressive poverty, had a lifelong sympathy for the blacks. His brief service aboard British "slavers" strengthened his conviction that slavery was a dirty and immoral business, and he consistently argued there could be no real freedom in America so long as blacks were in bondage. Apparently he attempted to express his feelings in a poem which at the outbreak of the Revolution he sent to a fellow naval officer, asking him "to put the enclosed into the hands of the celebrated Phillis the African Favorite of the Muse and of Apollo—should she reply, I hope you will be the bearer."

Phillis saw in the dignified person of Washington the symbol of independence, and a few months after he came to Cambridge in 1775 to assume command of the American forces, she sent him a long elegiac poem, with the hope "your Excellency" would triumph "in the great cause you are so generously engaged in." Not yet accustomed to the accolades of the public, Washington wrote to Joseph Reed on February 10, 1776:

> I recollect nothing else worth giving you the trouble of, unless you can be amused by reading a letter and poem addressed to me by Mrs. or Miss Phillis Wheatley. In searching over a parcel of papers the other day, in order to destroy such as were useless, I brought it to light again. At first, with a view of doing justice to her great poetical genius, I had a great mind to publish the poem; but not knowing whether it might not be considered rather as a mark of my own vanity, than as a compliment to her, I laid it aside, till I came across it again in the manner just mentioned.

On February 28 he belatedly acknowledged it to the author:

> Mrs. Phillis: Your favour of the 26th of October did not reach my hands 'till the middle of December. Time enough, you will say, to have given an answer ere this. Granted. But a variety of important occurrences, continually interposing to distract the mind and withdraw the attention, I hope will apologize for the delay, and plead my excuse for the seeming, but not real neglect.
>
> I thank you most sincerely for your polite notice of me, in the elegant Lines you enclosed; and however undeserving I may be of such encomium and panegyrick, the style and manner exhibit a striking proof of your great poetical Talents. In honour of which, and as a tribute justly due to you, I would have published the Poem, had I not been apprehensive, that, while I only meant to give the World this new instance of your genius, I might have incurred the imputation of Vanity. This and nothing else, determined me not to give it place in the public Prints.
>
> If you should ever come to Cambridge, or near Head Quarters, I shall be happy to see a person so favoured by the Muses, and to whom Nature has been so liberal and beneficent in her dispensations. I am, with Great Respect, etc.

There is a story that the two had a half-hour visit at Cambridge a few days before the British evacuated Boston. Reed managed to quickly get the poem into the *Pennsylvania Magazine* of April 1776. A sample of the style will suffice:

Fix'd are the eyes of nations on the scales,
For in their hopes Columbia's arm prevails.
Anon Britannia droops the pensive head
While round increase the rising hills of dead.
Ah! cruel blindness to Columbia's state!
Lament thy thirst of boundless power too late.
Proceed, great chief, with virtue on thy side,
Thy ev'ry action let the goddess guide.
A crown, a mansion, and a throne that shine,
With gold unfading, WASHINGTON! be thine.

Oddly the triumph of Phillis Wheatley did not alter Jefferson's fixed notion that Negroes were mentally inferior to whites. Even though he subsequently modified his stand by saying possibly after three generations of culture and education they might attain the intellectual capacity, he brushed aside the phenomenon of Phillis. The blacks had produced a Phillis Wheatley but not a poet, he contended, and dismissed her 1773 poems as "below the dignity of criticism." Franklin saw her in London that year but briefly noted: "I went to see the black poetess and offered her any services I could do for her." Ornate poetry by anyone had little appeal for the practical Franklin, who preferred his own lusty drinking songs to homilies or elegies.

Phillis had some views of her own about the capabilities of her race. With an intransigence equal to Jefferson's she published two volumes of verse, "The Negro Equalled by Few Europeans."

A free woman herself since 1771, she married a free Negro, John Peters, in 1778. The marriage was beset by unhappiness. It would have been difficult for anyone who had enjoyed such fame when not yet twenty to settle into the domestic pattern. Peters, according to tradition, was not equipped to confer "happiness upon such a gifted companion." Color is hardly the criterion. The mind of Phillis Wheatley would have found few whites in eighteenth-century America who could have matched it stride for stride. Her three children died in infancy, and she separated from Peters. She lived alone, dying, impoverished and forgotten, in 1784—a year after America's independence had been made fast by treaty with England. She was thirty-one.

Annis Boudinot discovered the Muse in Princeton, New Jersey—a small crossroads stage stop, whose principal claim to fame in 1755 was its college. That year, when she was nineteen, Annis married Richard Stockton, a young lawyer six years her senior. Phillis Wheatley at two was just becoming aware of her African world.

The Boudinots were of French Huguenot descent. Annis was born near Philadelphia, where her father Elias had some success as a goldsmith. In the 1740s he was lured by the prospect of copper to New Brunswick, New Jersey, and his savings were lost when the venture failed. So he began again in Princeton as a silversmith; the family was living in a small house rented from the Reverend Aaron Burr when Richard became interested in Annis. There is a hint that the Stocktons, as extensive landowners in the area, were not enthusiastic about the wedding. As searchers after status they saw little promise in the lovely and gracious girl. It was a monumental miscalculation which Richard luckily refused to share. Annis wrote it all down:

> I found me all thy own in spite of those
> Whose cold unfeeling minds would bid us part
> . . . .
> Methought without restraint you lean'd your head
> On this fond breast, and rested every care:
> My hand you took and from the circle led
> My willing steps to breathe the vernal air.
>
> Thro' various scenes we rov'd, lovely and gay;
> Of books we talk'd, and many a page compared:
> Thy works of genius softened by the lay
> Of *her* who all thy leisure moments shared.

She called it "The Dreamer." It fitted nicely, for there would be, through most of her life, a gossamer glow about Annis.

With the death of her father-in-law in 1757 she became mistress of the mansion house which had for almost a half-century been known as "The Stockton Place." To its rows of catalpa and chestnut trees she and Richard added two tulip poplars at the entrance—the traditional "bride's trees." He went along with her suggestion they assume "literary" names; she would be "Emelia" and he "Lucius." Such pseudonyms had a tinge of practicality, for presumably they allowed letter writers to express themselves without inhibition. Hence they were a fragile safeguard against alien eyes that frequently peeked into private correspondence before it reached the addressee. Ultimately, as Annis formed her circle each adopted, or received from her, a suitable name, occasionally using them to hide synthetic flirtations at which more sophisticated characters in nearby Philadelphia would have snorted. But it was part of Annis's make-believe world, and she peopled it with garlanded images such as Watteau painted.

In 1760 Scottish author James Macpherson published "Fragments of Ancient Poetry Collected in the Highlands of Scotland . . ." and embarked on a literary hoax of monumental proportions. His technique, not uncovered until after his death a comfortable thirty-six years later, was quite simple. To basic lines echoed by many generations of Highlanders he supplied copious contributions of his own. The fusion purported to be an epic written by a third-century Gael, Ossian. It sent a surge of romanticism through France, Germany, and America, as Ossian alias Macpherson recounted the fictitious exploits of his father, Fingal. Fingal's abode was called "Morven," and the enchanted Annis conferred the mist-hung name on "The Stockton Place"—and it has borne the picturesque title ever since.

If in retrospect some of her whims seem silly, the beautiful and gentle woman could banish doubts with a flick of her fan. If there was some affectation in selecting white myrtle as her talisman, her adoring husband did not notice. In 1766 when his health broke under the strain of his law practice and physicians urged him to take a vacation abroad, he was loath to leave her. It was impractical for her to accompany him since their four children were so small: Julia, seven; the twins Mary and Susan, five; and Richard, two. Lucius Horatio would arrive in 1768 and Abigal in 1773.

As a man of substance the tall, good-looking Stockton, an

excellent horseman and swordsman, moved with ease in London's fashionable circles. "I saw all your Duchesses . . . so famous for their beauty," he wrote Annis, "but . . . I had rather ramble with you along the rivulets of Morven or Red Hill and see the rural sports of the chaste little frogs, than again be at a birth-night ball." "I see not a sensible, obliging tender wife, but the image of my dear Emelia is full in view. I see not a haughty imperious ignorant dame, but I rejoice that the partner of my life is so much her opposite." He told her he was often asked if he did not prefer the elegant excitement of England to provincial life in Princeton. "No, my dearest Emelia, the peaceful home that God has blessed me with at Princeton, you and the sweet children you have brought me are sources from which I receive my highest earthly joys."

She idolized him, writing long letters sprinkled, and sometimes overwhelmed by, lengthy poems. "Your verses . . . give me great pleasure," he said appreciatively. The last stanza of "An Epistle to Mr. Stockton" provides a glimpse of Annis's style and sentiments:

> But if the powers of genius ever heard
> A votary's prayer, and e'er that prayer prefer'd,
> On me may wit and elegance bestow
> Some emanation bright, some softer glow,
> Some sweet attractive that my heart may twine,
> Stronger than beauty, with each nerve of thine.
> For, oh, I find on earth no charms for me
> But what's connected with the thought of thee.

He was always searching for plants and shrubs to lend color to the grounds of Morven—"a little box of flower seeds and the roots that will do at this season, with the hope that these will please you for the present, but I really believe you have as fine tulips and hyacinths in your little garden as any in England." He informed her he was making "a charming collection of bulbous roots" and, sharing her admiration for Alexander Pope, sent her into ecstasy by saying, "I design to ride to Twickenham . . . to view Mr.

Pope's garden and grotto . . . and . . . I shall take with me a gentleman who draws well to lay down the exact plan of the whole."

Stockton had tried to shy away from public office in New Jersey. "The publick is generally unthankful," he had written Joseph Reed, his former law student, "and I will never become a servant of it, till I am convinced that by neglecting my own affairs, I am doing more acceptable service to God and Man." Still in 1758 he drew up a petition protesting the quartering of troops in Princeton homes during the French and Indian War; he was one of the first to challenge, in conversation at least, Parliament's authority to tax the Colonies in the absence of American representation. When some of his colleagues at the bar felt New Jersey should not send delegates to the Stamp Act Congress in New York, he dissented: "We shall not only look like a speckled bird among our sister Colonies, but we shall say implicitly that we think [the Stamp Act] no oppression."

His views were sought in English governmental offices, and he prefaced a response to a question put by an undersecretary of state with the statement he had nothing to ask of the government, and therefore "dare speak my sentiments without cringing. Whenever I can serve my native country I leave no occasion untried." Despite this forthright declaration he preferred the gentler things in life, and when he came back to Morven in September 1767 he was more absorbed in the artifacts he collected for the facsimile of Pope's grotto than in the political situation.

The design for the elaborate garden became a project of paramount importance for the couple. Meticulously they related Morven to Twickenham, planting the cedars of Lebanon, cypresses, yews, Spanish chestnuts, mulberries, boxwood, and royal walnuts in Pope's pattern. As often as possible they planted the shrubbery personally, giving it the meaning Annis was to describe after her husband's death as the "fragrant bowers planted by his hand."

In 1770 the Boston Massacre's shock wave reverberated through America, and as events piled on events even the calm of

Princeton was shattered. In July 1770 the students demonstrated against "the base conduct of the merchants of New York in breaking through their splendid resolutions not to import [British goods]." So noted James Madison, then an undergraduate. He added: "The letter [of the New York merchants] to the merchants of Philadelphia requesting their concurrence [in breaking the resolutions] was lately burned by the students of this place in the college yard, all of them appearing in their black gowns and the bell tolling."

Like many lawyers Stockton preferred a course of moderation at this stage. The Boston radicals like Sam Adams would not let up the pressure, and by 1773 were pressing for independence. Stockton, who accepted appointment to the New Jersey Supreme Court in 1774, proposed "An Expedient for the Settlement of the American Disputes" to Lord Dartmouth later that year. It envisioned a commonwealth status, whereby America would be self-governing but still owe allegiance to the crown. He stayed aloof from the Committee of Safety, which held its provincial session in Princeton in August 1775. Even though Washington had taken command of the Continental forces and Annis's brother Elias was actively involved in the New Jersey Committee of Correspondence, sending powder to the beleaguered Bostonians, and similar missions, Stockton persisted in the belief that reconciliation was possible. In this his thoughts paralleled those of John Dickinson and others who were sitting in the Continental Congress. As the situation grew worse, and the confrontation between British and Americans expanded, Stockton accepted appointment as a delegate to the Congress, and took his seat on June 28, just a few days before independence was declared.

The tremulous two weeks in June before he went to Philadelphia must have been agonizing for him. His friend, Governor William Franklin, who had been appointed by the crown as the royal governor of New Jersey some years before, was driven out of office and confined in Connecticut. His new son-in-law, Dr. Benjamin Rush, was a firebrand for separation from England. Rush, fourteen years older than his bride, Julia, had known the

Stocktons since he was a student at Princeton. Now as a prominent Philadelphia physician, he was anticipating being named a
Pennsylvania delegate to the Congress. Annis most certainly reflected her husband's misgivings about taking the final step. As
chief justice of New Jersey he judiciously weighed the alternatives, and it is said that not until he heard John Adams make a
forceful argument for independence, did he reach the decision
and affix his signature to the Declaration. Annis, now an attractive forty, thus became the wife of one signer, and the mother-in-
law of another when Rush added his name.

Morven had lost its serenity, but added a new element for
Annis in the excitement of being caught up in a war. A whole
fertile field for poetry lay open to her pen, offering countless
themes. By November 1776 the spacious house lay directly in the
path of the war, as Washington's troops, suffering a double defeat
in New York, retreated toward Pennsylvania. Silver and valuable
objects of art were buried in the garden, and Annis, as an afterthought raced over to Princeton's Whig Hall to rescue some important documents which President Witherspoon of the college
and other evacuees had forgotten. This feat earned for her the
honor of being named the only woman member of the Whig Society.

As the Stocktons moved out on November 29 they left their
twelve-year-old son Richard and a servant in the mansion, probably to satisfy a legal technicality of occupancy to avoid confiscation. It was a curious decision and a strange time to be thinking of
points of law, matters that must have seemed even more baffling
to young Richard, who was given the unenviable assignment. He
must have had mixed emotions as he watched his father and
mother and the other children drive off to take refuge thirty miles
away in Monmouth County. Although their destination was
"Federal Hall," John Cowenhoven's place, Monmouth County
was a Tory stronghold; why Stockton selected it instead of joining
the refugees following Washington across the Delaware into
Bucks County, Pennsylvania, is still a mystery. During the second
night Stockton and Cowenhoven were pulled out of their beds by

loyalists and handed over to the British at Perth Amboy. Stockton, as a signer, was taken to the Provost Jail in New York, where he was shackled and denied food for twenty-four hours, spared from starvation only by scraps. He was freed in a few days, but took the oath to "remain in a peaceful Obedience to His Majesty and not take up arms, nor encourage Others to take up arms, in Opposition to His Authority." This was the oath prescribed by Sir William Howe as a condition to a full pardon, and assurance that those subscribing would be allowed to enjoy their property in full liberty. In January the Stocktons were back at Morven, which had suffered fairly extensive damage at British hands. "God be thanked that it is not worse with us," Annis wrote to her friend, Elizabeth Graeme Fergusson, "but I assure you that it is quite bad enough."

Benjamin Rush wrote to Richard Henry Lee from Princeton on January 7, 1777, and told him the town "is indeed a deserted village. You would think it had been desolated with the plague and an earthquake as well as with the calamities of war. The College and church are heaps of ruin. All the inhabitants have been plundered. The whole of Mr. Stockton's furniture, apparel, and even valuable writings have been burnt. All his cattle, horses, and hogs, sheep, grain, and forage have been carried away by them. His losses cannot amount to less than five thousand pounds." The British got some assistance from the Americans in wreaking havoc on Morven. On February 3 Washington's General Orders carried this admonition:

> Any officers, or soldiers of the American Army, who are possessed of Bonds, or other papers, belonging to Mr. Stockden are strictly ordered to deliver them to the Adjutant General at Head-Quarters.

It had been naive to think burying silverware and jewelry in the flower beds would do anything more than inconvenience invaders. The east wing of Morven had been burned, and the library so cherished by Annis and Richard stripped, many of its

treasured volumes defaced or stolen. One trunk of valuables escaped detection, and two of Annis's best-loved books, Young's
Night Thoughts and the Bible, survived. She found letters Stockton had written to her over the years tucked into some straw used
by soldiers for bedding. The portraits of her and Richard had
been slashed and unceremoniously tossed outside.

Stockton came in for some criticism, but so many Jerseyites
had recently vacillated between the winning sides that only his
prominence made his oath-taking unusual. Since the British were
too preoccupied to make propaganda from it, there was no general knowledge of his defection. Rush, who most certainly would
have excoriated such conduct in anyone else, was too closely
bound by affection to the family to publicize it, and even in Congress only casual comments were made off the floor. Annis had a
desperately sick husband on her hands. President Witherspoon
told his son that there was some local reaction to Stockton's conduct among Princetonians, but added that he "is not well in
health" and dismissed as "very doubtful" a story circulating that
Stockton claimed he was planning to take the oath when he was
captured. In December 1777, he took the oath of abjuration and
allegiance prescribed by the New Jersey legislature, and, having
divested himself of the Howe formula, was back in good standing.
Still he kept away from involvement in any political affairs, concentrating his energies on recovering his health and his estate.
Morven was repaired, the portraits restored, and about 1780 the
charred east wing was rebuilt.

While Stockton's health improved he became concerned
about a severely chapped lip that refused to heal, and from Philadelphia on November 30, 1778 wrote Annis: "My mind is in a
continued state of uneasiness about it—for your sake and that of
the dear children, as well as my own, I trust God that I may be
relieved" and on December 9 informed her he had an operation
performed the previous day. She immediately left to be with him
at the Rush home, where he was staying. The relief proved only
temporary and as 1780 drew to a close, Annis told Elizabeth
Graeme Fergusson she was "confined to the chamber of a dear

and dying husband, whose nerves have become so irritable as not to be able to bear the scraping of a pen . . . or even the folding of a letter." Her intimate thoughts she put in verse:

> While through the silence of the gloomy night
> My aching heart reverb'rates every groan,
> And watching by the glimmering taper's light,
> I make each sign, each mortal pang my own.
> . . . .
> Oh! could I take the fate to him assigned,
> And leave the helpless family their head!
> How pleased, how peaceful to my lot resigned,
> I'd quit the nurse's station for the bed.

Although Annis's grief was genuine when Stockton died, one gets the impression—perhaps unfairly—that he had posthumous value as a theme for her poetry. Understandably she would urge "Ye stately Elms! and lofty Cedars! Mourn" in the immediate wake of the funeral, but a "Pastoral Elegy" included in her correspondence with her sister muse, Elizabeth Fergusson, who had become "Laura" some time before, which still kept Stockton in his character as Lucius, seems a bit maudlin:

> Can Laura forget that this day
> Brings fresh to my woe-pierced mind
> The hour that tore me away
> From Lucius, the constant and kind?

There is the uneasy feeling that in doggerel like this, emotions are tailored to fit words, and the vanity of the poet is better served than the person supposedly honored. At least Annis had the good sense not to overdramatize her loss to a point where she went into seclusion. On the contrary she expanded her horizons, dutifully turning out on each anniversary of her husband's death an appropriate verse but filling the other 364 days with children, grandchildren, and the excitement of America's victory over Britain. In Princeton the dowager became known as "The Duchess," and Morven—ablaze with candlelight—became the spacious scene for entertaining such celebrities as Washington, Rochambeau, and scores of others. It is inevitable that Washington would wind up as a central figure in her poems.

Shy as she was, she was aware that an ode to Washington might bring her talents to a wider audience than the literary circle which the years had narrowed. She could hardly forget that one of her first efforts, a salute to Colonel Schuyler when he passed through Princeton in 1758 after having escaped Indian captivity, got into print in several local newspapers. And she could argue purity of motive by pointing to lines she had written in praise of Washington after the Battle of Princeton. When the future was still quite indefinite she had hailed him then:

> ... Thou the basis of this mighty fabric
> Now rising to the view, of arms, of arts
> The seat of empire in the western world.

Possibly this was the lost ode which Washington acknowledged in a letter to Elias Boudinot, her brother, on February 28, 1779:

> I find myself extremely flattered by the strain of sentiment in your sister's composition. But request it as a favr. of you to prest. my best respects to her, and assure her, that however I may feel inferior to the praise, she must suffer me to admire and preserve it as a mark of her genius tho' not of my merit.

On hearing that Cornwallis surrendered at Yorktown, she was moved to another poetic tribute. "Pardon this fragment," she wrote to her brother Elias, "but when the fit is on me I must jingle," and enclosed the fruits of her inspiration. Later she developed them in a lengthy pastoral which she ponderously titled "Lucinda and Aminta." This was published in the *New Jersey Gazette* of November 28, 1781, and she got up enough courage to send it to the triumphant general on July 17, 1782. Washington replied promptly and with encouraging warmth:

Philadelphia, July 22, 1782

Madam: Your favor of the 17th, conveying to me your Pastoral on the subject of Lord Cornwallis' Capture, has given me great satisfaction.

Had you known the pleasure that it would have communicated, I flatter myself your diffidence would not have delayed it to this time.

Amidst all the complimts. which have been made on this occasion, be assured Madam, that the agreeable manner, and the very pleasing Sentiments in which yours is conveyed, have affected my Mind with the most lively sensations of Joy and satisfaction.

This Address from a person of your refined taste, and elegance of expression, affords a pleasure beyond my powers of utterance; and I have only to lament, that the Hero of your Pastoral, is not more deserving of your Pen; but the circumstance, shall be placed among the happiest events of my life.

I have the honor, etc.

In the summer of 1783, Princeton became the refuge for Congress, seeking escape from the embarrassing demands of discontented soldiers in Philadelphia. Elias Boudinot was now its president and made Morven his residence, a circumstance that delighted Annis. She presided over private dinners in her home and was exhilarated to see the town come alive with new stores and new faces. Handsome and gracious, the forty-seven-year-old dowager was especially thrilled by the news that Washington, at Congress's request, was coming to Princeton to give his views on the subject of defense, specifically the size of a standing army. He arrived on August 23, accompanied by Mrs. Washington, and stayed at "Rockingham," in nearby Rocky Hill. Three days later he rode into Princeton to the cheers of the crowd and the collegians as he made his way to Nassau Hall, where the Congress was sitting. Although there was no formal banquet, it is probable that he dined at Morven, since Annis's brother as presiding officer of the Congress would most likely have extended the invitation. Whether he did or not, Annis was transported by his presence and dashed off another poetic tribute she hastily headed "Morven, August the 26":

> With all thy country's blessings on thy head
>   And all the glory that encircles man,
> Thy deathless fame to distant nations spread,
>   And realms unblest by Freedom's genial plan;
> Addressed by statesmen, legislators, kings,
>   Revered by thousands as you pass along,
> While every muse with ardour spreads her wings
>   To greet our hero in immortal song;
> Say, can a woman's voice an audience gain,
>   And stop a moment thy triumphal car?
> And wilt thou listen to a peaceful strain
>   Unskilled to paint the horrid wrack of war?
> For what is glory—what are martial deeds—
>   Unpurified at Virtue's awful shrine?
> Full oft remorse a glorious day succeeds,
>   Thy motive only stamps the deed divine.
> But thy last legacy, renowned chief,
>   Hath decked thy brow with honours more sublime,
> Twined in thy wreath the Christian's firm belief,
>   And nobly owned thy faith to future time.
> Thus crown'd, return to Vernon's soft retreat;
>   There, with Amanda, taste unmixed joy.
> May flowers Spontaneous rise beneath your feet,
>   Nor Sorrow Ever pour her hard alloy.
> And, oh, if happly in your native Shade
>   One thought of Jersey enters in your mind,
> Forget not *her* on Morven's humble glade
>   Who feels for you a friendship most refin'd.

If Washington shared this with Martha she may have wondered how she got the new name Amanda. He could hardly have been excited about the poem, whatever its merits. Throughout the year he had been regaled with tributes from all corners of the Colonies. Still he quietly reveled in the new-found glory, and he received the garlands with suitable modesty. Someone who saw him at this time noticed "his front" was "uncommonly open and pleasant, the contracted, pensive phiz, betokening deep thought and much care, which I noticed on Prospect Hill, in 1775, is done away." His weight was up to 209, a well-balanced match for his six-foot, three-inch frame. So as he read Annis's apologetic note which accompanied the ode, he was almost playful in the studied abandonment with which he answered:

> You apply to me, My dear Madam, for absolution as tho' I was your father Confessor; and as tho' you had committed a crime, great in itself, yet of the venial class. You have reason good, for I find myself strangely disposed to be a very indulgent ghostly Adviser on this occasion; and notwithstanding "you are the most offending Soul alive" (that is, if it is a crime to write elegant Poetry) yet if you will come and dine with me on Thursday and go through the proper course of penitence, which shall be prescribed, I will strive hard to assist you in expiating these poetical trespasses on this side of purgatory. Nay more, if it rests with me to direct your future lucubrations, I shall certainly urge you to a repetition of the same conduct, on purpose to shew what an admirable knack you have at confession and reformation; and so, without more hesitation, I shall venture to command the Muse not to be restrained by ill-grounded timidity, but to go on and prosper.

Then follows a strange, for Washington at least, paragraph:

> You see Madam, when once the Woman has tempted us and we have tasted the forbidden fruit, there is no such thing as checking our appetites, whatever the consequences may be. You will I dare say, recognize our being the genuine Descendents of those who are reputed to be our great Progenitors.

Washington was always attracted to lovely women, but kept his emotions tightly controlled, constantly conscious of his image and reputation and the vows that bound him to Martha. Not many times since he wrote his first impassioned love letters to Sally Fairfax, had he acted this kind of role. After suggesting she dine with him—not mentioning Martha in the process—he sallies forth with a passage that must have made Annis flutter with the possibility of a romantic flirtation. He continues:

> Before I come to the more serious Conclusion of my Letter, I
> must beg leave to say a word or two about these Fine things you
> have been telling in such harmonious and beautiful Numbers.
> Fiction is to be sure the very life and Soul of Poetry. All Poets
> and Poetesses have been indulged in the free and indisputable
> use of it, time out of Mind. And to oblige you to make such an
> excellent Poem, on such a subject, without any Materials but
> those of simple reality, would be as cruel as the Edict of Pharaoh
> which compelled the Children of Israel to Manufacture Bricks
> without the necessary Ingredients. Thus are you sheltered under
> the authority of prescription, and I will not dare to charge you
> with an intentional breach of the Rules of the decalogue in giving
> so bright a colouring to the services I have been enabled to
> render my Country; though I am not conscious of deserving any
> thing more at your hands, than what the purest and most disin-
> terested friendship has a right to claim; actuated by which, you
> will permit me, to thank you in the most affectionate manner for
> the kind wishes you have so happily expressed for me and the
> partner of all my Domestic enjoyments. Be assured we can never
> forget our friend at Morven; and that I am etc.

It is as easy to read too much into this letter, as it is, considering
Washington, not enough. Certainly if Annis did dine alone with
him, and was inclined to interpret his warm words as any kind of
a special invitation, he had—either intentionally or unintention-
ally—left the door partially open. He was to remain at Rocky Hill
until November, and the prospect of seeing the attractive Annis
frequently was pleasant to contemplate, even if it never got beyond his imagination. In all likelihood it was a brief romantic
interlude that never passed the metes and bounds of sentimental
sentences. At any rate, we have no indications of how the dinner
party went, or whether it even took place.

In January when he was back at Mount Vernon she wrote to
him apparently seeking reassurance about her talents as a poet
and he answered in his characteristic formal style:

> It would be a pity indeed, My dear Madam, if the Muses should
> be restrained in you. I have only to lament that the hero of your
> poetical talents, is not more deserving of their lays. I cannot

however, from motives of false delicacy (because I happen to be the principal character in your pastoral) withhold my encomiums on the performance for I think, the easy, simple and beauteous strains with which the Dialogue is supported do great justice to your genius, and will not only secure Lucinda and Aminta from Wits and Critics, but draw from them, however unwillingly, their highest plaudits, if they can relish the praises that are given, as highly as they must admire the manner of bestowing them.

Mrs. Washington, equally sensible with myself, of the honor you have done her, joins me in most affectionate compliments to yourself, the young Ladies and Gentlemen of your family.

With sentiments of esteem, regard and respect, I have the honor, etc.

While he was president of the Constitutional Convention in Philadelphia in the summer of 1787 she sent him another "poetical performance" which he acknowledged with usual modesty and declaration of unworthiness, adding, "I have Scarcely a moment in which I can enjoy the pleasures which result from the recognition of the many instances of your attention to me or to express a due sense of them. . . . The friendship you are so good as to assure me you feel for me, claims all my gratitude and sensibility, and meets the most cordial return."

As mistress of Morven she had much to occupy her time. The gardens won the admiration of Michaux, Louis XVI's botanist, when he stopped at Princeton on his plant-collecting tour of America; and like dedicated gardeners they exchanged information and Annis received from him Persian-plum seeds. In 1788 when Richard, Jr., married, his wife became the lady of Morven; but Annis continued to supervise the "outdoor family," as the slaves tending the grounds were affectionately called. Her daughters, all now wed, were much like her in beauty and grace and at least one, Julia, had the capacity to evoke in her husband, Dr. Rush, the consistent adoration she inspired in the late Richard during the twenty-six years of their marriage. The anniversary of his death was ritualistically observed ("this day, from all the world retired"), and she was "mournfully" pleased to copy for Abigail, who had been only eight when Richard died and was now twenty, "your dear, and ever lamented father's letters. Your tender years when he left us prevented you from forming any adequate idea of your loss in such a parent." Still Richard's shade must have cringed at the bathos of the "Elegiac Ode" she turned out on the seventh anniversary:

> And what so potent as a lover's tomb?
> And what can preach so earnest as the grave?
> The world shut out, within myself at home,
> All other preachers at a distance leave.

Since it was hardly immortal poetry Annis penned, one had to be gratified by the remembrance—and, since she was so prolific, constantly aware that virtually anything or anyone might send her poetic pulse soaring. In 1782 when the French Minister Luzerne staged a lavish party in Philadelphia to honor the birth of the Dauphin, the "lovely Infant" got a baroque ode. Six years later the "Destruction of the Trees by Isicles" got an appropriate elegy.

If her son-in-law, Rush, had not been such a violent critic of Washington it is possible, during his summer stay in Philadelphia in 1787, they might have had a convenient place to enjoy each other's conversation and company. On the other hand, on days when the Convention was not sitting, the general relaxed in the countryside west of the city, and seems to have had no inclination to make the comparatively short trip to Princeton.

That he obviously enjoyed her is reflected in a letter from Mount Vernon in August 1788, responding to a "plain prose" note she had sent earlier that month, with her usual saccharine salute. He searched for a new way to say thanks, and produced a lumbering paragraph larded with references to the Epicureans and Cicero, and the classical allusions he knew would please her. The worth of his letter to posterity is in the next paragraph:

> The felicitations you offer on the present prospect of our public affairs are highly acceptable to me, and I entreat you to receive a reciprocation from my part. I can never trace the concatenation of causes, which led to these events, without acknowledging the

mystery and admiring the goodness of Providence. To that super-
intending Power alone is our retraction from the brink of ruin to
be attributed.

Eventually politicians would adopt God as an American, and assume that in quest of our "manifest destiny" everything we did
was by divine right. But Washington's note of thanksgiving here,
coupled with Lincoln's later reminder that it might be better for
Americans to be on God's side instead of presuming He was on
theirs, puts history in a clearer perspective.

Washington told Annis he thought "you Ladies are in the
number of the best Patriots America can boast" and asked
"whether they are not capable of doing something towards intro-
ducing federal fashions and national manners? A good general
government, without good morals and good habits, will not make
us a happy People; and we shall deceive ourselves if we think it
will . . . Is it not shameful that we should be the sport of European
whims and caprices? Should we not blush to discourage our own
industry and ingenuity; by purchasing foreign superfluities and
adopting fantastic fashions, which are, at best, ill suited to our
stage of Society?" Although he knew she shared his thoughts on
the subject, he did not think "promulgation" of such an idea
"would work . . . reformation."

His election to the presidency in 1789 brought forth a long
letter from her and "The Vision, An Ode." "I bless myself—I
bless posterity—but I feel for you," she rhapsodized in the note,
and confessed an "ardor that almost censured my delicacy—
which impelled me to seize your hand and kiss it, when you did
me the honor to call on me in your way to York town." Even
though she knew he would now be very busy, she said she was
confident she would see more of him, and tactfully included "my
dear Mrs. Washington, whom I sincerely love." Although the ode
was a bit much, as a short selection will show:

> I saw great Fabius come in state,
> I saw the British Lion's fate,
> The Unicorn's despair

Washington professed to find it "elegant" in an acknowledgment whose brevity he excused because of the press of other matters.

Annis was among the distinguished Jerseyites who greeted him as he passed through Trenton en route to his inaugural in New York. While she has been credited with composing "Welcome, Mighty Chief," which the young ladies lining Assunpink Bridge sang as he crossed it, the author was Major Richard Howell. She was not to be denied, and on May 1, 1789 sent him a poem, "The President General," in which she included herself as "The Muse of Morven," with "tears of pleasure" and "gratitude's delightful glow" in her bosom. She drafted the "heroes' spirits" enshrouded by "the blue mists" "on Hudson's whitened plain"

> Each in his cloud of awful state
> Pronounced thee good as well as great,
> And filled thy cup of fame.

Washington must have been withering under this barrage; yet he managed to get off a very brief note of appreciation.

If he was too prudent to become more than platonically involved with Annis, Princeton's President Witherspoon, widowed in 1789 at sixty-seven, would have gladly become a substitute. Not long after he buried his wife, Witherspoon laid siege to Morven's Muse, to the amusement of her children and their friends, one of whom called him "the venerable Adonis" and asked "Has he yet thought it expedient to propose himself? I find the report travels far and wide." Then she added these spritely lines:

> This little God of Love is a roguish elf:
> He makes old age look foolish as himself.
>   'Gainst sixty-two
>   Oh, luckless lot—
>   His bow he drew
>   And true he shot
> Twang—went the string
> Whiz—flew the dart
>   On a *gray* goose quill
>   To an old man's heart.

Annis was bemused by it all, but Witherspoon was not one to dally. He went off to Philadelphia and married the twenty-four-year-old widow of Doctor Dill. Had she wed Witherspoon she could have boasted, if it so pleased her, that she was the wife of two signers and mother-in-law of a third. She remained content with what she had, and it is most likely—life and death being such uncertain things—she wanted to hold herself in readiness in case anything happened to Martha Washington.

The Washingtons visited her at Morven in 1790, and she was exalted. Happily she subdued the Muse so far as the president was concerned, and there is no further record of any odes floating out of Morven to crown his brow. In 1796 when she reached sixty, she moved out of her beloved home to make way for the increased younger generation; when Washington next visited her she was boarding with a friend in the neighborhood. Her health began to give way and by 1799 she could no longer walk; without a horse and carriage at her disposal, she was isolated. Washington's death that December, less than two weeks before the exciting century ended, seemed to be the close of a final chapter for her. On February 6, 1801, she died, "happy, full of peace and joy," said Dr. Rush.

Local legends grew about her memory. One was that her favorite white myrtle died at Morven when she did, and has never been successfully regrown. Even skeptics do not contest this too seriously, for Annis Boudinot Stockton added such a patrician charm to her little corner of history, she is entitled to a bit of fantasy. It would satisfy her romantic spirit to count the eminent men of letters who were to emerge from the little college she knew so intimately. Perhaps she was permitted to take that white myrtle with her after all.

In the happier, younger days when the white myrtle was in full flower, Annis wrote these lines to Elizabeth Graeme:

> Permit a sister muse to soar
> To heights she never tried before
> And then look up to thee.

Thus "Emelia" paid homage to "Laura," one year her junior. It was not simply a gracious gesture, for Elizabeth had spent months in England, traveling the countryside where the great poets had walked and thought and composed. Tall, attractive, and highly literate, she had shared a stagecoach with Laurence Sterne of *Tristram Shandy* fame and been presented to George III. Her bearing was aristocratic and she wore her learning lightly. In 1737, the year she was born, her father, Dr. Thomas Graeme, acquired from his father-in-law, Sir William Keith, the manor house and 1,200 acres near Horsham, some twenty miles north of Philadelphia. For an accomplished poet it seemed to afford a perfect pastoral setting.

If nature lavished gifts on Elizabeth with one hand, it snatched something in return with the other. Her trip to England in 1764 was to mend a broken heart. She had been engaged to Franklin's son, William, but when he went to London with his father another girl caught his fancy and he married her. "Miss Betsy Graeme," Franklin wrote from London to his wife on February 14, 1765, "lodges not far from me, and is pretty well." He had evidently been quite fond of the young woman whom he expected to be his daughter-in-law, for she later told Benjamin Rush, "I have some of the kindest and fondest letters from Dr. Franklin wrote to me when he wished me to have been a member of his family, which had had [sic] vanity taken place, and I had had a mind to have shewn them, would have been circulated thro all the anecdote writers in Europe and America under the article traits of Dr. Franklin's Domestic Character."

The word of William's change of heart came like a bolt from the blue. His early letters from Europe, of course, could give no indication of what was yet to happen to him, so she, at twenty, could still dream of a future filled with him and their shared interests in history and literature. "How have I long'd to inform you," he wrote in December 1757, "of the Pleasure I enjoy'd in visiting Windsor, its Castle, and its shady Retreats. Places you yourself recommended to me, and which I have often heard you rapturously speak of, tho' your Knowledge of them was purely

Ideal. The enchanting Scenes at Vauxhall, is another Theme on which I could dwell for Hours together. What would I not have given for a Power of instantaneously transporting you to that delightful Spot!" But it was as a twenty-seven-year-old, and alone, that Betsy saw these sights, enthralling her friends back home with her interesting letters despite her leaden spirit. She translated Fénelon's *Telemaque* into English verse as a diversion, and worked spasmodically on a metrical version of the Psalms; eventually the magic of England and the help of the great London physician, Dr. Fothergrill, restored her buoyancy.

The death of her sickly mother brought her back to the Philadelphia area, and the manor house her grandfather had built in 1721. There is a certain grimness to the exterior of brown fieldstone, because the building is high and narrow and unrelieved by any artistry. Sir William probably felt the simplicity would please the passing Quakers, and, since he was deputy governor of the province, this had political merit. As a non-Quaker, however, he let the interior reflect his love of luxury, and carefully screened guests were entertained lavishly in the beautifully appointed rooms. He had selected a site so far from Philadelphia to discourage government officials from bothering him with the minutiae of state, and this contributed to his ouster by the Penns in 1726. Keith stayed on for a time, but then conveyed the property to his son-in-law and stepdaughter and returned to England. There his expensive tastes brought him to debtor's prison, where he died in 1749.

As mistress of Graeme Park Elizabeth kept up Sir William's tradition of hospitality, and since her physician father had a spacious town house in Philadelphia, she regularly held Saturday soirees to which kindred souls were invited. Unlike the famed French salons, where the hostesses wanted only men present, Elizabeth welcomed her sister "muses" as well. Benjamin Rush, nine years younger, was enraptured with the catholicity of Elizabeth's knowledge, and recalled that in her sparkling conversations "her body seemed to evanish, and she appeared all mind." She was easily the equal of the best male minds, and superior to most.

The manuscript journal of her travels in which she had been "all eye, all ear, and all grasp" passed from hand to hand, and added its bit of luster to her reputation as the city's lady of letters.

Death once more cut into her family circle in 1766, when her sister, Mrs. Charles Stedman, died. Her aging father grew crotchety and demanding, and more time was spent in the melancholy loneliness of the manor house, as she concerned herself with his care, becoming more or less resigned to the single life. Then on December 6, 1771 Rush brought a young Scot to one of her "Attic evenings." Henry Hugh Fergusson was eleven years younger than Elizabeth's thirty-four, but the age difference seemed to matter only to her father, who strongly opposed any romance—the more so because no one knew much about the man. But the young woman felt she could not let this possibly last chance for her future happiness slip through her fingers, and four months later in April 1772 they were quietly married in Old Swedes' Church in Philadelphia. Dr. Graeme died later that year; so Fergusson became co-owner of Graeme Park. Then in 1775 he sailed for Scotland, supposedly on business, and Elizabeth was left to languish in silence.

In October 1777 when the British occupied Philadelphia, she learned Fergusson was with them in a civilian capacity. As the Americans were encamped a few miles north of Germantown, she asked Washington to permit her husband "to come out and remain at Graeme Park" for thirty days. He gently but firmly rejected the request, surmising Fergusson's "intent to return at the expiration of that time into the Quarters of the Enemy." "I confess," he added, "it appears to me very odd, that a Gentleman who has been so long absent from his family should wish to remain so short a time with them." But he placed no restriction on Elizabeth's travel to Philadelphia to see him there. She had hoped to persuade him to align himself with the American cause. Far from convincing Fergusson, however, she was made the scapegoat of a scheme that was to make her own loyalty suspect.

While in residence in Philadelphia Elizabeth had been a member of Christ Church, and thus knew the eloquent pastor,

Reverend Jacob Duché, who had so electrified the first Continental Congress with his prayers in 1774 it named him chaplain. When Congress fled the city to avoid capture in 1777, Duché stayed behind. Undoubtedly as an Anglican minister he felt in no danger, and British officers attending the service on their first Sunday in Philadelphia in September 1777 heard him offer the traditional prayers for the royal family. This gesture did not save him, for he was arrested and carted off to jail. A day later he was released, but what transpired in the interim can only be guessed. On October 8, a few days after Washington was deprived of a victory at Germantown by a mixup in movements caused by fog and some incompetence on the part of a few field officers, Duché wrote him a long letter, urging him, as head of the army, to rescind the Declaration of Independence and sue for peace.

It is virtually certain Elizabeth had no idea of the content of the letter when Fergusson asked her to deliver it to the general. Washington forwarded it to Congress, labeling it a "ridiculous, illiberal performance," and added: "I made a very short reply by desiring the bearer of it, if she should hereafter, by any accident, meet with Mr. Duche, to tell him I should have returned it unopened, If I had had any idea of the contents, observing at the same time, that I highly disapproved of the intercourse she seemed to have been carrying on and expected it would be discontinued."

When Duché's letter was made public in Congress, he was loudly denounced; in November he sailed for England and an obscure chaplaincy. Fergusson was given a post by Sir William Howe as commissary of prisoners. From Graeme Park's isolation a frightened Elizabeth wrote to Rush at Morven, where he was visiting his wife and new-born son. He replied almost immediately with a mixture of compassion and tactlessness, commiserating with the successive bereavements she endured followed "by a misfortune (worse in some respects than death)" of separation "from a husband."

Your account of Mr. Fergusson in your letter of this evening in some measure precludes my offering you any consolation drawn from the sources mentioned in my last letter. I can only look forward to a peace with Great Britain, which will probably (as in all wars like the present) include acts of indemnity . . . This may once more restore Mr. F_____ to his family and country. In the meantime, my dear afflicted friend, rest assured that you possess an unbounded share of sympathy of your friends and of every friend of human excellency, and that your name will never be mentioned in company or upon any other occasion without exciting (with an involuntary sigh) a glow of the highest esteem and warmest affection from everyone that has ever known you. . . .

It is in some measure to renew your grief to tell you of the happiness I enjoy in the society of my dear Julia. I have not a wish that is not gratified in her. Many thanks to you for your congratulations on the birth of our dear boy.

Elizabeth had previously sent to Annis some of the letters her late mother had written to her when she was in England, and Annis was so moved by them she had shared them with her daughter Julia and Rush. So he continued:

It afforded us some pleasure to find that he possesses one quality which your mother tells us you possessed in your infancy . . . He is so good-tempered that he seldom or never cries. He spends his whole time in sleeping, eating, and pulling his mama's caps and handkerchiefs to pieces.

Yes, my dear madam, I was the man who introduced Mr. F. into your acquaintance. Ah!—but the drama is not yet closed. All may yet end well, for "all is for the best." His office will enable him to show mercy to our countrymen in captivity, and this may prepare the way for his future reconciliation with his country. Can I serve you in diverting the attention of the legislature or Council of Pensylvania to your property if anything is intended against it? Most of the gentlemen of the Council are of my acquaintance. Many thanks for your remembrance of my wife in the pound of green tea. With the best compliments to Miss Stedman [Elizabeth's niece], I am, dear madam, yours sincerely,

B. RUSH

But, despite Rush's cheerful observation about things being for the best, for Elizabeth they became decidedly worse. The British had decided to leave Philadelphia in June 1778, and Fergusson intended to leave with them. She was in town to plead once more with him when the Carlisle Peace Commission arrived from England. This extraordinary group had been put together in Westminster, and empowered to negotiate peace with the Colonies. Most of those chosen had some ties, however vague, indicating a strain of sympathy for America; but a wary Congress on April 22 had resolved that any persons treating with the Commission were forthwith to be regarded as enemies of the United States. Two of the Commission members were George Johnstone, a Scot who had been governor of West Florida and had a reputation in Parliament for being a partisan of the Colonies, and a close friend of Johnstone, Adam Ferguson, a prominent professor of moral philosophy at Edinburgh and, more immediately, a relative of Elizabeth's husband. Pennsylvania officials had already ordered Henry Hugh Fergusson to appear before the State Executive Council in Lancaster on June 24 to answer to a charge of high treason—an order he certainly had no intention of obeying. But the alternative was confiscation of any property he had in the state, which included his marital share (one-half) of what was Elizabeth's.

The Commission was authorized, if it ever got around to negotiating, to agree to the suspension of all offensive statutes passed by Parliament since 1763; yet Congress was adamant that Britain must recognize American independence. Johnstone decided to try personalized contacts with certain members of Congress, based on his own background as a former colonial governor and his Parliamentary reputation. Robert Morris, the financier, who had hesitated until the last minute before signing the Declaration of Independence because he was not certain it was the proper course of action, received a seemingly high-principled communication which said, "I think that Washington and the president [of Congress] have a right to every favour that grateful nations can bestow if they could once more unite our interest and spare the miseries and devestation of war. I wish, above all other things, to see you, and I hope you will so contrive it." The delicate wording was capable of dual interpretation, and if Washington and others took offense at the hint that English honors and emoluments could lead them to betray their trust, Johnstone could pretend righteous indignation and claim he most assuredly had no such intent. For Joseph Reed, who had grown critical of Washington's generalship and was regarded as ambitious, a different plan of action was devised. A simple letter merely requesting a meeting was sent to Reed, who got it at Valley Forge; on June 14 he drafted a reply which Washington thought too cordial. The general suggested care lest it conflict with the official position Congress might want to assert. He did think there was no great harm in Reed's idea of acknowledging Johnstone's compliments with praise for the Commissioner's support of America in Parliament, and Reed and the general probably laughed at the suggestion in Reed's letter that if Great Britain frustrated his "humane and generous purpose" he could "come to America, the future asylum of the brave and virtuous from every quarter of the world. She will think herself honoured to receive into her bosom so illustrious a citizen. His eloquence will not then be spent in vain, nor his eminent worth pass unrewarded."

Into this game of cat and mouse, poor Elizabeth was drawn. Johnstone had brought her from England a snuffbox with Washington's portrait in the lid. Although he had not previously met her, he was aware of her marriage to Fergusson and her relationship to the Stedman family—one of whom, a Philadelphia lawyer, was an avowed Tory at whose home Johnstone was staying. Upset by the imminent departure of her husband, and her feeling that since he was still a British subject he could not be guilty of any treason, Elizabeth seemed a likely choice for the mission Johnstone had in mind. When he overheard her say, at Stedman's place, that she intended to go to Lancaster to ask the Council to drop the high treason charge against Fergusson, Johnstone explained he was anxious to talk to Morris and Reed, and she said she thought Reed was at Lancaster. She later testified Johnstone

said he "should be particular glad of Mr. Reed's influence . . .
Mrs. Ferguson, says he, and I think he looked a little confused, if
this affair should be settled in the way we wish, we shall have
many pretty things in our power, and if Mr. Reed, after well
considering the nature of the dispute, can, conformably to his
conscience and view of things, exert his influence to settle the
contest, he may command 10,000 guineas and the best post in the
government, and if you should see him, I could wish you would
convey that idea to him. I own I felt hurt and shocked, for I
regarded the hint as indelicate, and from that moment Mr. Johnstone appeared to me in a different point of light." Johnstone
started to leave the room, but she said she stopped him. "Do you
not think, Sir, that Mr. Reed will look upon such a mode of
obtaining his influence as a bribe (I really made use of that plain
term). Do you think so, Madam? I really, Sir, should apprehend
so. By no means, Madam: this method of proceeding is customary
to all negotiations; and one may honourably make it a man's
interest to step forth in a cause." She disagreed and, she said,
doubted that Reed could be influenced to act against his judgment. Johnstone obviously thought there was no point in continuing the dialogue and withdrew.

But two days later, Elizabeth saw the British army leave. Possibly because she saw her last hopes of regaining her husband go
with them, she sent word to Reed she must see him personally "as
writing will not do . . . Be so obliging as to appoint the place; but
I could wish to avoid passing through the camp [Valley Forge];
but any little cottage or farmhouse would be agreeable to me to
see you in." Since she thought he was still at Valley Forge, her
mysterious request took a circuitous route before it reached him
in Philadelphia, where he had come on the heels of Arnold and
the American army of occupation. Since, in Reed's words, she
was "a lady of family and reputation," he called on her that
evening.

Her preoccupation was with her husband's proscription, and
the opening phase of the conversation was on that subject. Then,
Reed said, "we imperceptibly slid into that of the British commis-

sioners" and ultimately to the Johnstone offer. "I found an answer was expected, and gave one: That I was not worth purchasing, but such as I was, the king of England was not rich enough to do it."

Elizabeth was now at the mercy of everyone. Unwanted by her husband, she faced the double frustration of losing him and her property, too. Instead of going to Reed openly to protest the treason charge, she put on paper a statement that for what she had to tell him "writing will not do" and suggested a meeting at some inconspicuous place. Possibly she had second thoughts about the concern she voiced to Johnstone about his offer being a "bribe," the more so, when he, as an experienced public official, denied such an interpretation and explained that was the way in which negotiations were carried on. In any case her first concern was the treason indictment and its implications for her own future, but she must have realized that if Reed showed any interest in the Johnstone proposal she would have acquired an ally with sufficient influence to have the treason matter dropped. By letting it slip into the conversation as a casual afterthought, she probably felt, if it backfired, it would be regarded as only incidental to the real reason for the meeting, and she could escape the danger of being an intermediary. It was risky business, since the Duché affair was less than a year old.

Reed did not rush into print with the offer. He could have made political capital for himself by doing so, but rejoined Washington and fought at Monmouth on June 28, and went back to Congress on July 15. "In the meantime," he said, "I was deliberating what steps I ought to pursue. On the one hand, the duty I owed my country seemed to demand a full disclosure; on the other, a reluctance to expose the lady to a criminal prosecution, or popular resentment, and myself to the imputation of vanity and ostentatious integrity, kept me silent except to General Washington and two or three other gentlemen." But he learned that Congress on July 9 had directed its members to lay before it any letters received "from any of the British commissioners, or their agents, or from any subject of the king of Great Britain, of a public nature." He complied on the eighteenth, and his account of the oral offer made to him, without mentioning Elizabeth by name, was published in the *Pennsylvania Packet* of July 21. On August 11, Congress resolved it would have no more to do with Johnstone as a commissioner. The latter resigned from the Commission on the twenty-sixth and said he would issue a statement later. On October 5, shortly after he had sailed for England, the *New York Gazette* carried a piece in which he said he had left with Adam Ferguson "indisputable evidence that no act of mine, by word, writing, message, or conversation with any person, whatever, could have been conceived by . . . Joseph Reed . . . as an attempt, or having a tendency, in any manner whatsoever to corrupt his integrity." He reaffirmed this denial in the Commons on November 26, and when the alleged proof never came to light, Elizabeth was in a deeper quandary than before. She made her own sworn statement in February 1779, and Reed published a lengthy one in September. This time he was less concerned about protecting Elizabeth.

Despite the soundness of her legal argument that her husband had never taken an oath of allegiance to America or Pennsylvania, and hence could not have betrayed his loyalty since it was nonexistent, the Council—of which Reed was president—ordered the interests of both confiscated.

It was an anomaly. No one seriously questioned Elizabeth's steadfast devotion to the American cause. Yet the political atmosphere in Philadelphia demanded a victim, and she was sacrificed. Graeme Park fortunately was not sold, and largely through the dedication of Benjamin Rush it was restored to her in 1781. During the agonizing years between, her nephew, John Young, a loyalist, said she was so "much attached" to the rebels, "she would not complain, believing it to be the necessary consequences of the measures they were pursuing."

She never saw Fergusson again. In 1787 she asked Rush to intercede for Young, and Rush replied he was "fully of opinion that Mr. Young will meet with a cordial reception from his former fellow citizens in Pennsylvania and that there will be no difficulty in getting his attainder taken off by the council of the State. He may either devote himself to farming at Graeme Park or study the law if he prefers public and active life." Young, who indicated he espoused the rebel position in 1775 largely to please his aunt, had been captured while trying to join up with the British in 1776. In 1780 he purchased a commission in the British Army; to all intents and purposes, he appears to have had no interest in farming or practicing law, and is believed to have died in the service of the king.

With her faithful companion, Eliza Stedman, Elizabeth lived out the rest of her life in the old manor house, adding to her reputation for kindliness by her small charities in the neighborhood, despite the fact that she was almost impoverished when she died in 1801, the same year her close friend, Annis Stockton, passed away. She was affectionately known as "Lady" Fergusson, a title won by her own dignity and courage and underscored by the melancholy mien of the homestead. Graeme Park, after Miss Stedman's death, was sold for a small sum as a poor house in 1836, but was back in private hands by 1855, and was described by a visitor as

> a two-story stone double house, sixty feet by twenty-five feet, rooms wainscoted; an iron chimeny-back in the south room second story has a date of 1728 on it; very heavy banisters, and stairs of oak; rooms not very large, but finely finished, with ceiling mouldings, etc. . . . It was uninhabited in 1855, except by a miserable insane old woman, who could not speak intelligibly, and who locked herself in an upper corner room, and went to Mr. Penrose's for her victuals.

Eventually it was acquired by the Historical and Museum Commission of Pennsylvania, and has now been restored its former grandeur. As befits such an ancient house, brooding like something out of the Brontës, Elizabeth Graeme Fergusson's ghost has been reported walking by the pond. If the theory that ghosts come back to set something evil in their lives aright holds true, one wonders what the tragic muse's sin might have been that requires expiation. Life dealt pretty harshly with her during her earthly occupancy of the place.

Patrician and Slave

The Women in Thomas Jefferson's Life

French tourists like the Marquis de Chastellux often made snap judgments of the people and places they saw in America. But there was something to substantiate his observation that upper-class southern women in the late eighteenth century "have little share in the amusements of the men, beauty here serves only to find husbands . . . and it is in general the young ladies' faces that determine their fortunes. The consequence . . . is . . . they are often coquettish and prudish before marriage, and dull and tiresome afterwards." In a way they were victims of the system as much as the black women who were their slaves.

The system developed almost imperceptibly. Slavery had been recognized in Massachusetts some years before Virginia and Maryland converted it into an institution. Even the placid Pilgrims took women and children of belligerent Indians as slaves, and despite John Elliot's worried protest that selling "souls for money seemeth to me dangerous merchandise," deemed it all a part of their Christian adventure. "There is a little squa that Stwart Calacot desires," reported Colonel Israel Stoughton after a successful raid, "to whom he hath given a coate. Lifetenant Davenport also desires one, to witt, a tall one that hath three stroakes upon her stummack, thus ! ! !". The more godly John Winthrop wrote to the equally godly William Bradford he had given sanctuary to the wife of a Pequot sachem, a woman "of a very modest countenance and behavior" who pleaded that the English "not abuse her body." Compact farms made it unnecessary to have more than a few slaves, and New Englanders with their Yankee nose for profit, sold most captives off to the West Indies or occasionally traded them for "moores," as the blacks were called.

There were some awkward moments, as when an owner of a comely black woman decided to breed her with another Negro. Unceremoniously she pushed the man from her bed, indignantly stating that such an idea was "beyond her slavery." And when Goodwife Mendame of Duxbury seduced an Indian she was sentenced "to be whipt at a cart's tayle through the town's streets, and to weare a badge with the capital letters AD cut in cloth upon her left sleeve . . . and if shee shall be found without it abroad, then to be burned in the face with a hott iron." Massachusetts had very liberal attitudes toward premarital sex, and equally liberal divorce laws, since it weighed the biblical admonition to "increase and multiply" against the brimstoned sentences about fornication and adultery, and struck a pragmatic compromise. It winked at the former and glared harshly at the latter; so the aggressive "goodwife" was punished because she had a husband at the time she found the Indian irresistible.

The proprietary interest diverse Christian sects have claimed in Jesus inevitably led to theological discussions about the precise status of the Negro. As a non-Christian and a non-Jew, he was a heathen, and hence, it was widely felt, inferior to the white. Morgan Godwyn's *The Negro's and Indian's Advocate*, published in 1680, examined the question in some detail. While Godwyn made a lengthy defense of the blacks as not being the descendants of

Ham, the accursed son of Noah, he was not helpful in improving their status because he quoted a West Indian as saying "that Negro's were beasts, and had no more Souls than Beasts, and that Religion did not concern them." What happened if they were "gospelized" and became Christians? Godwyn had another vague authority who remarked to him that baptism did no more good to a Negro "than to her black Bitch." Chief Justice Samuel Sewall dissented from such views. In 1700 he published a tract, *The Selling of Joseph*, which caused consternation among New Englanders who had comfortably concluded that Godwyn's witnesses were correct. In 1719 when Judge Sewall presided at the trial of a man charged with killing his slave, he said heroically:

> The poorest Boys and Girls in this Province, such as are of the lowest condition, whether they be Indians or English or Ethiopians—they have the same Right to Religion and Life that the Richest Heirs have. And they who go about to deprive them of this Right, they attempt the bombarding of Heaven, and the shells they throw will fall down on their own heads.

Most of his fellow citizens, however, by that time had accepted the theory that Indians and "Ethiopians" were in the lowest order, and in 1705 Massachusetts became the only New England colony to prohibit sexual relations between Negroes and mulattoes and Englishmen or members of "any other Christian nation."

Pennsylvania Quakers seldom troubled themselves with theology, since they looked upon ministers as blockheads who muddled direct communications with Heaven. If a black person was a slave they cheerfully would buy or sell him without any concern about his Christianity or conversion. If he was a free black he was entitled to the same privileges as anyone else, and the Quaker Assembly underscored this by refusing to interfere with the growing number of interracial marriages in the city. Pennsylvanians, on the whole, preferred indentured white servants because they produced more and cost less to maintain. Still it was from Philadelphia that the most strident voices would call for the abolition of slavery, and there in 1780 the first emancipation statute would be enacted.

In the South slavery developed against a wholly different background. Tobacco, rice, and cotton demanded vast acres and many hands. Indentured servants, white and a few blacks, offered no long-range solution, for in Virginia and Maryland, as soon as their terms were up, they claimed their small patches of ground and began to eke out an existence on their own. South Carolinians felt the problem even more acutely. Wetlands so ideal for rice were small inducements to men who dreamed of being independent farmers some day. So in the last quarter of the seventeenth century they looked hard at the methods used in the sugar and cocoa fields of the West Indies. To these, and to the vast coffee plantations of South America, millions of African blacks had been transported. Toughened against the sun and more resistant than Indians to malaria, yellow fever, and measles, their labor and sweat were turning huge profits for their owners. Thus it was to South Carolina the first large import of black Africans were brought.

In the beginning there was no thought of life servitude. But these strangers in a strange land, frightened and rebellious against an alien culture, and worshipping their ancient idols, made it easy for equally frightened whites to justify harsh laws. From this point it was just a step to declaring them property. Maryland set the example by holding them bound to their master for life, and in Virginia and South Carolina the pattern was followed. In rapid succession statutes declared that a white woman who married a slave became a slave herself, and children born of a slave were to be slaves regardless of the father's status.

The dehumanizing process was not an innovation of the South. It began in Africa, where for centuries tribal chiefs had sold their own people into slavery. The Portuguese, discovering this practice in the midsixteenth century, expanded the market. The French and English were among the seafaring nations who became interested, and after being momentarily ousted from Africa by the Dutch, the English came back in 1672 to establish the Royal African Company—whose accomplishments so pleased Charles II that a new coin, minted from gold it had sent back to London, was named the "guinea" and the elephant seal of the corporation impressed upon it. By 1713, when it acquired Spain's share, Britain became the largest slave trader in the Western world.

While there were some incidents of white raids on African native villages to get slaves, these were comparatively rare since it was not at all expensive to bargain with tribal leaders. New Englanders who got into the trade relied chiefly on the West Indies; small vessels, less than fifty tons and carrying a master and a crew of eight, did a brisk coastal business. Newport, Rhode Island, became the foremost slave port in the Colonies. Most southern dealers and the larger plantation owners preferred shipments brought in by the English, although conditions aboard were so wretched due to overcrowding that almost a quarter of the human cargo died en route. Between 1600 and 1800 an estimated 9 to 10 million blacks were moved by slave ships to the Western Hemisphere, but not more than about 450,000 were taken to the North American mainland. Concern over the increasing number of Negroes led several colonies to pass laws prohibiting further imports, but these were vetoed by the Privy Council in London as an infringement on the lucrative English slave trade—something of an anomaly since the British never recognized the legality of slavery.

So long as southerners had only first generation Africans working the fields it was easy to maintain the convenient theory that whites were inherently superior. The brightest person can appear helplessly stupid in a foreign land if he cannot communicate; Christianity and communication gave the colonists the margin of difference they sought. But as the second and third generations of blacks were born in America, grew up with the language and customs, and adopted the white man's religion, the falseness of the distinction became more apparent. So the whites turned to the law to shore up the barriers. As in Massachusetts, it was decided that whatever baptism might do for blacks in the hereafter, it was to have no impact on their earthly bonds. To reinforce the distinction between black and white, sexual intercourse was prohibited—a statute the vast majority of blacks could have earnestly wished enforced, since the whites were invariably the aggressors. Because blacks could not testify against whites, and the courts gingerly avoided the affairs between masters and slaves, only the poorer whites were likely to be ensnared when caught in the act.

Plantations created their own myths. Whether medium-sized, with perhaps 50 to 100 slaves, or vast, like "King" Carter's reputed 335,000 acres and 1,000 slaves, they were self-sufficient. Their similarity to the feudal baronies in medieval England was striking, with slaves acting the part of serfs. Almost subconsciously the parallel suggested the age of knighthood, with its codes of chivalry, martial spirit, and the exaltation of fair damsels. Emphasis was placed on family, and even Thomas Jefferson, who in the evening of a fulfilled life would disdain any lengthy recital of his ancestry, was eager in his youth to acquire a coat of arms. Since the tobacco aristocracy was established by many whose English backgrounds were of the lower social orders, the situation was not without its amusing side. Still, out of the whole cloth was woven a remarkable sense of pride which, through a contagion of spirit, was to manifest itself in 1861 and sustain an entire region through the four tragic years of the War between the States, against overwhelming odds in northern manpower and resources.

The romantic part of the fantasy, however, had a frustrating effect on countless white women who lived in the mansion houses of the plantations. Like princesses trapped in towers they found themselves circumscribed by conventions, and isolated on pedestals where few wanted to be. Like the Queen who reportedly gritted her teeth in the bridal bed and muttered "All for England," these "fragile flowers" were expected to bear children, not out of passionate love, but from a sense of duty. Passion was a characteristic of the "savage nigger girls," and it was in the slave quarters that men of the plantation went for excitement. If the black woman became pregnant there was no embarrassment, since the laws enslaved the child. The presence of half-brothers and half-sisters as servants apparently did not discomfit legitimate children; and most wives accepted, however grudgingly, the fact that their husbands were frequenting the beds of Negro women. It was there that the sons of the masters were initiated in the art of sex, and college students in the North were invited to spend pleasant summers as "studs" to improve the slave stock.

Josiah Quincy, visiting from Massachusetts in the late years of the eighteenth century, wrote:

> The enjoyment of a negro or mulatto woman is spoken of as quite a common thing; no reluctance, delicacy or shame is made about the matter. It is far from uncommon to see a gentleman at dinner and his reputed offspring a slave to the master of the table. I myself saw two instances of this, and the company very facetiously would trace the lines, lineaments and features of the father and mother in the child, and very accurately point out the characteristic resemblance. The fathers neither of them blushed or seemed disconcerted. They were called men of worth, politeness and humanity.

Mary Boykin Chesnut, wife of an ardent secessionist during the Civil War, recorded the remarks of a Confederate wife:

> I hate slavery. You say there are no more fallen women on a plantation than in London in proportion to numbers; but what do you say to this? A magnate who runs a hideous black harem with its consequences under the same roof with his lovely white wife, and his beautiful and accomplished daughters? He holds his head high and poses as the model of all human virtues to these poor women whom God and the laws have given him . . . Mrs. Stowe did not hit the sorest spot. She makes Legree a bachelor.

To which Mrs. Chesnut added her own thoughts:

> There will never be an interesting book with a Negro heroine down here. We know them too well. They are not picturesque.

Only in fiction do they shine. Those beastly Negress beauties are
only animals.*

Inured as they might be to their husbands' adventures with
black women, wives were highly sensitive about attentions paid to
other ladies in their own social circle. William Byrd II of Westover, who gave Virginia, along with a distinguished list of descendants and a splendid mansion, a bubbling diary comparable to
Pepys's, discovered this at a party in Williamsburg. "I played at
(r——m) with Mrs. Chiswell," he wrote in 1709, "and kissed her
on the bed till she was angry and my wife was also uneasy about
it, and cried as soon as the company was gone. I neglected to say
my prayers which I should not have done, because I ought to beg
pardon for the lust I had for another man's wife. However I had
good health, good thoughts and good humor, thanks be to God
Almighty." One of Byrd's delightful qualities was that remorse
was always momentary. He was always falling in love with
women of every type, size, and description. "The struggle between . . . the King and the Parliament in England was never half
so violent as the Civil War between this hero's principles and his
inclinations," he painstakingly noted in his encoded diary, em-
ploying the third person as if it gave more objectivity to his
thoughts and deeds. Highly exuberant, he somehow always managed to reconcile the frequent triumph of his "inclinations" so
they "happily" supported his "principles." By the standards of his
time he was a kindly master to his slaves, and in pursuit of his
particular happiness, Negro women were just a part of his sexual
adventures. As a forty-three-year-old widower in London he acquired a mistress; when she was late on one occasion, he seduced
the maid, and upon the arrival of the mistress cheerfully carried
on with her. Subsequently he dismissed his mistress because of
infidelity.

---

* There was more jealousy than truth in this caustic comment, but among the
black women who followed Sherman's troops through the Carolinas and Georgia
there was a trail of tragedy that shocked even the sympathetic Northerners. Hundreds of little children were found slain or abandoned along the roadsides because
they had become too much of a burden on their mothers during the exhausting
march. Even such brutal statistics must be kept in perspective. Child abuse has been
a persistent problem in every era, and not the exclusive crime of a particular race.

Byrd was hardly typical. Several long stays in England, where he had been educated, gave him a cosmopolitan air, literary tastes of the first order, and an incurable romanticism. He regarded himself as a religious man, and after a night on the town in London came back to his lodgings "about eleven and said my prayers. I kissed the maid 'till my seed ran from me." He summed up his situation as a plantation owner thus:

> Like one of the patriarchs I have my flocks and my herds, my bond-men and bond-women, and every sort of trade amongst my own servants, so that I live in a kind of independence on everyone but providence . . . we sit securely under our vines and fig-trees.

When he died in 1744, a more trenchant observer of life in Virginia had just passed his first birthday.

Thomas Jefferson never knew his father, Peter, who died a few months before he was born. A solid, quiet man who built a sizeable estate, Peter Jefferson had been a friend of Byrd. To the perceptive Tom, as he grew to manhood, slavery assumed ominous proportions:

> The whole commerce between master and slave is a perpetual exercise of the most boisterous passions, the most unremitting despotism on the one part, and degrading submissions on the other.

He hoped the day would not be distant when total emancipation would take place, but wanted no integration of the races:

> Deep rooted prejudices entertained by the whites; ten thousand recollections, by the blacks, of the injuries they have sustained; new provocations; the real distinctions which nature has made; and many other circumstances will divide us into parties, and produce convulsions, which will probably never end but in the extermination of the one or the other race.

He wanted Virginia to provide for the education of the blacks, although he had little confidence in their ability to learn such sophisticated theories as "the investigations of Euclid" and because "in imagination they are dull, tasteless and anomalous" anticipated no great things. Jefferson recommended that, once given basic training in the art of civilization, the blacks be shipped back to Africa or out west, where they could establish a homogeneous nation. "In music," he granted, "they are more generally gifted than the whites, with accurate ears for tune and time, and they have been found capable of imagining a small catch. Whether they will be equal to the composition of a more extensive run of melody, or of complicated harmony, is yet to be proved."

While he admitted there should be

> great allowances for the difference of condition, of education, of conversation, of the sphere in which they move . . . yet many have been so situated, that they might have availed themselves of the conversation of their masters; many have been brought up to the handicraft arts, and from that circumstance have always been associated with the whites. Some have been liberally educated, and all have lived in countries where the arts and sciences are cultivated to a considerable degree, and have had before their eyes samples of the best works from abroad. The Indians, with no advantage of this kind, will often carve figures on their pipes not destitute of design and merit. They will crayon out an animal, a plant, or a country, so as to prove the existence of a germ in their mind which only wants cultivation. They astonish you with strokes of the most sublime oratory; such as prove their reason and sentiment strong, their imagination glowing and elevated. But never yet could I find that a black had uttered a thought above the level of plain narration; never seen even an elementary trait of painting or sculpture.

He traces out his thesis in the physical differences between black and white:

> Are not the fine mixtures of red and white, the expressions of every passion by greater or less suffusions of colour in the one, preferable to that eternal monotony, which reigns in the countenances, that immovable veil of black which covers all the emo-

tions of the other race? Add to these, flowing hair, a more elegant symmetry of form, their own judgment in favour of the whites, declared by their preference of them as uniformly as is the preference of the Oran ootan for the black woman over those of his own species. The circumstance of superior beauty, is thought worthy attention in the propagation of our horses, dogs, and other domestic animals; why not in that of man?

Despite the seemingly patent snobbery, Jefferson was examining the problem, to all intents and purposes, with judicious scholarship and reflection. Relentlessly he pursued the differences, even to the variations in body odors. Such postulates have led many of his modern biographers to denounce, with surprising vehemence, the persistent story that Jefferson had illegitimate children by his slave girl, Sally Hemings. Almost to a man they contend that miscegenation was so abhorrent to him that such a liaison would have been totally out of character.

Perhaps, but Sol Feinstone is of the strong opinion that Jefferson's constant insistence on the complete separation of blacks and whites was a cover-up for his relations with the beautiful mulatto. After all, Jefferson, so remarkably talented that he mastered an extraordinary catalogue of subjects, was also a master of duplicity. There is a philosophical detachment in countless topics which came under his scrutiny and were explored with his highly objective mind. If he could rise above his personal passions and prejudices to find the level of truth, he saw no need to bare his own soul in the process. In this he sacrificed warmth to wisdom, and only in his personal letters of the most intimate nature do we get a glimpse of emotion. His pen, capable of majestic passages in so many realms, would never have been able to write the simple, candid sentence Byrd jotted one evening: "I kissed a Negro girl."

There was no particular reason for him to record such an event even if it happened. The difficulty lies with posterity rather than with him, for we come to expect of our heroes that they share with us such moments. Quite rightly Jefferson the philosopher felt no obligation to satisfy our curiosity about Jefferson the lover. The fascination about his alleged relationship with Sally is that historians have made it almost as much a storm center of debate today as Jefferson's political enemies in 1800, using some of the heated adjectives which his champions then employed to denounce the rumors as "vile." It should be noted that scholars who rely on a politician's character as a key to his conduct are frequently naive locksmiths.

On October 2, 1802 a literary magazine, *The Portfolio*, gleefully showed its Federalist bias by this little gem, which it blandly said was "Supposed to have been written by the Sage of Monticello":

> Of all the damsels on the green
> On mountains, or in valley
> A lass so luscious ne'er was seen
> As Monticello Sally.
>
> Yankee Doodle, who's the noodle?
> What wife were half so handy?
> To breed a flock of slaves for stock,
> A black amour's the dandy....
>
> When pres'd by load of state affairs,
> I seek to sport and dally,
> The sweetest solace of my cares
> Is in the lap of Sally.
>
> Yankee Doodle, etc.
>
> What though she by the glands secretes;
> Must I stand shill-I-shall I?
> Tuck'd up between a pair of sheets
> There's no perfume like Sally.
>
> Yankee Doodle, etc.

The fragmentary descriptions we have of Sally state that she was "mighty near white," striking in appearance with black hair worn down her back. She was a half-sister of Jefferson's late, dearly loved wife—having been one of several sired by his father-in-law,

John Wayles. Her mother was Betsey, begotten of an African black by an English sea captain. At Wayles's death, Betsey and her children came to Monticello as part of Martha Wayles Jefferson's inheritance.

We know very little about the ten years of this marriage, save that Jefferson, in retrospect, described the period as "ten years of unchecquered happiness." She was a twenty-three-year-old widow when Jefferson, thirty, married her on January 1, 1772. Her health was fragile, and it appears that each of her six pregnancies made her progressively weaker. It was after she had delivered her sixth child by Jefferson—having had one by her deceased husband—that she went into the decline that some months later snuffed out her life. Three of the six children died in infancy. "My dear wife died this day at 11-45 A.M.," he wrote in his account book for September 6, 1782, but it remained for his eldest daughter in later life to describe his grief:

> As a nurse, no female ever had more tenderness or anxiety. He nursed my poor mother in turn with Aunt Carr and her own sister, sitting up with her and administering her medicines and drink to the last. For four months that she lingered, he was never out of calling; when not at her bedside, he was writing in a small room which opened immediately at the head of her bed. A moment before the closing scene, he was led from the room almost in a state of insensibility by his sister, Mrs. Carr, who, with great difficulty, got him into the library, where he fainted, and remained so long insensible that they feared he never would revive. The scene that followed I did not witness; but the violence of his emotion, when almost by stealth I entered his room at night, to this day I dare not trust myself to describe. He kept to his room three weeks, and I was never a moment from his side. He walked almost incessantly night and day, only lying down occasionally, when nature was completely exhausted, on a pallet that had been brought in during his long fainting fit . . . When at last he left his room, he rode out, and from that time he was incessantly on horseback, rambling about the mountain, the least frequented roads, and just as often through the woods. In those melancholy rambles, I was his constant companion, a solitary witness to many a violent burst of grief.

Among all the Jefferson memorabilia, nothing of Martha remains except a brief letter of August 8, 1780 in which, as the wife of Governor Jefferson, she pledges her support for a war relief project begun in Pennsylvania, a receipt she signed, and some notations about household items at Monticello. No portrait, no lock of hair, no gown, and not a single letter she ever wrote or received from her husband.

No one knows why. Some of his biographers confide he wanted to insulate her memory from his public life. It is a logical conclusion, since he was still smarting from a legislative resolution of the previous year calling for an investigation of his last year as governor of Virginia. Even though his supporters prevailed, and managed to get resolutions of appreciation for his services adopted, he saw in the perfunctory tribute a strain of ingratitude. He had inscribed on Martha's tombstone a line from the *Iliad* as a pledge her love would remain sacred to him and its flame burn undiminished by death. With unabashed romanticism, his admirers have taken the tombstone tribute as conclusive evidence Jefferson never thereafter was seriously involved with any woman. Homer's words, if such was the case, were more durable than his own subsequent statement: "The earth belongs to the living and not to the dead."

In 1802 a former friend and client, John Walker, provided Jefferson's political enemies with a statement that Jefferson had on various occasions between 1768 and 1779 tried to make love to his wife, but was successively repulsed. The story was broken by a hack writer, James Callender, who had done some journalistic hatchet work for Jefferson when the latter was secretary of state. Significantly, it also was Callender who first disclosed the tale about Jefferson's implacable enemy, Alexander Hamilton, and Mrs. Reynolds. In that instance, Jefferson's biographers note with pride, the man from Monticello passed no judgment on Hamilton's misadventure. Such silence might have been prompted by nobility, vulnerability, or political sophistication. Whatever, Hamilton was more successful with Mrs. Reynolds than Jefferson with Mrs. Walker.

The recital, replete with rebuffs, was hardly a tribute to the young lawyer's magnetism or technique. Walker sketched the incidents: Jefferson, in 1768, shocking Mrs. Walker with his advances during the absence of her husband; in 1769 renewing his "caresses" and placing "in Mrs. W's gown sleeve cuff a paper tending to convince her of the innocence of promiscuous love," which she "on the first glance tore to pieces"; the bachelor Jefferson excusing himself from his male companions on pretext of a headache, and slipping into Walker's room "where my wife was undressing or in bed"—a move she "repulsed with indignation & menaces of alarm & [Jefferson] ran off"; the married Jefferson visiting the Walkers with his bride, taking advantage of Mrs. Walker's routine to intercept her in the hall, clad only "in his shirt ready to seize her on her way from her chamber—indecent in manner." If the revelation of ancient ardors seemed belated, Walker explained somewhat fuzzily that his wife kept silent for "fear of its consequence which might have been fatal to me." Presumably this meant that since he regarded Jefferson as such a good and close friend, news of the persistent siege would have precipitated either a heart attack or a duel. Jefferson, running for his second term as president, faced this and Callender's allegations about his relations with Sally Hemings by announcing: "I plead guilty to one of their charges, that when young and single I offered love to a handsome lady . . . It is the only one founded in truth among all their allegations against me."

Sally Hemings was fourteen when she accompanied Jefferson's younger daughter to Paris in 1787. He had been named minister to France two years earlier by friends in the Continental Congress who feared the gloom in which he enshrouded himself after the death of his wife might destroy him. The assignment proved an ideal tonic. He had the opportunity to make his prodigious reading about Europe come alive, and, more important, to meet two captivating women.

For all the easy breadth of his mind, Jefferson had fixed notions about women. Parisian women, as a group, bored him. He thought their high fashion artificial, and their intrusion in political discussions annoying. His ideal, perhaps best represented by his late wife, was a quiet, cultured, and domestic type. Still he rejoiced in the company of Abigail Adams, who blended his idea of domesticity with a sharp perception of politics. She was in London with John, who was busy setting up shop as minister to Great Britain; and Jefferson, at her request, was buying objets d'art, shoes, and even a corset for her daughter. The light banter that filled his letters showed how much he appreciated her friendship. Then into his life came a lovely twenty-seven-year-old, blue-eyed blonde, Maria Hadfield Cosway.

She had been born in Florence, Italy, to English Protestant parents, but became such an ardent Catholic that her frantic mother rushed her off to England in 1779 when she began to talk of becoming a nun. A talented artist and musician, set by her mother's design in the best social circles of London, she was quickly besieged with eager and eligible suitors who found her beauty enhanced by the charm of her Italian accent. She was sufficiently spoiled and egocentric to leave the matter of marriage up to her mother, who, after examining the assets of the swains, chose Richard Cosway, a short, odd-looking man seventeen years her senior, who acquired a sizeable fortune through his skill as a painter of miniatures. They were married in 1781 and by the time John Trumbull, who was sketching Jefferson for his painting of the signing of the Declaration, introduced the Virginian to them in Paris in the summer of 1786, the Cosways were suitably bored with each other. Like scores of others before him, the forty-three-year-old Jefferson was entranced by Maria. Inept he may have been in his quest of Mrs. Walker, but now, mature, cosmopolitan, and highly sophisticated, he was appreciative of the unbounded freedom accorded by French custom to married women; and Cosway was generously cooperative. They spent long hours together visiting a wide variety of places celebrated in French history and art. It is idle to speculate whether they became lovers in the physical sense, but there is no doubt of Jefferson's intensity, and the affair added new dimension to his writings. The philosopher-statesman now measured his thoughts by and about Maria, and when they were reduced to correspondence they vibrated with passion, shimmering descriptions, and such carefree passages as: "I am but a son of nature, loving what I see & feel, without being able to give a reason, nor caring much whether there be one." He examined his feelings in an imaginary dialogue between his "Head and Heart," a soliloquy of rare skill. It would have helped posterity considerably if Maria had paid more attention to English during her formative years. Despite her parentage, she was much more at home with Italian, and it is hard to determine the depth of her own emotions. If he pleads for a long letter, she coyly responds with four lines; if he neglects to write, she scolds him; when he explains that his "long silence" was due to a trip to Turin, Milan, and Genoa and asks:

> Why were you not with me. So many enchanting scenes which wanted only your pencil to consecrate them to fame . . . a castle and village hanging to a cloud . . . a mountain cloven through to let pass a gurgling stream.

she impatiently ignores his word-pictures:

> Do you deserve a long letter, my dear friend? No, certainly not, and to avoid temptation I have a small sheet of paper . . . How long do you like to keep your friends in anxiety! How many months was you without writing to me? And you felt no remorse? I was glad to know you was well, sure of your being much engaged and diverted, and had only to lament I was not a castle hanging to a cloud, a stream, a village, a stone on the pavement of Turin, Milan, and Genoa. . . . Oh, if I had been a shadow of this Elysium of yours! How you would have been tormented!

When she returned to Paris in 1787 something of the former magic was missing, possibly lost by her studied neglect of Jefferson amid a constant swarm of admirers. If it was a calculated step to bring him closer, it was the wrong strategy. As the time for her departure neared, she testily blamed him:

If my inclination had been your law, I should have had the pleasure of seeing you more often than I have. I have felt the loss with displeasure.

They spent her last evening in town together and she asked him to have breakfast with her, then hastily wrote him a note cancelling it:

To bid you adieu once is sufficiently painful, for I leave with very melancholy ideas.

He did not get the word in time and turned up at the appointed hour only to find her gone. From London she told him:

I left Paris with much regret, indeed, I could not bear to take leave anymore. I was confused and distracted. You must have thought me so when you saw me in the evening.

And a few days later another letter:

And what did you think of me? I did it to avoid the last taking leave. I went too early for anybody to see me. I cannot express how miserable I was in leaving Paris. How I regretted not having seen more of you. And I cannot have even the satisfaction to unburden my displeasure by loading you with reproaches.

There was a gentle rebuke in his gallant answer:

This spared me, indeed, the pain of parting, but it deprives me of the comfort of recollecting that pain . . . But in your case it was not any fault, unless it be a fault to love my friends so dearly as to wish to enjoy their company in the only way it yields enjoyment, that is, en petit comite. You make everybody love you. You are sought and surrounded therefore by all. Your mere domestic cortege was so numerous, *et si imposante,* that one could not approach you quite at their ease, nor could you so unpremeditatedly mount into the phaeton and hie away to the Bois de Boulogne, St. Cloud, Marly, St. Germain, etc. Add to this the distance at which you were placed from me. When you come again, you must be nearer, and more extempore.

Her close friend Angelica Schuyler Church, accompanied by Trumbull, came to Paris shortly after Maria left. Jefferson had never met Hamilton's beautiful and irrepressible sister-in-law before, and Maria asked:

> What do you think of her? She calls me her sister. I call her my dearest sister. If I did not love her so much I should fear her rivalship. But no, I give you free permission to love her with all your heart and I shall feel happy if I think you keep me in a little corner of it, when you admit her even to reign queen.

Jefferson was impressed with Angelica. She had brought her daughter to Paris to study at the same convent where his Patsy was enrolled. So without assuring Maria of any place in his heart he replied:

> I find in her all the good the world has given her credit for. I do not wonder at your fondness for each other. I have seen too little of her as I did of you.

Trumbull took back to London his portrait of Jefferson, and Maria was annoyed that the Virginian had not sent with either Angelica or him any message. She sent him a tart letter, asking his permission to obtain a copy of Trumbull's sketch: "It is a person who hates you that requests this favor." Trumbull made one for each of the ladies, and informed Jefferson he thought Maria wanted hers to scold. Jefferson meantime had opened a correspondence with Angelica:

> Come then, Madame, to the call of friendship . . . Your slender health requires exercise, requires amusement, and to be comforted by seeing how much you are beloved everywhere . . . If you will install me as your physician, I will prescribe to you a journey a month to Paris.

Angelica responded with her clever touch:

> Mrs. Cosway and I are enjoying the quiet of the country, the

plays and songs, and very often wish that Mr. Jefferson was here, supposing that he would be indulgent to the exertions of two little women to please him, who are extremely vain of the pleasure of being permitted to write him, and very happy to have some share of his favorable opinion. Adieu, my dear sir, accept the good wishes of Marie and Angelica. Mr. Trumbull has given us each a picture of you. Mrs. Cosway's is a better likeness than mine, but then I have a better elsewhere, and so I console myself.

Almost immediately he answered:

The memorial of me which you have from Trumbull is the most worthless part of me. Could he paint my friendship to you, it would be something out of the common line . . . I never blame heaven so much for having clogged the ethereal spirit of friendship with a body which ties it to time and place. I am always with you in spirit; be you with me sometimes.

She had said she was planning to return to America for a visit, and he suggested they make the voyage together:

Think of it then, my friend, and let us begin a negotiation on the subject. You shall find in me all the spirit of accomodation with which Yoric began his with the fair Piedmontese. We have a thousand inducements to wish it on our part. On yours perhaps you may find one in the dispositions we shall carry with us to serve and amuse you on the dreary voyage.

They could not arrange their schedules but thereafter saw each other on occasion when Angelica moved to Philadelphia, and they exchanged letters across the years, although Jefferson's subsequent feud with Hamilton strained their relations—a circumstance he lamented in a long, reflective letter to her. Similarly his political battles with Adams cost him the friendship of his cherished Abigail. Maria was upset when she learned he was going back to America:

is it true? and is it possible! Oh then I give up the hopes of ever seeing you again.

She spoke of a projected trip to Italy she was contemplating. He urged her to come to the United States with Angelica, or to sail across with him. She apparently pondered the idea but finally wrote:

> You are going to America and you think I am going with you. I thank you for the flattering compliment. I deserve it for I shall certainly be with you in spirit.

He declined the invitation she had extended to join the Cosways and go to Italy because business of state called him home:

> I am going to America, and you to Italy. The one or the other of us goes the wrong way, for the way will ever be wrong which leads us farther apart.

When his ship put into an English port en route home, they made half-hearted gestures to see each other once more; but she pleaded a cold and he made no attempt to go to her. Despite the fact they never met again they maintained contact through letters. Maria's earlier religious ardor found expression in later years when she took her ailing husband to Lodi, near Milan, and nursed him in a convent through a long illness. She founded a college for women in conjunction with the Church of Santa Maria della Grazie there, and was honored for her good works by the emperor of Austria, who made her Baroness Cosway of Lodi. That her affection for Jefferson was not forgotten is shown poignantly in one of the last letters, wherein she said she was:

> Happy in self gratification of doing my duty, with no other consolation. In your Dialogue your head would tell me, "that is enough," your heart perhaps will understand. I might wish for more. God's will be done.

She was to survive Jefferson by eleven and a half years.

The celebrated "Head and Heart," which he had written for her in the golden Parisian days, is illustrative in its title of their different approach to religion. Maria felt it through her heart;

Jefferson appraised it through the head. Much of his appeal for women lay in a gentleness and kindliness which closely approximated an ideal of Christianity. With him it was almost an instinctive quality, and hardly something he would ascribe to religious merit.

Sally Hemings and her brother, James, who were with him in France, were not slaves while there, for French law did not recognize such a system. Had they chosen, they could have left him. He paid them each a salary, and spent almost as much on Sally's clothes as those of his daughters. He had her tutored in French and provided her with a room away from the servants' quarters so she would be protected against the ribaldry and dangers there.

When she arrived in Paris in July 1787, she was a frightened child of fourteen. Abigail Adams remarked Sally required more care than Jefferson's younger daughter, whom she was supposed to be attending. By sixteen, however, she can be assumed to have acquired considerably more sophistication, and it was then—in 1789—that she is alleged to have become his mistress. The question of whether she was or was not is hardly of earth-shaking importance today, apart from a possible substantial increase in the number of his descendants, and the interesting speculation about the proliferation of his extraordinary genes. Jefferson denied it; but other great men, drawing a clear line between their private and public lives, have had no compunctions about denying things they reasonably felt were none of an inquisitive public's business. It would have no bearing on his qualifications as president. He could afford to sate the appetite for gossip by conceding, however obliquely, the Walker affair. It was mildewed, and Mrs. Walker was white. Moreover, such a concession lent credence to his denial about any relationship with Sally, who, before, during, and after the Callender "exposé" was still bearing children— every birth, as Professor Winthrop Jordan noted in 1968, nine months after Jefferson was on the premises at Monticello. Only the first child, if we credit Sally's son, Madison Hemings, was conceived elsewhere. He said his mother told him that was accomplished in Paris after she had become

> Mr. Jefferson's concubine, and when he was called home she was enciente by him. He desired to bring my mother back to Virginia with him but she demurred. In France she was free, while if she returned to Virginia she would be re-enslaved. So she refused to return with him. To induce her to do so he promised her extraordinary privileges, and made a solemn pledge that her children should be freed at the age of twenty-one years. In consequence of his promises, on which she implicitly relied, she returned with him to Virginia. Soon after their arrival, she gave birth to a child, of whom Thomas Jefferson was the father.

If Jefferson needed to reconcile his desires with his distaste for miscegenation, he had only to recall the happy experiences of his late father-in-law and his mentor, George Wythe of Williamsburg —the two men he most admired.

It was said that when John Wayles turned to his slave Betsey Hemings after the death of his third wife, such a strong bond of affection united them she was his wife in fact, if not in law. Sally was reputed to have inherited her mother's affectionate nature, and Jefferson must have sensed that she could offer steadfast companionship in his sitting room as well as in bed. If there was a bargain struck in Paris, Sally demonstrated foresight that bespeaks considerable intelligence.

No suppositions are needed to delineate Wythe's infatuation with Lydia Broadnax. After the death of his second wife, she took over the management of his home in Williamsburg, and not only shared his bed but many of his interests. Having become a master of Latin and Greek, through the inspiration of his own mother and by dint of self-effort, Wythe was proof positive of what anyone who tried could accomplish. He not only became a lawyer, he became the most eminent lawyer in Virginia, and the magnitude of his mind and his own philosophical sweep was the most powerful influence in the shaping of Jefferson's thought. A signer of the Declaration of Independence, he also held various offices in Williamsburg and Virginia. Of Lydia we know considerably less, except that, like many black women who had been domestic servants in the eighteenth century, she was refined and highly intelligent. Wythe, a vigorous opponent of slavery, gave her freedom, thus elevating her status and ensuring that the child she was carrying by him would be born free. They named him Michael Brown, and lavished affection upon him. Wythe taught him Latin and Greek as well as other subjects in which the lawyer was proficient, and to ensure that the boy would have the finest formal education available, made provisions in his will to that effect, and charged Jefferson, as one of his executors, to see they were fulfilled.

Ironically it was this will that undid Wythe's carefully laid plans. A grandnephew named Sweney was named to succeed to Michael's inheritance in the event of the young man's death. While brooding over what he deemed an injustice, the envious Sweney forged Wythe's name to several checks, and fearing prosecution, sprinkled arsenic in the coffee and over strawberries which Lydia was preparing to serve. Michael died instantly. Wythe, although almost eighty, lived long enough to disinherit Sweney. Lydia alone survived, but since she was black (despite being a free Negro), she could not testify against a white person; so Sweney went free. Virginia, by dint of this restriction on evidence, was forced to helplessly watch the murder of its distinguished citizen go unrequited. Jefferson, usually mild-mannered, spoke as both president and private citizen, when in 1806 he denounced the crime as "an instance of depravity . . . hitherto known to us only in the fables of the poets." Sweney was convicted of the check-forging charge, but on appeal this too was dismissed.

Undoubtedly there were instances where white ladies of the plantation had dalliances with black men, but the high risks involved on both sides discouraged such promiscuity. Jefferson, without elaboration, stated that black men preferred white women; but almost certainly the allusion was to less "fragile flowers" such as tavern maids or their equally hardy sisters on the fringe of the frontier, where itinerant ministers were shocked out of their senses at the abandon with which flimsily dressed maids frolicked with all kinds of men. Hemmed in by conventions and the need for economic security, only the boldest of plantation mistresses would have ventured for an integrated affair, since a pregnancy would precipitate many complications. A widow, safely past the fertility stage, was the most likely candidate for this kind of romance.

On July 4, 1776, one-fifth of all Americans were in some form of servitude—most, by far, slaves. Rough estimates fix the latter as numbering 41,000 in the North and over 350,000 in the South. With sentiment crystallizing for some form of abolition above the Mason-Dixon Line, hopes for freedom made blacks there more interested in the Revolution than their brethren in Maryland, Virginia, Georgia, and the Carolinas. Some 5 percent were free Negroes, and among these were a number who distinguished themselves in the ranks of northern militia units and the Continental Army. Unwilling to arm slaves and promise them freedom if they enlisted, the southern states subjected their blacks to the temptations of British proposals that they flee their plantations and serve under the British flag, with guarantees of protection and freedom. Many did, and while some discovered more hardships than they had endured as slaves, the British kept their word and evacuated them to England when their own forces were withdrawn. Virginia's royal governor, Lord Dunmore, had conceived the idea for an "ethiopian Regiment," and some 800 slaves managed to reach his quarters in Norfolk. Scores were intercepted in futile attempts, including two women who were captured with seven men in mid-December, 1776, in an open boat. Dunmore's move aroused anger. The *New York Journal* published this poem, addressed to Dunmore and referring to the report that a Negro woman in New York had named her child Dunmore.

> Hail! doughty Ethiopian Chief!
> Though ignominious Negro Thief!
> This Black shall prop thy sinking name,
> And damn thee to perpetual fame.

While the regiment was doomed by a high mortality rate due to smallpox and rigors for which it was ill prepared, its formation exhilarated blacks. In Philadelphia there were rumors of some blacks jostling whites on the street and boasting that when "lord Dunmore and his black regiment come, . . . then we will see who is to take the wall."

It seems strange to us that at a moment in history when Americans were giving eloquent expression to the rights of man, so many in our midst would be denied those rights. The burden did not fall entirely upon black shoulders, for there had been heavy traffic in buying and selling whites. During the colonial period some 20,000 convicts were transported to America, nearly all of them dumped into Virginia and Maryland. Scottish soldiers taken prisoner in the Jacobite rebellion were sold for £20, and Irish vagrants rounded up were a drug on the market at £4. The majority of these Scotch and Irish did not last more than a year— death having written their destiny in the undernourished and diseased condition in which they often arrived.

Still the white man and woman could cling to the thin thread of hope that in time their color would redeem them. For the blacks the prospect was remote.

Sally Hemings probably never sought for herself the freedom she reportedly claimed for her children. At Jefferson's death she was listed in the inventory of his estate as an "old woman" valued at "thirty dollars." She was fifty-three.

Jefferson, who died on July 4, 1826, the fiftieth anniversary of the Declaration of Independence, lived up to the agreement Sally is said to have demanded in Paris. In one way or another the children who reached their twenty-first birthday during his lifetime disappeared from Monticello to begin their lives elsewhere, and the others were freed by his will. But he released only five such slaves—all Hemingses—and the ninety-five others, including Sally, passed as part of his property. Possibly even in the hour of death he was anxious not to lend substance to the stories about Sally which had been so widely circulated, and in which she was said to be his mistress. He might have given his daughter Martha private instructions to liberate her after the publicity attendant upon the settlement of his estate had passed. In any case, Sally was released by Jefferson's daughter in 1828 and lived with her son Madison in Albemarle County, Virginia, until her death in 1835. They shared a house rented by a younger son, Eston. Perhaps the final irony was that the census taker in 1830, listing the occupants of the house, described Eston as the head of the family and white. In keeping with the practice at the time the others were just recorded by age and sex. For some reason, however, in noting Sally as a woman, somewhere between fifty and sixty, he felt impelled to add that she was white.

Sources and Resources

Where there are co-authors, readers have a right to know who wrote what. This book was inspired by an idea of Sol Feinstone, and involved many lengthy discussions, and some differences of opinion between us on a few points, which served to give balance to the whole. The task of final writing was left to me, but reflects our long and considered judgment about the women here portrayed.

As with any work of this nature, an incalculable debt is owed to scholars past and present who have ploughed a number of fields. Some are acknowledged below, but it is important to remember the libraries and historical societies which have preserved America's heritage through devoted care to manuscripts and books. Our mutual friend, Dr. Whitfield J. Bell, Jr., can personify the learned societies through his leadership of the eminent American Philosophical Society. Ms. Mary Jane Herre, reference librarian of the West Shore Public Library, Camp Hill, Pennsylvania, stands individually and symbolically for the libraries, large and small, to whom we are very grateful.

JOSEPH J. KELLEY, JR.

A Partnership of Minds

John and Abigail Adams were not only fortunate in each other, but in descendants who appreciated their worth, and shared their sense of history.

232

Their grandson, Charles Francis Adams, editor of *Letters of Mrs. Adams, the Wife of John Adams*, Boston, 1840, lamented in a perceptive preface that the great men of the Revolution were judged mainly by their public papers in which they were "conscious that they were acting upon a theatre, where individual sentiment must be sometimes disguised, and often sacrificed, for the public good . . . We look for the workings of the heart, when those of the head alone are presented to us." With Abigail there was never any doubt that her letters mirrored her heart and her head. In 1841 C. F. published in two volumes, *Letters of John Adams, Addressed to his Wife*. In 1876 *Familiar Letters of John Adams and His Wife, Abigail Adams, during the Revolution* . . . appeared. But scholars and readers alike had to rely on what C. F. said they said, and as late as 1946, Adrienne Koch and William Peden, in *Selected Writings of John Adams and John Quincy Adams* (Knopf, New York) expressed the general frustration: "Since scholars have not been permitted to study the originals from which Charles Francis Adams worked, there is no way of evaluating the kind of editing done." The next year, Stewart Mitchell edited *New Letters of Abigail Adams, 1788–1801*, breaking the monopoly C. F. had enjoyed. Now the massive collection of Adams papers has been opened to the public through the magnificent volumes thus far published by Belknap Press, Harvard, under the general editorship of L. H. Butterfield, beginning in 1961 with the *Diary & Autobiography of John Adams*. The significance of this monumental step is attested by the fact that President John F. Kennedy reviewed the initial four volumes in the *American Historical Review* of January 1963 and paid deserved tribute to Mr. Butterfield, his coworkers, the Massachusetts Historical Society, Harvard, and *Life* magazine for their contributions. It is safe to say that had President Kennedy lived to see the subsequent volumes in this extraordinary series, he would have been equally rhapsodic. In 1963 the first two volumes of the *Adams Family Correspondence*, which include the letters of the remarkable Abigail from December 1761 to March 1778, were published; in 1973 two more volumes carried it to September 1782.

Abigail awaits her definitive biographer. While we wait, she best comes alive in the *Correspondence*, with its copious notes, and Page Smith's *John Adams*, 2 volumes (Doubleday, New York, 1962), far and away the best biography of the man who became the second president and the fascinating woman who was his wife.

Best of Wives—Best of Women

Elizabeth Schuyler Hamilton will probably never attract a biographer, and must be content to be studied in the shadow of her famous husband. As the text indicates, she would be content. Such letters as passed between Alexander and her will appear in the *Papers of Alexander Hamilton* (Columbia, New York, 1961–), the nineteenth volume (1973) of which brings his life up to December 1795. When the series presumably ends with his death in 1804, Elizabeth's long, courageous widowhood, which, so far as I know, has lain forgotten since Allan McLane Hamilton's *Life of Alexander Hamilton* (Scribner's, New York, 1911), may depend on the slender thread of this chapter for remembrance. The perils of descendants writing of their progenitors are too well known to scholars to require flashing yellow lights, but A. McL. Hamilton had the good sense to incorporate a fair number of

Elizabeth's later letters, and since there was no need to gild this lovely lily, it is fairly safe to assume his book set them down as she wrote them.

My Dear Child

Deborah Franklin shares a gravesite with her husband, Benjamin, in Christ Church Burial Ground, Arch Street, Philadelphia. One is tempted to say that it is the longest Franklin remained in any one place, but, given the fact that his spirit permeates the city, it is impossible to be sure. At any rate Deborah, who took an active interest in the church, should feel relatively at home, and be equally happy that virtually all the letters she wrote, as well as half of the massive collection of her husband's writings, are nearby in the collections of the American Philosophical Society. Together with Yale University, the Society is sponsoring the definitive *Papers of Benjamin Franklin*, volume 17 (Yale, 1973) of which carries the celebrated man through to December 31, 1770. This series is the best place to study Deborah, unless, as the authors have been privileged to do, one can spend some time with Dr. Whitfield J. Bell, Jr., librarian of the Philosophical Society and one of the original editors of the *Papers*, and author of a number of books on personages of the American Revolution. Carl van Doren's unsurpassed *Benjamin Franklin* (Garden City, New York, 1941) gives her more space than most of his biographers; Bernard Fay's *Franklin, Apostle of Modern Times* (Little, Brown, Boston, 1929) and his *The Two Franklins* (Little, Brown, Boston, 1933) touch her lightly. No definitive biography of Deborah is available, and she has inspired few articles, all of which is unfortunate, but perhaps inevitable because the drama of her life was acted out on a virtually empty stage.

The Traitor's Lady

Peggy Shippen's role in the treason plot has been debated for almost two centuries, with the pendulum now leaning to the conspiracy theory. Whatever the truth may be, the balance is currently tilted by belief in Burr's story that she admitted to acting, when the plot failed. While the Shippen family charged Burr invented the tale in revenge for having been rebuffed when he made advances, and Burr's own trial for treason at a later date gave them popular support in a half-hearted way, Peggy must have been a consummate actress to fool such an intelligent audience as witnessed the histrionics. Lately she has commanded close attention by sound historians. James Flexner's *The Traitor and the Spy* (Harcourt, Brace & Co., New York, 1953) and Milton Lomansk's *Beauty and the Traitor: The Story of Mrs. Benedict Arnold* (Macrae Smith, New York, 1967) are among the better accounts. Lomansk is particularly good on the afteryears, as readers of the *American Heritage* of October 1967 may recall. Carl van Doren's *Secret History of the American Revolution* (Viking, New York, 1941) is indispensable, as is anything van Doren wrote on the period. There are a number of biographies of Arnold which accord Peggy varying degrees of space in proportion to the authors' sense of her importance.

Annis Stockton and the Muses

Annis Boudinot Stockton, the Muse of Morven, is in and out of the correspondence of Washington, Benjamin Rush (her son-in-law), and other notables. Her beauty is perhaps better measured by her daughter Julia's, which Charles Willson Peale captured, than by the primitive painting now at Princeton. Washington's celebrated letter to her, in a rare moment of levity, flirtation, or admiration (Washington's biographers interpret it differently), is in Sol Feinstone's collection. Alfred Hoyt Bill's *A House Called Morven* (Princeton, 1954) gives an excellent account of Annis and her home; Elizabeth Ellet's *Women of the American Revolution* (New York, 1850) III, 13–34 offers a briefer version of her life. L. H. Butterfield, in two articles in the *Princeton University Library Chronicle,* VI (1944–1945), 1–15, and VII (1945–1946) 19–39, printed some of her unpublished poems and letters; as editor of *Letters of Benjamin Rush* (Princeton, 1951), 2 volumes, he states (107n) that she had "marked literary taste," a compliment she would have treasured, coming as it does from one of the foremost scholars of the period.

Phillis Wheatley can be found in a very brief account in M. Herzberg (ed.), *The Reader's Encyclopedia of American Literature* (New York, 1962), page 1215, and gets one-line recognition in a variety of other works, but deserves much more. Washington's letter to her, dated February 28, 1776, can be found in Fitzpatrick, *Writings of Washington* (Washington, 1931) IV, 360; John Paul Jones's letter is described in Lincoln Lorenz's *John Paul Jones* (Annapolis, 1943), pages 15–16. Benjamin Quarles, *The Negro in the American Revolution* (North Carolina, 1961), a classic work in this field, gives due recognition to this accomplished woman. The most recent edition of her works is probably C. F. Heartman (ed.), *Phillis Wheatley: Poems and Letters* (New York, 1915).

Elizabeth Graeme Fergusson's home, Graeme Park, has now been restored and opened to the public by the Pennsylvania Historical and Museum Commission in Horsham Township, Montgomery County, Pennsylvania; but the brilliant and ill-starred lady, who reputedly wanders ghostlike on the grounds, may be in search of a biographer who will do her justice. Meantime she must settle for something less than a full-scale treatment. Simon Gratz, "Some Material for a Biography of Mrs. Elizabeth Fergusson, *née* Graeme," *Pennsylvania Magazine of History & Biography* XXXIX (1915), 257–321 and 385–409, remains the most complete account; but Van Doren's *Secret History of the American Revolution, supra,* deals extensively with her implication in the Tory plots. Thomas A. Glenn's *Some Colonial Mansions and Those Who Lived in Them* (Philadelphia, 1899), pages 367–98, is helpful; and Carl and Jessica Bridenbaugh's *Rebels & Gentlemen* (Reynal & Hitchcock, New York, 1942) discusses her in the literary world of colonial Philadelphia.

For prefatory material in this chapter dealing with Anne Bradstreet and the Puritans, the best introduction is Samuel Eliot Morison's *The Intellectual Life of Colonial New England* (Cornell, 1960, reprinted by New York University, 1956).

Patrician and Slave

William Byrd provides a delightful introduction to sex in the South in the pre-Revolution era, and one of the best bibliographies of what he wrote and what has been written about him can be found in P. Marambaud, *Wil-*

liam Byrd of Westover (Virginia, 1971). Louis B. Wright, an outstanding historian of colonial America, has edited much of Byrd's writings, and furnishes a fine introduction to him as a man of letters in *The Prose Works of William Byrd of Westover* (Harvard, 1966). Page Smith puts a number of things in perspective in his *Daughters of the Promised Land* (Little, Brown, Boston, 1970), and George F. Willison's *Saints and Strangers* (Reynal & Hitchcock, New York, 1945) is a minor masterpiece about the activities of the Pilgrims. The Puritans, long misunderstood and hence casting an erroneous shadow over American morality, are gradually emerging from whited sepulchres in the more definitive studies. The relationship between Jefferson and Sally Hemings is an indispensable item in virtually every major biography of the former, and objectivity is often transformed into fierce partisanship when the subject is broached. The last word will, as in practically anything, never quite be written; but Dr. Fawn Brodie, one of the brightest and best of our historians, has recently written a balanced account which just about sums up all there is to know to date about Jefferson's private pursuit of happiness with Sally. It may be found in *Thomas Jefferson: An Intimate History* (Norton, New York, 1974). At the risk of being human about the whole thing, one cannot help but think that Monticello, remote and beautiful, was an ideal spot.

Index